THE PROJECT IN INTERNATIONAL DEVELOPMENT

The project has become fundamental to international development and humanitarian practice, playing a key role in defining objectives, funding streams and ultimately determining what success looks like. This book provides a much-needed overview of the project in international development guiding the reader through the latest theoretical debates and exploring the core tools and stages of planning and design.

The book starts with an overview of the role of the project through development history, before taking the reader through the stages of a standard project management cycle. Each chapter introduces the stage, the most common tools used to support that phase of planning, and the critical debates that exist around it, with examples to illustrate discussion from around the world. The book explores the many challenges to working effectively in contemporary aid contexts, including the role of politics and the pressures wrought by the demands to demonstrate quantified results. Throughout, the book argues for the need to see the project as a form of governmentality that arranges resources and people in time and space, and that extends neoliberal forms of managerial control in the sector.

Ending with suggestions for innovation, this book is perfect for anyone looking for an accessible and engaging guide to the international development project, whether student, researcher or practitioner.

Caitlin Scott is Associate Professor (Senior Lecturer) in Development Management and Practice at the School of Global Development at the University of East Anglia (UEA), United Kingdom.

The Project in International Development

Theory and Practice

Caitlin Scott

Routledge
Taylor & Francis Group

LONDON AND NEW YORK

Designed cover image: © Chaofann / Getty Images

First published 2023
by Routledge
4 Park Square, Milton Park, Abingdon, Oxon OX14 4RN

and by Routledge
605 Third Avenue, New York, NY 10158

Routledge is an imprint of the Taylor & Francis Group, an informa business

© 2023 Caitlin Scott

British Library Cataloguing-in-Publication Data
A catalogue record for this book is available from the British Library

ISBN: 978-1-138-38481-1 (hbk)
ISBN: 978-1-138-38482-8 (pbk)
ISBN: 978-0-429-42741-1 (ebk)

DOI: 10.4324/9780429427411

Typeset in Bembo
by Apex CoVantage, LLC

Contents

List of Figures   *vi*
Acknowledgements   *vii*

1   The Project in International Development   1

2   Project Management in the Aid Sector   22

3   Project Inceptions   45

4   Project Planning: From Logframes to Adaptive Management   78

5   Monitoring: Indicators, Adaptation and Learning   114

6   Evaluation and Impact   139

7   Conclusion   166

    Index   *173*

Figures

1.1	An illustration of projects in relation to programmes	12
1.2	Characteristics of humanitarian projects	15
2.1	A basic project cycle	29
2.2	Project time in cycle theory and reality	34
2.3	An illustration of a project in the aid chain	37
3.1	Data and sources	51
3.2	Categories of stakeholders	54
3.3	Stakeholder power/interest grid tool	55
3.4	A problem tree	61
4.1	What is planning?	81
4.2	The 'Rosetta Stone of logframes'	84
4.3	The logical flow of the components of a logframe	86
4.4	A basic logframe format	86
4.5	A results chain for a vaccination programme	87
4.6	Logframe for a reading project	89
4.7	Example of a fourth-generation results framework	92
4.8	Sweeping unexpected change under the logframe carpet	95
4.9	Logframe versus theory of change-based approaches	97
4.10	Theory of action and theory of change	99
4.11	Diagram of theory of change for a children's rights project	101
4.12	Decreasing spheres of control over project	103
5.1	Monitoring diagram showing the relation of monitoring questions to levels of the logframe	118
5.2	Detailed indicator table	123
5.3	The importance of reflecting on assumptions when monitoring	124
5.4	Beware of machine-like monitoring	133
6.1	OECD evaluation criteria and questions	142
6.2	New logic model for Oxfam Ghana health campaign	155

Acknowledgements

This book is the product of some twenty-plus years of engagement and concern with how development is done. As an anthropologist and aid worker, I have been fortunate to have conversations and encounters with people in communities around the world, from chats with teenage boys on the pavements of Medellín, Colombia, to edifying conversations with elder women under Kenyan trees, to debates about the difference between an output and an outcome with colleagues in Eastern Europe. These encounters were shaped by both research and work in the sector, and their complex and multifaceted nature inspired a querying of how development works in practice, which this book attempts to address.

The book is also shaped by and draws on teaching work for project management modules at the University of East Anglia School of Global Studies (previously International Development). This includes the work of past and present colleagues, including Daniel McAvoy, Sebastian Taylor, Steve Russell, Brendan Whitty and David Girling. Colleagues including Kavita Ramakrishnan, Kirsten McConachie, Ludek Stavinoha and Brendan Whitty provided encouragement and advice via an informal writing group, as did mentor Martin Scott. Particular thanks go to Catherine Jere for her encouragement to pursue this book in the first place and support since. I am also grateful to the School of Global Studies for the seed funding and time to do this work. Like most projects, writing the book did not go according to plan, and I am obliged to Laura Camfield for her support and flexibility around this and enabling me to get it done. Lastly, the School's ever curious and creative students, for whom this book is largely written, have been a constant source of energy and inspiration.

I am very grateful to Silva Ferretti for permission to use some of her excellent drawings. Cathy Shutt did a remarkable job editing, for which I am very appreciative.

Invariably, as writing a book is never only a professional endeavour, I am greatly indebted to my family. For their unfailing tolerance, support and humour, the book is dedicated to Malcolm, Isabella, Callum and Odin.

1 The Project in International Development

Introduction: Projects and Tools in Development

The project is one of the most common and characteristic features of contemporary development, shaping how aid is both conceived of and delivered. As a means of planning specific pieces of work to deliver a predetermined objective over a short time period, it has been called both a workhorse (Picciotto 2020) and a privileged particle (Hirschman 1994) of the development process. It has remained relatively stable in its form over more than fifty years of development efforts of planned change to improve living standards and wellbeing.[1] It is also largely taken for granted as a vehicle for the allocation of resources, since most grants are administered via projects. So central is its place in the firmament that it has been conceptualised as a commodity with its own political economy (Freeman and Schuller 2020; Krause 2014). Indeed the project is so useful that despite the existence of other modalities in aid, as a way of thinking and mode of governmentality, there is no obvious alternative to it, even though project failures have been the subject of analysis and debate for decades (Hira and Parfitt 2004; Hirschman 1994; Ferguson 1994; Ika et al. 2010; Rondinelli 1983). Many attempts have been made to improve the systems and tools through which projects are enacted, as discussed in this book. It is a symptom or indicator of its success and resilience as well as its adaptability that the project remains so central.

Projects are also ubiquitous in modern life, as a means of achieving everything from the production of a new car to organising changes in personal circumstances, to the extent that almost anything can be subject to projectification (Jensen et al. 2016). In the machinery of development today, the project is both a standardised and standardising frame for work. As the basis of grants both small and large, the project is enacted through the use of a range of tools and concepts that embody many of the central premises of modern forms of management and production. As a management form, the project is thus a vehicle for other rationalities of management, such as a standardised commodified view of time, an emphasis on understanding change through linear models of causality, and of simplistic and direct relationships between inputs and outputs. Supporting the correct formulation of projects is an abundance of guidance about using the tools of project management. Much of this emphasises the use of the correct tools and concepts, from stakeholder analyses to logframes and indicator metrics, all part of the growing lexicon of development management.

DOI: 10.4324/9780429427411-1

These tools are the subject of significant debate, as specialists seek to improve these technical methods for addressing the problems that development tries to address.

The book treats these tools as central to the project as it is currently practiced and articulated. Practitioners and scholars of development today regularly speak of concepts such as goals, logframes and impact, but insufficient attention has been given to where these concepts and tools have come from and what the implications of their intellectual history are for ideas of development as a progressive endeavour. Yet few texts attempt to consider the project with the attendant range of tools, or provide a critical discussion of these, in one place. This book fills that gap. Putting these tools front and centre of the project allows the aspiring development practitioner not only to understand something about the range of tools used in project cycle management but also allows a critical analysis of the implications of them as a whole.

Focusing on the tools also allows for a different approach to addressing the problem of the gap between the theory or design and practice in implementation of the project. This has long been a topic of concern to both academics and practitioners. For critical perspectives such as those of Ferguson (1994), development projects typically never fulfil their objectives because these are immaterial to its real effects, of depoliticising development. Many scholars have followed in the wake of this analysis of development projects as part of an 'anti-politics machine' (Ferguson 1994). This has led to approaches that look at how projects enact a process of rendering technical (Li 2007), whereby development endeavours transform complex social and political issues and dynamics into isolatable and stable parts that they seek to change. The argument advanced here is that the tools of the project play a key role in depoliticising development and rendering development into a technical apparatus that acts as an instrument of governance and governmentality.

The tools of project management do the work of rendering technical by applying the semantics of engineering to the process of turning social and political issues into technical ones, throwing a technocratic veil over political issues. They then provide a set of approaches and instructions to enact that transformation. Firstly, the concept of tools provides a metaphor that suggests to the project planner that deciphering the problem of poverty before them is one that can be fixed with a pre-existing scientific approach. This aura of simple yet scientific reassurance proposes that they can grasp and fix the issue effectively. They introduce a notion derived from mechanics and engineering that is reassuring in its connection to modernity, that underlines the possibility of a correct fix that is universal.

Secondly, the toolkit at the planner's disposal provides a series of methods and approaches that allow them to assess each of the many different aspects of the situation that the project will encounter. For each stage of the project, a different set of tools is available to calibrate the problem. Each of these tools will allow the planner a means to engage with the problems in front of them and reconfigure these into ones which are amenable to intervention, however politically tense or historically deep. Some tools allow the measurement of poverty, via household surveys that assess the depth and spread of low income, and thus generate data on livelihoods to which a solution can be proposed. The logframe reveals how the intervention will produce the desired changes, and the indicators in the logframe will enable planners, donors and implementing staff with a means to verify and communicate exact levels of progress. A theory of change will be situated wholly in the present, and while acknowledging some of the factors that are external to the process and that may impact it, nonetheless seek to articulate how a series of actions will turn into a series of improvements. A complex set of evaluation tools will be available for assessment of impact at the end of the project.

These tools are a familiar part of the language of project management; yet they have been hidden in plain sight, made invisible by their ubiquity and even mundanity. As Graeber noted, processes of bureaucracy can be dull to study, even for anthropologists, as paperwork doesn't open onto anything but itself (2015: 51–52). However, their ubiquity does not make these tools any less powerful. On the contrary, and as I argue here, the tools are a key means by which the project is not just a form of governance (Li 2016), but governmentality (Foucault 2007).[2] The project's rules and tools serve to frame a set of possible actions and coordinates, as well as established rules for 'the conduct of conduct' (Gordon 1991). The tools are the rules, then, for disciplining and establishing correct behaviour in the fields of development intervention. This makes the tools a critical part of the anti-politics machine, of the process of rendering technical, as the tools provide a set of instructions.

Rules of governance necessarily have ethical dimensions, yet these tools help dissolve the larger and more profound political and ethical questions that frame development projects. There is no need for individual ethical or political questioning, if time were available or hierarchies rendered that feasible anyway. Instead the tools render the complex power relations of the development encounter into a series of tasks and steps, in which actors' roles are specified in relation to the performance of specific tasks, rather than their positionality in relation to a series of questions of colonialism, nationality, or gender.

The professional tools and the project's ascription of roles to individuals within them are also related to the advance a particular neoliberal form of governmentality. As Foucault noted, governmentality has a specific relation to political economy (2007: 108; Dean 2010). The rise of neoliberal ideologies since the end of the Cold War saw the expansion of market logics into areas that were previously the domain of the state. New public management (NPM) methods were adopted to bring the rationalities and efficiencies of the market into the management of the state (Pollit 2001). Goods and services once provided by the state have been privatised and outsourced, on the premise that market forces necessarily produce greater efficiency because the profit motive acts as the best incentive. Exemplified by the rise and use of the logframe, these ideas had a sharp ascendancy and impact within aid from the 1980s onwards (Biggs and Smith 2003; Kerr 2008; Roberts et al. 2005). Today, their impact is most apparent in the rise of audit culture (Power 1999; Strathearn 2000) within the sector, which enacts a system of surveillance and control through extensive use of metrics, which scrutinise the work of projects and their practitioners in the name of accountability and efficiency (Scott 2022). These accountabilities trickle down the 'aid chain' (Wallace et al 2007) and shape the day-to-day activities of the aid worker to involve copious reporting burdens (Hindman and Fechter 2014).

Mind the Gap

The book argues that these tools in their increasingly standardised and standardising forms in use across the aid sector have a series of disciplinary effects. The focus on results that accompanied the NPM concern with efficiency described previously has often been précised under the rubric of the 'results agenda' (e.g. Eyben 2015). The results agenda is a term which broadly encompasses the increased pressures placed on aid to demonstrate results from interventions, in line with the Paris Agenda for Aid Effectiveness (OECD 2005). This brought an increased focus on metrics as a means of verifying whether or not development was procuring intended results, in what has also been phrased as results-based management (RBM). In turn, results – in order to be intelligible – needed to increasingly be subject to quantification, and analysis via a range of metrics found in the NPM arsenal – rankings, targets, quotas and rationalisations according to cost. This agenda and tools were inspired by the apparent failure of development projects, and other interventions, to achieve their desired ends. Their goal was to address this gap between intention and outcome, or theory and practice. We can discern two significant trends in approaches to diagnosing fault and correction to repair the gap between design theory and implemented reality. The first, which I term techno-managerial, has been concerned with the failure to use technical tools correctly, and locates problems with the contexts of development, problems to be rectified with greater control and scrutiny from the centre. A second trend I term techno-normative is composed of reforming efforts that have sought to find new and more progressive approaches that reflect the contextual diversity of aid, such as adaptive management.

In the first, techno-managerial school, problems with projects are diagnosed as being caused by a combination of a failure to use tools correctly and the messy contexts in which development has been done. Some of the classic management analyses of project failure are summarised in the 'notorious nine' typical problems and constraints (Gow and Morss 1988). These include the complex webs of political and socio-cultural factors that significantly affect outcomes; problems with implementing institutions, such as limited capacities, and which agencies are selected; the limitations of personnel in host countries and the short-term provision of qualified people; and shortcomings in technical assistance. Others include vagaries associated with decentralised administrative structures, unsuitable time frames and poor-quality information systems. The effects of these upon project management techniques are summarised by Turner et al. thus: "Unfortunately, the rigour that these techniques bring to project analyses has not been reflected in project results" (2015: 192).

The majority of problems are identified as arising from the operational contexts in which projects have taken place, rather than any weaknesses in the management techniques themselves. In this view, the implicit assumption is that if suitable controls could be made upon these contextual externalities, sound and effective management could prevail. As a Project Management Institute (PMI) review of projects in development contexts put it, these contexts bring many 'peculiarities' to the normal workings of project cycle management (Golini and Landoni 2013).

The responses this diagnosis of failure produced have been shaped accordingly: if management systems have gone wrong, but it is not their fault, then they must be made more exacting and controlling, within the diverse fields of expertise that populate development. This has led to more stringent management systems, the use of more precise tools, alongside an emphasis on results, and extended the logic of managerialism, whereby every aspect of a project is turned into a rationality which can be assessed and inspected, ever further. Over the last twenty years this has been spread through both global linkages of donors, international non-governmental organisations (INGOs) and small NGOs in the global south, which have become networks for the spread of managerialism, now considered 'pervasive' (Roberts et al. 2005; Wallace et al. 2007; Girei 2016).

This focus on results has led to a number of deleterious consequences (Eyben 2015; Gulranjani 2011; Yanguas 2018). With the increasing demand for all projects to be formulated according to the most precise and professional management concepts if they are to be funded, projects are today often short term, focused on narrow results and typically quantified. The spread of NPM systems means that projects today must report on copious indicators, made donors averse to risk, and ensured that systemic or structural change is off the agenda.

In response to these strictures and unintended consequences of the rationalisation of projects, critics within the sector have endeavoured to craft alternative approaches, which I call 'techno-normative' approaches, the second trend highlighted earlier. Some are inspired by political critique that emphasises the need to counter top-down planning with the participation of would-be 'beneficiaries', others formulating analytical tools with increased specificity for apprehending the complex contexts in which projects operate. These broadly emphasise the need for improved technical approaches, with new methods to reflect the varied context and unpredictable elements of aid (Biggs and Smith 2003; Hira and Parfitt 2004; Ika and Hodgson 2014; Gulranjani 2011; Rondinelli 1983). The goal of techno-normative approaches is still to find management-inspired solutions and create tools for this, but to re-shape these to acknowledge unpredictability and the unsuitability of linear planning for diverse, often unpredictable contexts. Many of the tools reviewed here include discussion of these reforming approaches. Yet, and despite widespread acceptance of the normative case for involving local peoples in planning, as well as the evidence of the benefits of adaptive management, the use of these tools remains at the discretion of wider ideological, geopolitical and economic agendas that ultimately shape aid from the top down, and which have not overall dislodged the project as a form. Instead, it has merely absorbed them into its ample toolkits.

Critical Perspectives

The central argument made in the book is that these tools are disciplining, shaping the content of the contemporary development project. These instrumental approaches preserve managerial control, as they shape what can be done, how and when, and by whom, according to a fairly rigid set of criteria. Even if the project does not deliver as intended, the possibilities for defining the project have been registered, as the language of project management populates the imaginary and its tasks occupy the day-to-day. The governmentality effects of these tools suggest how they are linked with a neoliberal agenda, which sees inputs and resources as commodities and which instrumentalises resources and relationships according to specific logics derived from theories of the market. In this view, neoliberalism can be broadly defined by the prioritisation of economic logics over others, including political ones (Davies 2016: 5–6).

Governmentality argument is rooted in critical perspectives on management from feminist, decolonial and other angles, which point to the unsuitability of universalising models of management for development (Cooke and Dar 2008; Girei 2017). Critical management studies (CMS) approaches argue that management regimes and their associated knowledge systems are antithetical to the kinds of change many people envision as the objective of development (Cooke 2008; Cooke and Dar 2008; Kerr 2008; Thomas 2000). These systems are seen to reproduce the structural features of the contemporary world order that recreate and reinforce the systems of inequality and domination that produce poverty, effect racial inequality and destroy the environment. While management science is typically presented as neutral and technical, this simply conceals its status as a product and sustainer of broader power relations and inequalities (Cooke 2008: 112). Even apparently progressive measures such as participation are here seen as little more than vehicles for co-optation (Cooke 2008).

Thus a key task is to uncover the ways in which management effects these structures of co-optation and explore how they construct subjectivities. The view of these tools as disciplining is derived from the Foucauldian notion of governmentality, a neologism for government rationality (Foucault 2007; Gordon 1991). This allows us to consider how the rules for process, are shaped. Analysing forms of governance involves thinking about power and how it operates, extending to an interest in the rules that shape behaviour and action, quite often implicitly, but that can at once both totalise and individualise (Gordon 1991: 3). These include disciplinary logics, that work through the mechanisms of planning and through the dissemination of ideas of economic rationality as the pinnacle of reason. Governmentality is thus about the concepts and discursive practices that create and shape new subjectivities and ways of thinking, producing self-regulating individuals who think of themselves in the correct fashions and terms and are self-managing to fulfil the dominant expectations.

These tools have a significant effect over what is done, how it is conceived, colonising the imaginary. The apparently universal and scientific technical renderings in the techno-managerial approaches to the project in fact draw on specific value systems and configurations. The relationship between means and ends articulated within project management is an instrumental one, which prioritises the uses or ends to which the resources or means can be put. Projects are based on a dominant capitalist conceptualisation of human and other resources in terms of inputs, that can then be used to deliver outputs, outcomes and so on. This framing of human resources rests on a prior understanding of human labour as a commodity, that can be traded in a market for labour and sold in the units that can become inputs. This use value necessarily dislocates other values, including those which might pertain in diverse cultural and social contexts. For example, the instrumental value of agricultural training is that it will facilitate an increase in yields that will in turn improve income and profit, an example of the kinds of ends which must be pre-approved in the project. Education can be thus formulated as a way of increasing 'human capital' that can contribute to gross domestic product (GDP), rather than achieving any goals of freedom, emancipation or other political transformations. The project supports, indeed demands, the use of instrumental reason in a manner in which resources are conceptualised, such as the linkage of an input to an output. As we will see in Chapter 2 in relation to who undertakes projects in the contemporary space, this commodification that the project demands also enables the financialisation of development.

It is one of the key elements of neoliberalism's success that governing activities are recast, reformulated and repackaged as "nonpolitical and nonideological problems that need technical solutions" (Ong 2006: 3). The project can thus be seen as a vehicle for dominant neoliberal agendas, not just in the kinds of goals or interventions extolled, but in how it is done and in how it is enacted. The project has these logics embedded in it, through its tools, and in the ways its management has been reformed over the last twenty years.

We can further see the effects of neoliberal governmentality in aid in relation to how individuals, including workers, are framed through its discourses and practices. A connection between the disciplinary and governmentality effects of the project is found through the work of NPM rationalities on the individual. Underlying the myriad technologies of NPM is a neoliberal view of the individual as an atomised agent. This rational, individualistic, selfish and rent-seeking 'economic man' – and the gendered specificity of this is notable (Marcal 2015) – has come to hold a central place not just in economic theory, at the centre of neoliberal economics, but also made its way into planning and human resource management. This is due to the manner in which NPM extends ideas of public choice and principal-agent theory (PAT). Implicit in the managerialist NPM approaches, and drawing on work by von Hayek in the 1930s and Buchanan and others in the 1960s, PAT holds that individuals are inherently selfish and rent-seeking, and are best managed by systems of control and incentivisation (Olssen and Peters 2005; Pollit 2016; Shutt 2016; Udehn 2002; Widmalm 2016). This view of rational man drew on methodological individualism, in which society is seen as a kind of aggregate of individuals behaving according to rational self-interest, extending from a long line of European thought, including in Hobbes' *Leviathan* (1651), according to which human nature leads to societies in which life is nasty, brutish and short without constraint. The fact that negative renderings of humanity such as PAT operationalise a deeply cynical view of humanity, and why it deviates so far from common views of ethics in society (Bøhren 1998), warrants more attention, particularly in the aid sector where social goals may well motivate workers (Honig 2018). Yet neoliberal rationalities for management enmesh and enlist aid workers in multiple ways, including the disciplining effects of short-term contracts in the employment market, and practices such as individual assessment, which turn individuals into self-managing disciplined and entrepreneurial selves in ideologies of meritocracy (Alvesson and Käremman 2004; Ong 2006; Kelly 2006).

Anthropological Insights

In looking critically at the project, and the gap between theory and practice, the book's approach brings insights from the anthropology of development. In recent decades, studies have drawn attention to the need to see projects as socially con-stituted events and processes, whereby certain kinds of rationalities are negotiated by the travelling logics of aid workers, and the technical renditions of problems that aid delivers (Mosse 2005a; Li 2007; Mosse and Lewis 2006; Rottenburg 2009). Anthropologists are typically less concerned with whether or not projects work, than with the social processes through which aid is enacted – although this can include how social relations are shaped in order to justify or hide appar-ent failures. The gap between the idea and the practice, such as the logframe being a tool for planning that has little bearing for locals (Wallace et al. 2007), is accounted for in the ways these processes are socially constituted, by relation-ships, documents, power relations and interpretations. These approaches involve looking carefully at how meanings are negotiated and constructed within project (Mosse 2005a) or policy (Green 2011) contexts, and draws attention to micro-processes in aid.

Ethnographic analyses of the project have seen it framed as a socially produced construct, an authorised framework which aid actors endeavour to show their work matches, such that their efforts should appear as instances of approved pol-icy (Mosse 2005a), and around which people also shape their own interests and careers (Sampson 1996). Other anthropological work has shown how projects are formed in response to different kinds of problem identification (Li 2007), which through their technical renderings repeatedly fail to take account of the historical and political.

These perspectives allow us to see how, through its technical framings, a project is designed "to take out history, to isolate the project from the continuous flow of social life" (Mosse 2005a: 47). This provides a key insight into how projects can fail. Because projects turn social and political problems into technical ones, excluding real political contestation and history, projects never really address the difficult prob-lems that communities face in the real political and historical terms in which locals experience them (Li 2007; Ferguson 1994).

A related point that underpins the conceptualisation of projects as depoliticis-ing technical endeavours is to understand the technical language through which projects are framed, and how technical categories and approaches which aid draws on to legitimate interventions are developed. Projects are often drawn from and operationalise specific policy constructs around specific fields of work and kinds of problems that are created and sustained by international networks of experts and actors. These networks of expertise produce pyramids of knowledge that distribute these pre-approved categories of problem, and of beneficiary that are considered morally and financially legitimate, and which are then enacted via projects carried out by a range of actors in the aid system (Green 2011, 2012). The simplifications and glossing over of wide diversities within the categories that aid systems construct are an important source of gaps between theory and practice.

Another set of concerns identified by anthropologists include how tools such as indicators are developed and constituted as social facts that privilege certain kinds of knowledge over others. As Merry (2016) argues in looking at indicators of gender-based violence, they do not reveal truth but instead create it, producing numbers which are decontextualised, homogenising and remote from local systems of meaning. They thus risk producing knowledge that is 'partial, distorted, and misleading', yet which is used to develop policy because its sources are seen as authoritative. As with the United Nations Millennium Development Goals (MDGs) that framed development as a specific set of limited and quantified outcomes (Fukuda-Parr et al. 2014), these simplifications and abstractions underline the power of numbers to produce unintended consequences by focusing attention to narrow goals, shaping and distorting thinking along the way.

Looking at how indicators function draws our attention to how other tools of the project also generate representations of knowledge, and how representations may be significantly at odds with the realities they are meant to represent. This issue of knowledge and accuracy has significant bearing in project inceptions, as considered in Chapter 3, but also throughout the project cycle. As we look at in Chapter 5, the ways in which local practices were both ignored and treated as a source of spreading Ebola during the West African pandemic in 2014 not only produced interventions that communities struggled to accept, but also exacerbated existing fears of authority (Parker et al. 2019).

The project has also been noted as a mode of governance, which organises people and resources in time and space. As Li notes in the context of neo-patrimonial, financially driven politics in Indonesia, projects play an important role in election spending, whereby government officials and politicians create projects because they are a vehicle to disburse funds for collaborators. These politically driven projects are largely ineffective in relation to their ends, but they are effective in depoliticising problems and extending networks of support (2016: 82, 92).

This conceptualisation of the project as a political tool, tied to specific ends for mobilising political support and allegiances as noted by multiple anthropologists, is instructive. However, the various anthropological approaches outlined do not specifically question the many and specific tools through which development projects are created. Neither Li's nor Mosse's approach take into account the typical kinds of tools that are used to design projects and which create the structure of the project as a technocratic tool, replete with procedures which frame, identify, demarcate and allocate in specific ways. I argue that if we are to take seriously the multiple technical renderings that aid performs, we must look deeper into the project's mechanisms to see how these categories are created and identified, how meanings are created, within what templates and with what tensions.

In exploring the project and its constitutive tools both from the perspective of a would-be practitioner and with a critical academic stance, the book functions on two registers. The first is explaining the nature of project management tools, brought together in one place. The second is derived from critical reflections on these tools, engaging with practitioners' debates and reflecting on the managerialist and techno-normative discourses that create order and structure. It also considers how more radical aims are undermined through critical anthropology, and the lens of governmentality.

The argument unfolds over the course of the book's chapters, reflecting the stages of the project cycle and the tools through which this is developed and enacted. Each chapter starts with a vignette of the theory of how the tools and the stage should function. This is contrasted with the typical realities produced by the facts of functioning in the aid chain, and with tools defined for the respective tasks. These juxtapositions of theory and reality demonstrate some of the ways in which project processes and tools diverge from the ideals that are portrayed in the anodyne, generic and standardised manuals for development that practitioners must engage with, and how a gap opens up between this technocratic ideal and the rather messier world of application. To understand this gap, we look at how the complex political processes, environmental challenges and cultural dimensions of development work make for a demanding systems in which practitioners and agencies are meant to deliver distantly designed processes. Alongside the accounts of how projects *should* be run are critical accounts of some of the many challenges that are encountered when trying to put these models into practice in the 'real world'. As we will see, individual tools generate a significant amount of debate – for example, around the logframe (e.g. Kerr 2008; Wallace et al. 2007; Gasper 2000) or evaluation approaches (Camfield and Duvendack 2014).

As I discuss further in Chapter 2, the governmentality effects that tools and programming manuals achieve is because they are written without context: they are presented in a generalised style, a specific kind of development speak that is stripped of context. This means that those using them need to understand how to run a focus group or conduct a survey effectively in one location, and how to go about developing indicators for agricultural projects in another. This presumes a level of capacity to interpret, and time and space in which to do so, that may be at odds with the hurried pragmatics of developing a proposal for grant funding. At a practical level, the varied tools produce their own technical disconnections. Many roles within aid organisations are technically very specific and separated into functional departments, or as they're often referred to in terms of effects, 'silos'. This means that staff working on one aspect of a project may be unaware of developments in another area.

As we see unfold, at every turn the disciplining forces of the tools shape and mould what is conceived of, and yet also clash with practical exigencies. The model of PCM which depicts a dynamic of cyclical learning and improvement is at odds with the realities in which learning opportunities are compromised by the focus on results. The tools through which projects are researched at inception need to provide strong quantitative data, and yet can completely ignore deeper cultural realities and social histories. To begin this process of exploration, we must first define the object of analysis.

Defining the Project in International Development Contexts

The fact that a significant proportion of aid is done in the form of a project is one of the reasons for this book, but what do we mean by 'a project'? The word or phrase *project* means "a piece of planned work or an activity that is finished over a period of time and intended to achieve a particular purpose" (Oxford English Dictionary). In development contexts, the World Bank notes that the project concept "essentially provides a disciplined and systematic approach to analysing and managing a set of investment activities" (Hira and Parfitt 2004: 32). This version explains that a project is typically focused on investing capital, providing services, strengthening local institutions, improving policies, or making plans for those.

In the 1960s, when development institutions were growing in the shadow of the Cold War, as arms of western influence to spread a capitalist version of industrial development and modernity, projects were at the forefront of delivering this agenda (Hirschman 1994; Ika and Hodgson 2014). At the time, development projects were a special kind of neatly packaged investment mechanism by which multilateral banks lent money for key infrastructural elements. They became "privileged particles of the development processes" (Hirschman 1994: 1), used to design and deliver electricity, irrigation, highways, railways and telecommunications developments, which dominant economic theory of the time, such as Rostow's (1991) 'stages to take off', held would spur the engines of growth via industrial development, and so put developing countries on the path to prosperity.

If the form of the project lent itself relatively easily to large engineering projects, given its origins in scientific and military contexts, the project as a form has proven remarkably adaptable. Projects have proven amenable to alignment with a range of policy formulations over the decades. In the 1970s, projects accommodated a shift in attention to agricultural foci and goals of national food sovereignty, with integrated rural development projects aligned to the green revolution, and subsequently taking their place within neo-liberal policy agendas such as structural adjustment of the 1980s (de Haan 2009; Williams 2012). Subsequent uses within the World Bank included as levers for policy instruments such as institutional reform within the Washington consensus of the 1970s and 1980s, building blocks for policy-led country assistance programmes afterwards, and remaining indispensable instruments of thematic reform programmes (Picciotto 2020: 478–480).

Over succeeding decades, major bilateral aid has sought to gain advantages from efficiencies of scale, and from coordinating aid efforts into more coherent outcomes according to reigning policy agendas through the Paris Agenda for aid reform and subsequent iterations of the aid effectiveness debate. This gave rise to new approaches, including direct spending support to national governments and other forms of larger-scale agreements (de Haan 2009; Williams 2012; Mosse 2005a).

Much aid must still be delivered in project form for implementation purposes, or simple accountabilities. In many instances imagined for this book, projects are carried out by non-governmental organisations (NGOs) or civil society organisations (CSOs), although private-sector actors are playing an increasing role too. Projects continue to have a role within more recent pushes to expand the reach of and integration to markets globally. A significant proportion of private finance is also delivered in the form of grants, which are often premised on programmes or project models, whereby a specific deliverable is proposed on the basis of a finite budget and within predetermined time frames. So while there is an association in some quarters of projects with individual pieces of work that surmise only narrow attention to single issues, their adaptable nature means that projects are likely to remain the privileged instruments of development enterprise (Picciotto 2020).

A project is typically considered different from a programme – in many cases, a project is a small part of a larger programme. For Oxfam a programme is "a set of strategically aligned, mutually reinforcing interventions . . . that contribute to a sustained positive impact on the lives of women and men living in poverty" (2010: 10).

A project in this context is a subset of this work, which contributes to some of these changes. It is also notable that projects may be conceived of simply as grants, or considered interchangeably with a grant, as slices or sections of programme work are often bundled up for funding purposes. This definition is not dissimilar to that set out for general and commercial contexts, whereby a programme is a "collections of projects with shared goals and objectives . . . and . . . resources . . . all of whose benefits must be realised for program overall to work" (Morris 2013: 17).

In an INGO context, project–programme relationships can look as per the diagram in Figure 1.1. In a hypothetical example, NGO BritAid works in Ruritania.

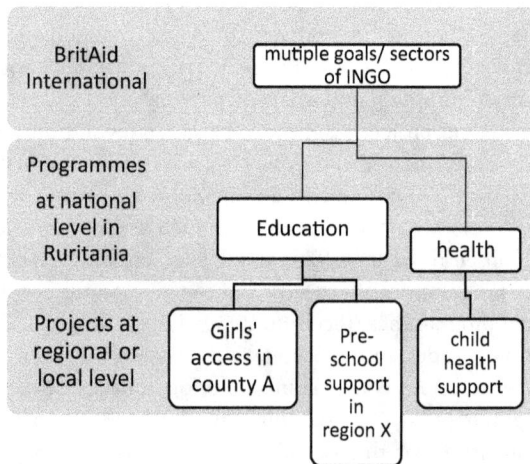

Figure 1.1 An illustration of projects in relation to programmes

Source: The author

BritAid has several thematic areas it works on, such as livelihoods, health and education. Within one country where BritAid has an office, two of these thematic programmes are running, education and health. These align to BritAid's analysis of what it can most effectively contribute to in Ruritania. Under its national education programme, which includes supporting preschools across two other regions, it has decided to support girls' access to education in county A. This has been packaged as a project, which has successfully received funding from the UK government's girl's education challenge fund. This project has a specific goal to increase girls' access to school by 40% over three years.

Key Characteristics of the Project in a Development Context

Like the project to increase girls' access to education in county A in Ruritania, the contemporary development project has several key characteristics. These include working to achieve a specific change-related aim, in relation to a specific group of people in a determined geographical area, within a specific time frame. This gives the development project a number of notable common features that are outlined as follows.

What: A Goal, Predefined Purpose

The goal of a project is usually stated as a broader change objective which should be achieved longer term. It is often a statement of change, that seeks to create some transformation to a central aspect or need in a group of peoples' lives. Changes are often expressed at two levels: one in relation to a goal, a vision or other longer-term objective that a project will contribute to, and the other a more concrete set of changes that can realistically be delivered by the project itself. For a climate adaptation project in Cambodia funded by the EU, for example, *the aim is to **reduce emissions and increase people's adaptation capacities**, contributing to a greener, low carbon, climate-resilient, equitable, sustainable and knowledge-based society.*[3]

The key outcome is in bold type, *the longer term goal* working on both emissions and people with a longer-term issue, namely climate change resilience.

In an example of Save the Children's child protection work (Thompson 2012), the goal of a project in Pakistan is "To ensure that the survival and protection needs of 280,000 flood-affected people, including approximately 235,000 children, are met in Swat, Dir and DI Khan districts (KPK province)".

In this example, specific needs are identified for a target group of people in a specific location. These are of survival and protection of people affected by flooding, including a pre-identified number of beneficiaries and within this, a large proportion of children. These people are located in three districts in one province, giving a fairly specific area of operation and intended impact.

When: Short, Predetermined Time Frames

A further key characteristic is that projects have a specific **time frame**, with a start and end date which is known in advance. This timing is typically three years, but can be as little as a few months, in the case of humanitarian projects, or up to five years. This relatively short time frame for attempting to produce change is one of the enduring features – and frustrations – of the project. It means that resources must be mobilised, staff hired, contracts and memorandums signed, and work then undertaken at a relatively fast pace. This can be challenging in any context but it is even more so given the many facets of social, political and environmental contexts that projects must grapple with in a given locality, and which often behave in different ways to what can be predicted in a classic risk analysis.

Who: Target 'Beneficiaries'

These changes are targeted at a defined group of beneficiaries – in the first example of reducing emissions and improving adaptive capacities, a wide section of Cambodian society is targeted, while in the second example they are a closely defined number of people in a specific location, albeit in relation to broadly stated needs.

Most projects outline in detail why specific people are in need. In the Save the Children example, the target population have been affected by floods in dramatic ways – survival and protection are key issues here. There is an inherent urgency to this aim. Moreover, the proportion of the total beneficiaries that are children is very high, and children are usually associated with vulnerability, in addition to their status as legal minors and economic dependents, which underlines their need for protection – both humanitarian in the form of shelter and food, but also safeguarding, as flood and other emergencies can produce risks to children of separation from families.

The fact that the intended beneficiaries are often, still, simply referred to as 'beneficiaries' is a sleight of hand in planning that underlines the presumed efficacy of the project, and that its intended outputs actually reach the intended population. This is important for, as we note throughout the book, intention is not the same as effect.

Where: Area of Intervention

The defined **area of intervention** of projects is often relatively small geographically. Projects tend to be delineated by implementation logistics to operate within a very specific area of a country or region where the common issue or problem is identified. This is often for both practical and tactical reasons. Problems can correlate with livelihoods that are linked to specific patterns of natural resource use, or ethnic or religious communities experiencing those problems who live in specific areas. Targeting just those areas is practical under such circumstances.

A project must be (in theory) realistic enough to cover that geographical area. This means thinking about the staff, be they directly employed or contracted or via a partner organisation, their working sites and transport possibilities. It is also related

Humanitarian projects: characteristics of interventions in 'special circumstances'

- These projects tend to run much shorter cycles of 3–12 months, or be 'hyper-**projectised**'.
- Focused on **direct delivery** of 'life-saving' materials to crisis-affected populations **based on inputs**.
- In such circumstances there may be **little or no connection** between the project and wider government and civil society circumstances, because of conflict or a natural catastrophe.
- These projects are rarely **sustainable**, without design to support continuation of the goals post-recovery, and beneficiaries are rarely consulted directly.

Figure 1.2 Characteristics of humanitarian projects

Source: The author

to administrative jurisdictions within countries. Many devolved systems have local administrative apparatuses that function at state and local levels, and which must be engaged with and through for any development endeavour.

Questions of Method

In writing the book, I draw on several sets of sources and research. One is my own experience. This includes time as a researcher, a consultant and a salaried staff member for several INGOs. Through these I learnt about the ways in which agencies structure and use monitoring and evaluation resources, in particular, at a time when new staffing and technologies reflected the growing importance of the results agenda. This included running training sessions around the world with a focus on results- and rights-based approaches, explaining to colleagues in regional and national offices how new formats designed in London were to be used to track and assess new work, and how to express ideas about results in ways that fit internal planning systems and strategies.

A second set of sources is my own more recent research that has started to answer these questions. This has involved interviews with some fifteen staff of various sized NGOs and foundations on the subject of planning and their experiences with tools such as the logframe. Some observational material has also been gleaned by participant observation around the sector, following debates around new tools and large topics in online blogs or email groups.[4] I also draw on original research around a project in rural Colombia. This 'project' was really an initiative, growing out of a mixture of research, activism, agricultural practice and community mobilisation around licit uses of the coca crop in the southern state of Cauca, Colombia. This initiative had grown from the ground up as the results of community action and found support from a US-based foundation working on the same issues. In so doing, a complex initiative arising out of a combination of efforts to bring peace to a region which had experienced the ravages of the drug trade and ethnobotanical research was gradually being transformed into a project for funding purposes. This, as we explore in Chapter 3 on project inceptions, is different for many of the NGO-led projects in the book which are designed from afar, but also offered insight into some of the processes that project packaging involved.

A third source is ethnographic analyses drawn from secondary sources, which has explored the project and associated perspectives, including work by Mosse (2005a, 2005b), Green (2011), Merry (2016), Li (2007, 2016), and on which I draw to bring forward the social realities and multiple perspectives around projects. As I discussed earlier, an ethnographic approach is essential to see how the interacting parts of the aid system fit together, from the would-be beneficiaries filtering and adapting what projects might offer, the management system and indicator bundles designed in senior office enclaves and the project workers in between trying to communicate between the two poles and the many levels between. A final source of material are the project planning manuals and tools to which the book makes multiple references. I discuss these further as a genre in Chapter 2, and refer to them in each chapter.

Plan of the Book

The book's plan follows the various stages of project development, sharing a selection of the main tools and debates about their improvements along the way. At the same time, each chapter explores the challenges and critiques that have accompanied these tools.

This exploration starts in Chapter 2 with a brief review of the history of development planning and some of the impacts of contemporary logic on development. The central model of project cycle management is explored, as it is according to this model that many development projects are implicitly or explicitly enacted. After exploring its stages, we consider how this management rendition of cyclical learning is at odds with the linear, often abruptly timed processes of a project grant and delivery, and some of the implications of this disconnect.

We then look at how instructions for project design are expressed in contemporary manuals and guidance documents, or toolkits. It is argued that the technical tools that respond to demands for clear results have changed the way aid is done, as project-based aid has increasingly been shaped by the logics of short time scales and quantifiable results. The relationships which govern project contracts are explored in relation to the aid chain, a hierarchical system in which funding has a central role. A focus on project management rather than progressive change has also allowed the private sector, using the language of management and efficiency, to become an increasingly significant actor in the sector, alongside the 'philanthrocapitalist' class of global billionaires who engage in limited kinds of ways with the goals of development.

Chapter 3 explores how projects come about in the 'real world' of development, from funding calls to programming streams and objectives within INGOs, and how this sometimes produces projects which are poorly aligned to local realities. These typical funding and design processes constitute important elements within which projects operate, from the specific concepts that donors prioritise to the predefined goals which projects need to align to. These strictures form part of the governance of aid and the disciplinary moulds within which aid must work.

The chapter then details the various tools typically used in project research and design phases, from general situation analyses gathering large stores of data to varieties of Political Economy Analysis to stakeholder analyses, with examples. In discussing these tools, reflection is offered on their limitations in practice as well as in theory. We also look at the attempts to make development planning more bottom up and participatory, through tools such as the problem tree, as well as attempts to make participation a core part of institutional agendas, with a case study from ActionAid. The chapter also discusses the sector's ambivalent relationship to culture, noting the absence of culture from planning guidance. The absence of such analyses has had many detrimental effects, contrasted with examples here and throughout the book of how anthropological insights can provide essential understanding of the complex interactions communities have with project interventions.

The fourth chapter explores the key planning tools used by most agencies in the core elements of project planning, such as the logframe and theories of change. Explaining the core terms such as goals, objectives and outcomes, it considers the widespread use of the logframe, and its variations across many decades of use. We also look at how the linear constructions and conceptualisations of cause and effect underneath the logframe gave way to theories of change and other more adaptive responses. These have risen to the fore in development discourse in recent years, derived from an awareness of complexity theory, and we look at examples of where project design has been adapted to be more responsive, seeing design as an active and not one-off process. However, the increased role of management demands is also shown to be evident in the shaping of fourth-generation results frameworks, which demand increasing detail of costs and targets.

The next phase of a project is monitoring, explored in Chapter 5. Here we look at mapping out the monitoring of implementation and progress towards objectives and the kinds of indicators needed for this, as well as the implications for system design. The chapter discusses typical approaches to project monitoring and the reality that this is often done more for donors than for management, and underpins single rather than double loop learning, or the possibility of learning from projects as they evolve. Case studies on adaptive and responsive planning underline the importance of participation from different stakeholders in these processes. We also consider some of the institutional challenges of making such dynamics between unequal actors flexible enough. Such monitoring is also framed as a crucial element of top-down surveillance that contemporary project management systems entail.

Chapter 6 considers the last stage of project management, evaluation systems and approaches. This starts with a review of the varied tools and approaches most common in the sector, from randomised controlled trials (RCTs) to process tracing, and situates these in relation to debates about mixed methods within what is often a quantitively focused results system. It explores some of the challenges to the use evaluative knowledge in development, including how a results-focused system discourages the openness necessary for learning. The demands of an audit-based system and its focus on results are contrasted with the need to learn from development work, and explore the challenges within agency systems and structures to creating a learning culture.

The book concludes by reviewing the centrality of the tools of project planning to the nature of projects in development. The gap between theory and practice in relation to the project shows the difficulty in taking a simplifying system to complex environments, and for chasing the multifaceted goals of development. The multiple negative effects of the results agenda, linked to the increasing projectisation of aid, suggest that the time has come to rethink how aid is disbursed and managed. This links to the role of the aid chain in performing an effectively disciplinary audit function. The hierarchies of aid and the power relations they entail in particular need attention and reform in light of calls for the decolonisation of aid and for development agendas to be refocused on systemic means of reversing the growing gap between rich and poor globally. Calls for epistemic reconfigurations around development serve to highlight the narrowing and disciplining effects of the contemporary tools of project management.

Notes

1 In the book I am concerned with development as imminent and deliberate or planned change, rather than immanent development, involving long-term structural changes to society. See Cowen and Shenton 1996. In so doing I refer primarily to the period since the Second World War and particularly work done in the wake of the establishment of the Bretton Woods institutions.
2 See Dean 2010: x for discussion on the various publications of Foucault's lecture on governmentality, originally part of his lectures into 'security, territory, population' at the College de France in 1978.
3 https://ec.europa.eu/europeaid/projects/cambodia-climate-change-alliance-ccca_en
4 Duncan Green's blog 'How Change Happens' and the PELICAN initiative are key examples.

References

Alvesson, Mats and Will Käremman 2004 Interfaces of control. Technocratic and socio-ideological control in a global management accounting firm, *Accounting, Organisations and Society*, 29, 423–444.
Biggs, Stephen and Sally Smith 2003 Paradox of learning in project cycle management and the role of organizational culture, *World Development*, 31(10), 1743–1757.
Bøhren, Øyvind 1998 The agent's ethics in the principal-agent model, *Journal of Business Ethics*, 17(7) (May), 745–755.
Camfield, Laura and Maren Duvendack 2014 Impact evaluation – are we 'off the gold standard'? *European Journal of Development Research*, 26, 1–11. DOI: 10.1057/ejdr.2013.42.
Cooke, Bill 2008 Participatory management as colonial administration, in S. Dar and B. Cooke, eds. *The new development management*, London: Zed Books.
Cooke, Bill and Sadhvi Dar 2008 Introduction: The new development management, in Sadhvi Dar and B. Cooke, eds. *The new development management*, London: Zed Books.
Cowen, M. and R. W. Shenton 1996 *Doctrines of development*, London: Routledge.
Davies, William 2016 *The limits of neoliberalism: Authority, sovereignty and the logic of competition*, Revised edition, London: Sage.

De Haan, Arjan 2009 *How the aid industry works*, West Stamford, CT: Kumarian Press.

Dean, Mitchell 2010 *Governmentality: Power and rule in modern society*, London: Sage Publications.

Eyben, Rosalind 2015 Uncovering the politics of evidence and results, in Rosalind Eyben, Irene Gujit, Chris Roche and Cathy Shutt, eds. *The politics of evidence and results in International development*, Rugby: Practical Action Publishing.

Ferguson, James 1994 *The anti-politics machine: Development, depoliticisation and bureaucratic power in Lesotho*, University of Minneapolis Press.

Foucault, M. 2007 *Security, territory, population: Lectures at the college de France 1977–1978*, Basingstoke: Palgrave Macmillan.

Freeman, Scott and Mark Schuller 2020 Aid projects: The effects of commodification and exchange, *World Development*, 126, 104731. ISSN 0305–750X.

Fukuda-Parr, S., A. E. Yamin and J. Greenstein 2014 The power of numbers: A critical review of millennium development goal targets for human development and human rights, *Journal of Human Development and Capabilities*, 15(2–3), 105–117.

Gasper, D.S. 2000. *Logical Frameworks Potential and Problems*. Teaching Material for ISS Participants, Rotterdram: International Institute of Social Studies of Erasmus University, https://repub.eur.nl/pub/50949/

Girei, Emanuela 2016 NGOs, management and development: Harnessing counter-hegemonic possibilities, *Organization Studies*, 37(2), 193–212.

Girei, Emanuela 2017 Decolonising management knowledge: A reflexive journey as practitioner and researcher in Uganda, *Management Learning 2017*, 48(4), 453–470.

Golini, Ruggero and Paolo Landoni 2013 *International Development Projects: Peculiarities and Managerial Approaches*, Pennsylvania USA: Project Management Institute Inc.

Gordon, Colin 1991 Governmental rationality: An introduction, in G. Burchell, C. Gordon and P. Miller, eds. *The Foucault effect: Studies in governmentality* (pp. 1–52), Chicago, IL: University of Chicago Press.

Gow, D. D. and E. R. Morss 1988 The notorious nine: Critical problems in project implementation, *World Development* 16(12), 1399–1418.

Graeber, David 2015 *The Utopia of rules, on technology, stupidity and the secret joys of bureaucracy*, Brooklyn, NY: Melville House.

Green, M. 2011 Calculating compassion: Accounting for some categorical practices in international development, in D. Mosse, ed. *Adventures in Aidland: The anthropology of professionals in international development*, London: Berghahn Books.

Green, M. 2012 Framing and escaping: Knowledge work in anthropology and in international development, in T. Yarrow and S. Venkatesen, eds. *Differentiating development*, Oxford: Berghahn Books Inc.

Gulranjani, Nilima 2011 Transcending the great foreign aid debate: Managerialism, radicalism and the search for aid effectiveness, *Third World Quarterly*, 32(2), 199–216.

Hira, Anil and Trevor Parfitt 2004 *Development projects for the new millennium*, London: Praeger.

Hirschman, Albert O. 1994 *Development projects observed*, Washington, DC: The Brookings Institution.

Honig, Dan 2018 Navigation by judgment: *Why and when top-down management of foreign aid doesn't work*, Oxford: Oxford University Press.

Ika, Lavagnon and Damian Hodgson 2014 Learning from international development projects: Blending critical project studies and critical development studies, *International Journal of Project Management,* 32(7). DOI: 10.1016/j.ijproman.2014.01.004.

Ika, Lavagnon, A. Diallo and Denis Thuillier 2010 Project management in the international development industry: The project coordinator's perspective, *International Journal of Managing Projects in Business*, 3(1), 61–93.

Jensen, A., C. Thuesen and J. Geraldi 2016 The projectification of everything: Projects as a human condition, *Project Management Journal*, 47(3), 21–34.

Kelly, P. 2006 The entrepreneurial self and 'youth at-risk': Exploring the horizons of identity in the twenty-first century, *Journal of Youth Studies*, 9(1), 17–32.

Kerr, Ron 2008 International development and the new public management: Projects and logframe as discursive technologies of governance, in Sadhvi Dar and B. Cooke, eds. *The new development management*, London: Zed Books.

Krause, Monika 2014 *The good project: Humanitarian relief NGOs and the fragmentation of reason*, London: University of Chicago Press.

Li, T. 2007 *The will to improve: Governmentality, development, and the practice of politics*, Durham, Duke University Press.

Li, Tania Murray 2016 Governing rural Indonesia: Convergence on the project system, *Critical Policy Studies*, 10(1), 79–94. DOI: 10.1080/19460171.2015.1098553.

Marcal, Katrine 2015 *Who cooked Adam Smiths dinner?* London: Portobello Books.

Mawdsley, Emma 2016 Development geography II: Financialization, *Progress in Human Geography*, 1–11.

Merry, Sally Engle 2016 *The seductions of quantification: Measuring human rights, gender violence and sex trafficking*, Chicago: Chicago University Press.

Morris, Peter 2013 Reconstructing project management reprised: A knowledge perspective, *Project Management Journal*, 44(5), 6–23.

Mosse, David and David Lewis eds 2006 *Development Brokers and Translators: The Ethnography of Aid and Agencies*, Boulder CO: Kumarian Press.

Mosse David 2005a *Cultivating development: An ethnography of aid policy and practice*, London: Pluto Press.

Mosse, D. 2005b Global governance and the ethnography of international aid, in D. Mosse and D. Lewis, eds. *The aid effect: Giving and governing in international development*, London: Pluto Press.

OECD 2005 Paris Declaration on Aid effectiveness, Paris: OECD OECD/LEGAL/5017. http://legalinstruments.oecd.org.

Olssen, Mark and M. A. Peters 2005 Neoliberalism, higher education and the knowledge economy: From the free market to knowledge capitalism, *Journal of Education Policy*, 20, 313–345.

Ong, Aihwa 2006 2010 *Neoliberalism as exception: Mutations in citizenship and sovereignty*, Oxfam: Duke University Press.

Parker, M., T, Hanson, A. Vandi, L. Sao Babawo and T. Allen 2019 Ebola, community engagement, and saving loved ones, correspondence, *The Lancet*. http://dx.doi.org/10.1016.

Picciotto, Robert 2020 Towards a 'new project management' movement? An international development perspective, *International Journal of Project Management*, 38(8), 474–485.

Pollit Christopher 2001 Clarifying convergence. Striking similarities and durable differences in public management reform, *Public Management Review*, 3(4), 471–492.

Pollit, Christopher 2016 Managerialism redux? *Financial Accountability & Management*, 32(4) (November), 0267–4424.

Power, Michael 1997 *The audit society: Rituals of verification*, Oxford: Oxford University Press.

Roberts, Susan M., John Paul Jones III and Oliver Frohling 2005 NGOs and the globalization of managerialism: A research framework, *World Development*, 33(11), 1845–1864.

Rondinelli, Dennis 1983 Projects as instruments of development administration: A qualified defence and suggestions for improvement, *Public Administration and Development*, 3, 307–327.

Rostow, W. 1991 *The stages of economic growth: A non communist manifesto*, 3rd edition, Cambridge: Cambridge University Press.

Rottenburg, Richard 2009 *Far-fetched facts. A parable of development aid*, Cambridge, MA: MIT Press.

Sampson, Steven 1996 *Weak States, Uncivil Societies and Thousands of NGOs: Western Democracy Export as Benevolent Colonialism in the Balkans*, in Sanimir Recic (ed.) Cultural Boundaries of the Balkans. Lund: Lund University Press http://www.anthrobase.com/Txt/S/Sampson_S_01.htm

Scott, Caitlin 2022 Audit as confession: The instrumentalisation of ethics for management control, *Critique of Anthropology*, 42(1), 20–37.

Shutt, Cathy 2016 *Towards an alternative development management paradigm?* Stockholm, Sweden: Report for the Expert Group for Aid Studies (EBA).

Strathern, M. 2000 Introduction: New accountabilities, in M. Strathern, ed. *Audit cultures*, London: Routledge.

Thomas, Alan 2000 Development as practice in a liberal capitalist world, *Journal of International Development*, 12(1), 773–787.

Thompson, Hannah 2012 *Cash and child protection: How cash transfer programming can protect children from abuse, neglect, exploitation and violence*, Save the Children UK. www.savethechildren.org.uk/content/dam/global/reports/education-and-child-protection/cash_and_child_protection.pdf.

Turner, Mark, David Hulme and Willy McCourt 2015 *Governance management and development: Making the state work*, 2nd edition, London: Palgrave Macmillan.

Udehn, Lars 2002 The changing face of methodological individualism, *Annual Review of Sociology*, 28, 479–507.

Wallace, Tina, L. Bornstein and J. Chapman 2007 *The aid chain: Coercion and commitment in development NGOs*, Rugby: Practical Action Publishing.

Widmalm, Sten 2016 After NPM, curb your enthusiasm over the principal agent theory, *Statsvetenskaplig Tidskrift*, 118(1), 127–143.

Williams, D. 2012 *International development and global politics: History, theory and practice*, London: Routledge.

Yanguas, Pablo 2018 *Why we lie about aid: Development and the messy politics of change*, London: Zed Books.

2 Project Management in the Aid Sector

In theory, the development sector deploys rational planning tools to ensure good management derived from models developed in industry and commerce. The project is typically seen as functioning in a cycle, that starts with the identification of a problem that needs solving. Practitioners then gather evidence of what needs to change for a specific group of intended beneficiaries. Based on evidence of what has worked elsewhere, a project approach is then developed in consultation with local staff and experts. The work the project will undertake is laid out in a logical framework, built on principles of scientific management, and which sets out how the planned series of inputs and activities as well as the series of effects will deliver the desired change and achieve the practitioners' goals. The logframe allows everyone involved, especially potential donors, to understand the core elements of the project. It also spells out the indicators that will be used to measure and manage the performance of projects and people along the way. Key project metric information will be conveyed to donors so that they can monitor progress in accordance with the plans against which funding was given. Professional project staff with suitable expertise will be hired to deliver the project and their time and activities mapped out on a Gantt chart or similar workplan that shows who is doing what, where, and when, and linked to a clear budget. A monitoring team will gather accurate data at regular intervals about how project implementation is going, allowing management to make small adjustments as needed, and report regularly on progress to the donor. At the end of the project, an impartial evaluation team will fly in and use rigorous methods to measure performance and the extent to which the project has met its objectives and goal. The evaluation may find some areas that could be improved, and potential learning points will be shared with the project team and relevant experts in the sector. They in turn will note the lessons and absorb them into their growing body of expertise to improve the next iteration of similar projects. If the results are good, the project may even be scaled up into a wider programme of work.

In reality, projects are often created because there is an opportunity being offered by a donor. Some assessment of the problem takes place, but a looming deadline means the project proposal is written by staff in another country. The objectives are aligned to the key 'buzzwords' or themes that the donor is prioritising, rather than what local staff or the intended beneficiary community identified as their priorities. The typical approach that the organisation uses is applied, without much consideration of the

DOI: 10.4324/9780429427411-2

local context. The numerous monitoring indicators that the proposal contained turn out to be onerous and difficult for local partners to collect data on, so only some of them get fully reported on, and it is difficult to measure performance. The project leads have to fill out regular reports trying to make sense of the data, which takes up a lot of time. At the end a small internal evaluation is done with a visitor from head office who wants to trial a new evaluation method, which involves complicated logistics and takes up a month of everyone's time. There are some learnings, but the report is quietly put on the shelf because the findings showed the project delivered much less change than expected. The funding agency says the project won't be renewed because a strategic review means they are no longer prioritising that issue or location, and on the ground, the project's limited effects are soon forgotten.

Introduction

The prior summaries of what should and could happen illustrate some of the ways in which reality departs from planning models. In theory, a project will unfold in a series of carefully planned and executed phases that allow for scientific management, with professional technical tools at each stage. In reality, in many projects' life cycles, time is in short supply, and donor priorities for project goals and requirements for reporting have a significant impact on the kind of work undertaken. At each stage of the project cycle, institutional realities derived from power relationships within the aid chain have a significant impact on what happens.

To review these issues, this chapter starts by exploring how project management systems came into the aid sector. This history shows how ideas about science and the possibilities of scientific management came to provide models for the complex processes of development. We then consider the model of project cycle management that this bequeathed to the aid sector. Thinking about the model in practice, the chapter discusses the tools, guidance and manuals through which project cycle management is meant to be enacted. An anthropological perspective is used to consider how they are written to present an apparently scientific version of objective reality, obscuring ambiguity. This in turn suggests that applying these tools to real-world problems requires much interpretation by development practitioners operating in what is often termed 'the aid chain'. We end the chapter by exploring the complicated power relationships that operate within this aid chain, shaping actors' realities and experiences of technical managerialism. Despite the efforts of techno-normative approaches to make planning fit practice better, these are also sustained in power relationships which extended conditions for governmentality. Governmentality's effects are visible in the precision of the tools for planning and in the manner in which individual workers are managed, through a mixture of socio-ideological and bureaucratic control systems (Alvesson and Käremman 2004).

Management Science: From the Factory to Aid HQ

The origins of the tools, technologies and other means of management with which projects are formed must be explored if we are to understand how and why aid work goes wrong. One of the key challenges is that the tools, and indeed the very concept of a project, have been imported into aid from very different origins. The project brings with it technical rationalities such as time management and the linking of time to specific outputs that originate in factory production systems. Its logframes, results and value for money frameworks demand a predetermined linkage of inputs to outputs and outcomes that is copied from planning contexts in which linear causality can be established with relative ease. Many of these tools and concepts presume a machine-like functioning of the world of social and economic change, and in so doing, tend to separate out very complex interrelated parts, without acknowledging their interconnectedness. A good deal of this is down to the history and origins of the project and the management tools around it.

Project planning techniques came into development in the 1960s, bringing with them a range of concepts and tools derived from corporate and military spheres. Rooted in the rise of scientific management from the early 1900s, the project's central role as a management form in development has grown steadily alongside the expansion of management sciences. The roots of this science are generally held to go back to Frederick Taylor's models for the refinement of factory production systems. Analysing the time taken on individual tasks within a factory setting, Taylor was able to propose means of making factories run at maximum efficiency by ensuring these ran alongside each other, without any idle or unproductive time (Adam 2003). This was essential to the factory owner, as factories ran on the basis of wages paid according to time, a development made possible by the expansion of standardised clock time across the US and UK in the late 19th century. Taylor's contemporary in this endeavour produced a workplan, the eponymous Gantt chart that detailed the order in which work was to be undertaken. This is in use today as the basis of time-based workplans (Wilson 2003) that accompany most project proposals, and whose use has been greatly aided by computer software.

The combination of Taylor and Gantt's work in streamlining factory efficiency demonstrates clearly how the goal of management is control (Alvesson and Käremman 2004). A genealogy of concern with the efficient or morally suitable use of time can be traced along Christian historical practices from monasteries in the 8th century onwards, and was given significant impetus by concerns of the Protestant reformation and with the rise of mercantile capitalism (Adam 2003). The correct use of time and metrics for productivity are central to management today, and one of the features of governmentality that the project as a form embodies.

These nascent ideas of scientific management were given refinement in the vast production systems of mid-20th-century America and codified in schools of management at major universities such as Harvard. In the early 1940s, one group of graduates was a cohort of so-called 'whiz kids' who would go on to use statistical analysis to streamline and improve efficiency. Amongst these was Robert McNamara, who applied these techniques to US efforts in the Second World War, the Ford Motor Company and the Department of State, for military campaigns against the Viet Cong. Amongst the hallmarks of his approach to assessing progress in the Vietnam War were enemy body counts published daily on the front of major US newspapers. While this approach was later decried for its simplistic and arrogant focus on metrics at the expense of other modes of expertise (Cukier and Mayer-Schönberger 2013; Muller 2018; Rosensweig 2010), in the 1960s a mastery of quantitative technologies was the cutting edge of management. These modern forms of scientific management made use of statistical analysis, tracking, monitoring and data analysis to discover optimum points for efficiency. By the late 1960s this approach had spread across Washington, DC, from the Pentagon to the World Bank, where PPBS (planning, programming and budgeting systems) were brought into use (Hirschman 1994). Indicative of the era, 1969 saw the establishment of the Project Management Institute (Kerr 2008), which fifty years later considers itself 'the world's leading authority on project management' (PMI 2021).

The prevailing ethos at the time was that "the scientific determination of correct investment choices seemed to be within reach" (Hirschman 1994: ix). Reflecting on his critical review of World Bank projects in the late 1960s, Hirschman noted that this less flattering perspective ran counter to the trends at the time: "In this intellectual atmosphere, it was to act as something of a spoilsport to call attention to very different, and much more problematic, levels of concern about projects" (ibid). If that was the case in the 1960s, it is no less the case now. As seen when exploring some of the tools in use in contemporary development planning and management, where one tool is found faulty, a more complex one often follows, underlining a commitment to the idea that a solution is there for the [scientific] finding.

The goal of ensuring management was as scientific as possible was also being pursued over at USAID, where consultants aiming to give staff "the position of a scientist, rather than a manager" (Fry Associates 1970: 48–49) developed the logframe, or logical framework matrix. Seventy years later, the logframe is still in use across the sector, albeit with modifications. A basic logframe summarises the intentions of a project, along with the means at its disposal to achieve those aims. The logframe matrix, based on four columns and four rows, encapsulates what you want to achieve and how your activities and the component parts will produce the outcomes or intended changes and goals. With the logframe and its associated indicators and reporting tools, projects are expected to "run rationally, according to set budgets, goals and time schedules" (Räisänen and Linde 2004: 103 cited in Kerr 2008: 97). While many adaptations of the logframe and its contents exist, as explored in Chapter 4, its key functions and internal logic are retained in contemporary 'results frameworks' required for measuring and managing project performance in the majority of grant giving today.

An early logframe was adopted in the British aid system in the 1980s, brought into use to better manage work across Overseas Development Agency (the precursor to the standalone Department for International Development [DFID], 1998–2021, now the Foreign Commonwealth and Development Office [FCDO]). In an introduction to staff at the British Council, a senior manager commended the logframe as a source of 'intellectual discipline' (Kerr 2008: 101). The possibility of rationalised control offered by project management systems included organisation and coordination of resources across time and space, including across functionally separate agencies. Project funding allocated to a specific set of ends could be linked with other new 'mediating technologies' (Kerr 2008: 99), including target systems, quotas and ranking, that were to become central to contemporary governance and management. Today lists, rankings, quotas, targets, league tables and reams of other metrics that characterise this New Public Management (NPM) are part of the everyday machinery of government, in use everywhere from hospitals to schools to universities (Muller 2018; Shore and Wright 2015), and they are now the basis for central internal structures of contemporary aid architecture and funding system.

The promise these systems make is to allow those in charge greater knowledge and control of the work they oversee. In the words of British Conservative politician Michael Heseltine in 1987, these methods were appealing to those in charge of governance:

> "When the literacies of the Civil Service and the generalities of their intentions are turned into targets which can be monitored and costed, when information is conveyed in columns instead of screeds, then objectives become clear and progress towards them becomes measurable and far more likely.
> (in Pollit 1993: 58, cited in Shore and Wright 2018)

These means of NPM emerged as a means of centralising control and using management science to govern at a distance as part of the apparatus of the increasingly privatised arms of the state (Fournier and Grey 2000; Kerr 2008; Shore and Wright 2015). The possibilities for scrutiny and surveillance of what was happening with public funds, via comparable data, with information neatly arranged in columns underlines the extent to which this is about making performance management easier for the managers, about a systematisation and streamlining of means of control. These new technologies for management at a distance were particularly relevant to international development as they offered the means to extend managerial control over significant distances of time and space. The project, with defined ends and a predetermined budget, could tie these elements together and provide both parameters and tools for tracking and management accountability.

In addition to the possibilities for surveillance, the 'literacies' in measurement systems that Heseltine refers to as useful for the practices of the civil service suggest the ways these systems have a pedagogic function, as systems of control that discipline and guide (Hogget 1996; Diefenbach 2009). This is a key effect that we see throughout the panoply of tools explored here that accompany the project. At every step of project development, criteria and standards are demanded that shape and guide what should be contemplated and how. Project funding formats and grant application forms specify the kinds of meanings that are expected, thus constituting a disciplining device (Duval et al. 2015), as is argued of the tools discussed here. The tools through which the data and concepts for filling out these forms are part of this linked process of disciplining, of exacting management control over what is done, where and how by demanding specific meanings, and ensuring these are part of wider systems of control. Amongst the technologies of NPM in use in development are target systems, quotas, ranking, project cycle management, logframe analysis and a raft of technical language of indicators. Today these technologies are widely used to ensure that development aid serves its intended purposes. Most professional development workers will be familiar not just with logframes, theories of change and project cycle management ideas, but often with a whole complementary suite of technologies specific to their subset of the sector.

The spread of these tools and systems for project management and evaluation accelerated through the early 2000s in the wake of growing clamours for aid efficiency and proof of efficacy under the Paris agenda, as well as increased reliance on grant funding of many aid agencies. The results agenda as imposed on the UK's DFID reflected the push for more control over aid, but also pressures to control foreign aid budgets as a result of the 2007–08 financial crisis. As Valters and Whitty note, this

> oriented DFID's vision to the short-term and narrow results of projects rather than wider processes of change. It has shifted the balance towards prioritising accountability to UK taxpayers over poor people abroad. It has been premised on the misleading idea that aid projects can be planned and implemented with certainty about the outcomes.
>
> (2017: 8)

The results agenda has led to the growth of monitoring and evaluation functions and approaches, as agencies compete to show their effectiveness in a shrinking pool of funding. One example of this is agencies stating how many beneficiaries they reach annually, with some larger INGOs developing comprehensive systems for tracking the aggregates of their work, in 'dashboards' of indicators that track project locations, number of beneficiaries, millions spent, millions saved and so on. Complementary to this focus on results and outcomes have been tools which demand agencies measure their cost effectiveness, such as value for money (see Shutt 2015).

One of the notable features of this focus on results has been that the measurement of impact is often narrowed to metric assessment; or that what counts is what can be counted. If donors want to know what their money has been spent on, it is easier to explain this in terms of thousands vaccinated rather than complex messy processes of right awareness training, for example, or engagement with drivers of systemic inequality that will take many years to produce change. This has meant that funding for strategic but 'messy' or complex work has often been harder to find. Critics have observed that the results agenda and the spread of managerial systems within development over the last twenty years has reduced scope for creativity and narrowed the ends to which development can work (Yanguas 2018; Mosse 2005; Eyben et al. 2013). As Rondinelli (1983) notes it is ironic that as problems have become more complex, planning systems have become more rigid. It has also tended to shift risk more onto development actors, as endeavoured in payment by results approaches, whereby aid is only disbursed upon achievement of pre-agreed outcomes (Clist 2016), as donors minimise their own risks (Yanguas 2018).

The broader but more subtle effects of systems of management power in and around projects are addressed by critical perspectives on management, as discussed in Chapter 1, that have sought to analyse the ways in which power relations are manifest in management, and to 'denaturalise' these and expose management science's ideological underpinnings (Alvesson and Wilmott 2012; Fournier and Grey 2000; Dar and Cooke 2008; Thomas 2000). While there has been some resistance to RBM within the aid sector, it remains to an extent the privileged purview of those who have the space, access and opportunity to engage with critical reflections. The fact that management is generally understood, and largely accepted, as a useful and important means of producing efficiency in a market-centric world is based on understanding this as a rational, neutral science. But this presentation of management as scientific, technical and therefore objective and neutral veils its role in sustaining inequality (Cooke 2008). For as critics of its role in development have argued, managerialism is designed to support political and economic interests that are directly contrary to the interests of poor people (Fine and Jomo 2006; McCourt and Johnson 2012). It can also contain and neutralise social change because it turns every problem into a technical one (Klikauer 2015).

Where technical tools of the project are presented as neutral, they are disconnected from the social, economic and political forces which created them. Mundane and everyday practices, such as those pursued in relation to projects, can have dehumanising effects, as ends are pursued instrumentally, and without due consideration of process. The logframe is perhaps most apparent in its pursuit of this logic of means and ends, but other tools also conceal as much as they reveal. Part of their allure is the apparent simplicity and logic with which management tools present their tasks. In the central tool we consider next, project cycle management, we see how planned change is presented as clear, logical and effectual.

The Project as a Series of Coordinated Actions: Project Cycle Management

One of the most common ways of conceptualising projects management is as a cycle. Since project cycle management (PCM) entered into use in the 1970s at the World Bank, it has become standard in the industry, used across the European Community and more (Baum 1978; Biggs and Smith 2003; Ika and Hodgson 2014; Picciotto and Weaving 1994). This cycle starts with potential implementers identifying a problem to be solved, then identifying a solution, supporting the implementation of the project, and finally, subjecting the project to some evaluation or assessment. At each stage of the cycle, a series of tools is often recommended, as explored in subsequent chapters.

Project cycles are frequently diagrammed, providing an appealing and visually clear appearance. A basic model is shown in Figure 2.1, a version of which is present in many technical guidance manuals, providing a central framework for structuring the tools that accompany each stage. The number of stages in the cycle can vary, so while the World Bank identifies six stages in its version, the model discussed here is four. The following sections walk through a simple introduction to how this is meant to work.

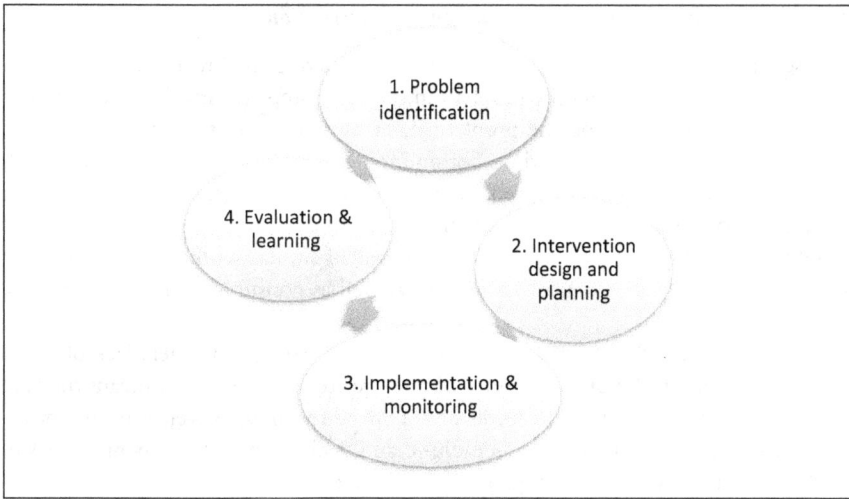

Figure 2.1 A basic project cycle

Source: The author

Stage 1: Identify Problem

The first step or start is defining the problem to be addressed, or the vision that is a response to a problem. This could be, for example, farmers' lack of access to credit or girls' dropout rates between primary and secondary school in a particular location. Any such symptoms of the problems need to be analysed, as does the broader situation. This might include wider structural problems such as economic marginalisation or environmental degradation that are root causes of the problem and that produce the visible problem a project is addressing.

At the first phase of investigating and defining a problem, common tools include a situation analysis, based on the latest statistical data on the sector to understand the scale and nature of the problem, such as how many people are affected, and reviewing what is going on at policy level nationally. This and other tools are discussed in Chapter 3, on project inceptions. Another simple tool inspired by critiques of top-down planning is a problem tree, that looks at those problematic root causes and can be used in a participatory process to understand these factors from within a local perspective. These can be complemented with one of various forms of political economy analysis (PEA), that look at the interactions between political and other forms of power, and identify who is involved in policy-making decisions and with what influence. From this data and analysis, a clearer definition and understanding of a problem can be achieved, and against this, a goal or objective formulated in relation to the solution needed. All this data and analysis will also feed into a background section of a written project proposal and be used to show that the project is intervening in a clearly defined problem, of significant scale and of which there is a good understanding.

Stage 2: Choose an Approach and Design an Intervention

The second key step is to design an intervention. Taking the broad kind of solution envisaged from considering the problem in step one, step two involves working out the best *approach* to solving the problem(s), or as many aspects of it as are feasible within the three-year (or so) time constraints. Examining exactly what approach is best suited should be considered via a review of the evidence of previous work undertaken on similar issues in the organisation and drawing on staff expertise. This should ideally also involve review of evaluations of similar work done globally, via systematic reviews of evidence if available, as well as consulting with local experts, staff and consultants.

The approach will determine what is done. If, for example, farmers' lack of access to credit is found to be one of a series of inter-related problems that means they are using an unimproved variety of seed, cannot afford fertiliser, as well as having problems with irrigation sources, then a multi-strand solution might be opening lines of credit to them through a cooperative, incorporate agricultural extension work on using new seed varieties, and irrigation measures such as digging new ponds for rain capture. Some form of self-help groups might also be created so that farmers can talk to and support each other in their efforts.

These various strands of activity will then be spelt out in the text of a logframe or other results framework, that sets out on paper to a donor what you intend to do to remedy the situation. This will set out the goal(s) and objectives of the project, as well as determine in what order which activities and inputs will be needed to realise those changes. Alongside the plans for the activities, the results framework needs to identify how the project will be monitored. Monitoring involves regularly checking on the project's delivery and whether or not it is delivering both activities and changes according to the intended plan. Planned changes may be underwritten by a theory of change, an articulation of how it is expected that the approach will produce the expected changes, complemented by a theory of action at a lower level that accounts for how interventions can accelerate this change. This theory of change might be that with the new ponds there will be more water, which in turn will provide more consistent irrigation which, coupled with the seeds and the newly available fertiliser, farmers will see increased yields from their crops and hence more profit and thus improved income and living conditions for them and their families.

Stage 3: Implement and Monitor (and Learn)

Once the project plan has been finalised and has funding or approval, the project is ready to implement. Unless it's rolling over from previous work, this often means hiring new staff, arranging new facilities, building new partnerships or relationships and sealed with contracts or memorandums of understanding that will enable the work of the plan to be carried out. Plans will need to be made according to the kinds of objectives to be achieved, and involve multiple strands of work and require several types of action. This might involve hiring some agricultural experts to train extension workers who will also work with farmers' associations, developing the credit arrangements and systems, perhaps with a mobile phone element for tracking payments and credit, and setting up the monitoring and evaluation system. Some work will be about the management of material inputs also, such as setting up distribution systems for the improved seeds, renting or building storehouses, and delivering new tools to project locations. Successful projects also involve building social and political alliances, so involve discussion and meetings to achieve broader aims with implementing partners, allies or counterparts. Some of this start-up work will also be about setting up the financial and support infrastructure to align with the project. Sometimes a baseline exercise will have been built into the plan, for example, to verify scant or partial data on farmers' existing levels of productivity and income. Such a baseline is essential for later determining to what extent planned improvements have made a difference so that performance can be measured and managed.

Once the project is underway, the monitoring and evaluation (M&E) plan is put into gear. This work will check whether the project is delivering as expected: are farmers' workshops being well attended, and are farmers interested in the new credit and seed as hoped and planned for? Measuring progress against logframe indicator targets at regular intervals, and holding regular meetings to review the evidence on performance, will allow adaptation of the implementation or overall plan as necessary (and possible). It might be that in one project area there is resistance to the plans and that efforts here are either redoubled, reconfigured or abandoned. To do your M&E, you may well have a specific member of staff appointed to manage the data and the systems for this process. If your project is part of a larger organisation or programme, data from your project may get aggregated to a wider set of data. Monitoring reports will also need to be planned for, at whatever intervals the donor has requested.

Stage 4: Evaluate and Learn

The final phase of evaluation and final learnings takes place as the project nears completion. After the two and a bit years have elapsed, and possibly with a mid-term review having taken place, you will be looking towards the end of the project and the need to conduct a final evaluation of the project and its successes, or otherwise. A final evaluation should allow all involved to understand to what extent the project made a difference. It will involve going back to the goal and outcome indicators in the original logframe and designing terms of reference for a consultant to assess progress towards these as well as analyse other aspects of project performance. Evaluations are often external to ensure impartiality or at least reduce bias, involve experts using rigorous methodologies, and usually required by donors. The evaluation terms of reference suggest evaluators should assess whether the project has met key OECD criteria, of relevance, efficiency, effectiveness, impact and sustainability. The planning for this may involve structuring visits, making data available and holding various meetings to discuss findings. The final evaluation is likely to offer lessons or learning, about what went right or wrong and what could be done better next time. This information should, in an ideal world, add to the professional expertise developed by all staff. You may be pleased with some outcomes and learn from those you're not. This can feed into the next phase of the project cycle and the next iterations of the project approach to be used, and so the cycle spins forward.

Manuals, Toolkits and the Search for Technocratic Perfectibility

One of the clearest ways in which management technologies and tools make their way into development is through manuals. Most agencies, from the UN to modestly sized charities, advocate the use of standard tools as spelt out in these guides, to ensure that projects are designed to the required standard. As demand for required results has spread over recent decades, an endless array of manuals and how-to guides have appeared to help practitioners with both general and specific tools, growing as technical specialists try to find new and improved ways of designing specific kinds of indicators, stakeholder analyses, or many other of the technical steps and tools of the trade. As noted by Kerr (2008) of the arrival of the logframe at the ODA, such tools are often accompanied by introductions which stress their importance. Two of the manuals I draw on here provide readers with pointers about how the instructions within them are to be used and interpreted; or we might say, instructions about the instructions.

The first is the second edition of the Save the Children manual *Toolkits: a practical guide to planning, monitoring, evaluation and impact assessment*, written by Louisa Gosling with Michael Edwards, a 2003 update to a 1995 volume. The first paragraph of the first chapter underscores where this has come from:

> When *Toolkits* was first published in 1995, many people saw planning, monitoring, review and evaluation as something imposed on them from outside, mostly by donors. There is still enormous pressure from donors, who increasingly impose stringent proposal and reporting requirements.
>
> (2003: 3)

However, it concludes that introduction by noting that good programme management is now "much more widely accepted by development practitioners" (ibid). The Save the Children toolkit re-introduces the idea of programming for improved effects within the child rights programming framework and devotes a whole chapter to involving people, with suggestions and caveats on how participatory processes can be used. It also at different points notes how exercises can be directed and managed, and identifies certain challenges that may be encountered (e.g. ibid: 61).

The gently propositional tone of this manual contrasts somewhat with that taken in the UNDP's 2009 *Handbook on Planning, Monitoring and Evaluation for Development Results*, which positions the role of planning more as a commandment.

In the Foreword by the then administrator, results-based management approach is explained as "tools which help us achieve goals". It carries on noting that this "requires us to embrace a culture of evaluation" (2009: i). In the opening pages, the handbook is explained as being for use as a reference throughout the programme cycle, and that its purpose is to explain the importance of various planning functions as well as to describe these (ibid: 3–5). It further underlines the importance of results-based management (RBM) and Management for Development Results (MfDR) that: "The culture of results orientation and the principles of RBM and MfDR must be embraced by all in order for UNDP to effectively contribute to human development". This sounds less of an encouragement than an instruction to follow certain disciplinary cultural guidelines within the organisation. It provides a good example of the ways in which RBM was imposed on the sector and within which it was impossible to disagree. This has echoes of the context of the observation made of project planning in the 1960s that to point out the risks of such systems was to go against the grain of the fashionable certainty around science (Hirschman 1994).

A few key points are relevant in relation to the origins, functions and effects of these manuals. The first is their apparent universality. These manuals have a very specific tone and language, designed to be both neutral and as universal as possible. The metaphor of a toolbox, neatly applied by Edwards and Gosling, continues in contemporary use. It implies the anodyne functionality of a plumber or electrician's toolbox, a set of instruments and approaches that with maximum utility and minimum fuss or further elaboration can accomplish the central tasks of producing sound and logical solutions to the myriad problems and challenges of development planning.

This leads us to a second observation about manuals, which is that they are written at a level of generality. This generality is typical of development writing. There is an imagined general development story to which writing is often pitched. This often takes on unique characteristics, that hover mid-air between idealisation and instruction. The anthropologist Mosse notes of the manuals created around a project he worked on for a decade in India, that they had an

> incentive to produce a coherent representation blurs the boundary between the normative and the descriptive, so that project planning manuals become cited and reproduced in project or donor texts as project experience. Of course this reproduces rather than resolves project contradictions.
>
> (2005: 164)

The blurring of the distinction between normative and descriptive means that the manuals present a model as if it were a representation of experience, as if what they were speaking of was exactly what had happened. In Mosse's view they thus represent or constitute a kind of official modelling of what this is supposed to look like, but which actually works to obscure much of the messy, contested and less successful elements of the process.

What this means is that the manuals themselves, by functioning in the level of generality, obscure the vast differences between theory and practice. Rather than being informed by a grounded reality, manuals persist in advancing myths of technologically managed development. Take how time is presented in the project cycle diagram as an example (Figure 2.2). In most project cycles, the lifetime of the project is represented as a looping cycle. At the pinnacle of that cycle is planning on the basis of the learning that emanates from the evaluations done at the end of the project, learning which should nominally inform the next iteration of the project.

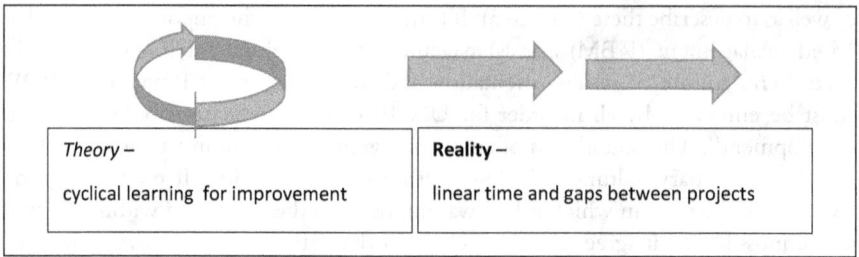

Figure 2.2 Project time in cycle theory and reality
Source: The author

However, in real life, projects are not delivered in a cyclical fashion. The model glosses over the fact that in reality, development projects inevitably occur in a linear manner through time. Learning lessons from evaluations, and between projects, is dependent on there being staff whose job it is to collect and synthesise that data and ensure it reaches the right people. At the end of a project, many staff come to the end of their contracts and leave, taking any learning they have acquired during the project process and from the evaluation with them, which they may or may not be able to apply where they work next. There may be a long time lapse between one project and another, by which time the favoured approaches may have changed. The findings of the evaluation may also be rejected, or as sometimes happens, withheld or hidden because they are simply too embarrassing for professional reputations. Moreover, learning itself is often a casualty or loss of the way RBM shapes aid today, as more effort is directed towards reporting than learning. The fact that in reality in project cycles the learning often falls between the gaps in projects and institutional ownership or responsibility, means that even this basic model for the project does not reflect reality.

A third point is that manuals are often built up as guidance for how to do things on the basis of a best-case scenario. That best-case scenario is stripped, a bit like a white-walled TV studio, of the specifics of culture, time and place, so as to be the perfect scene for the scientifically planned and instituted development. But reality does not take place in such laboratory-like conditions. Instead there are cultural habits, processes, tendencies, ways of thinking about time, environmental conditions, local and national politics, and so on, that are going to deeply affect the way actual work plays out. As Gasper notes, "Manuals are written to inspire confidence, but they do not mention the ups-and-downs of these methods in many organizations" (2000: 19). To this end, they perpetuate a myth around the relevance and utility of one-size-fits-all development approaches. This universalising tone of writing helps the tools dissolve the political and ethical questions that frame development encounters and projects. They render the complex power relations of the development encounter into a series of tasks and steps, in which actors' roles are specified in relation to the performance of specific tasks, rather than who they are in relation to a series of questions of race, nationality, rank and position.

Moreover, most manuals exclude any consideration of the cultural and organisational circumstances in which projects will actually be implemented. Culture is typically either ignored, as irrelevant to the technocratic progress being outlined or maligned, as a source of 'traditional' or harmful cultural practices which are inconsistent with rational progress and modernity. This is a key point, to which I return in the next chapter.

The simplified project planning model I outlined at the start of the chapter illustrates the ideal type that manuals present. In the book we look at the project cycle stages and elements of the project and look at various tools associated with each. As tools, we can consider what questions they ask practitioners to make or pose, what issues may be left out, and how their temporality may play out in the contexts of the project's life span. We can also think about how together these elements of the project produce effects about what we can do in development contexts within the funding and time frames available.

This does not mean that those producing such manuals are motivated by deceit; on the contrary, there is great concern to improve these constantly. Instead it is about the fact that they need to exist on a level of generality in which messy detail is barely acknowledged. This is partly about the institutional politics of representation, but also about the level and tone which manuals need to work at. As such development practices, although not uniform, are in their technocratic guide, stripped of the specifics which have helped to generate postulations and ideas. As we read then, we must be aware of this specific genre of writing and the blank space into which it often seems to be pointed. How does this blank space become real? How do the instructions, necessarily generic in their formulation, get interpreted and transformed into guidance for specific actions?

Many of the events through which these transformations happen are meetings, of various kinds, as projects are partly enacted through meetings. Thousands of these take place across the world daily, from small office meetings to large conferences and workshops. Meetings are thus important moments for the diffusion and discussion of the use of tools, and are also shaped by them. Technical specialists are dispatched or log onto video conferencing software to impart specialist knowledge to counterparts in field offices, country offices and regional hubs around the world. These meetings may offer a chance to "structure responsibilities for implementation" (Brown and Green 2017: 45), but what happens in these meetings, and how are new ideas and responsibilities translated and received? Meetings are also important moments in the development of the narratives and 'shared' views of projects. As Sandler and Thedvall (2017) note, meetings have a generative role, maintaining an organisation, and as sites and moments for the reproduction of power relations, may act as rituals of legitimation and space for trust building. Thus the meeting itself should be a focus of attention, particularly in the complex arrangements of power that the contemporary aid chain relies on.

Delivering Projects in the Aid Chain

Aid projects are funded by a range of both public and private sources, and delivered by an increasingly diverse set of actors. One of the key factors in understanding the institutional parameters of aid delivery, and how the various parts of the sector form an 'aid chain' (Wallace et al. 2007; Larsen 2010; Friberg 2015). This hierarchical view allows us to consider how the different organisations involved in this chain are staffed and relate to each other. A traditional view of projects in development might involve NGOs running small or medium size projects in rural areas of the world. Readers and others may envision this being enacted by a small team that knows the community well, talking to locals as they build a well or share improved farming techniques. The NGO staff might be local but are also likely to include foreign workers. This outfit is probably attached to or getting funding from an INGO based in the north. Back in the headquarters of that INGO, in London or Geneva, will be a cadre of experts in that technical field or specialism that the agency draws on to design programmes. These experts are in turn attending to debates at a global level about the best ways forward in rural agriculture and water sanitation, and probably attend conferences with UN experts, deliver papers at academic institutions and otherwise ensure they deliver expertise that in turn supports good work on the ground. That image may not be wholly unrealistic, but it is also only a small slice of the complex field of relations that characterises contemporary aid delivery.

Many public agencies and private foundations have very specific and limited goals which they support work on. Within these goals, different donors within the aid community choose their own geographical perspectives and preferences, aligning to the aforementioned global priorities such as SDGs but also reflecting national political and economic interests and foci. For example, Scandinavian bilateral agencies have often supported human rights and civil society funding, and the Swedish agency SIDA works across 15 areas, including education, agriculture and food security, peace and inclusive societies, democracy and human rights (SIDA 2022). Meanwhile in the UK, priorities for FCDO work have recently included global health security, including spending on vaccines and pre-Covid initiatives such as GAVI; girls' education, economic development and trade, and humanitarian assistance (Raab 2021).

Alongside such bilateral donors are multilateral bodies such as the European Commission, parts of the United Nations and private organisations such as the Gates and Soros foundations. Within many countries there are also smaller trusts and foundations which give to specific projects, and many abroad. We look at different actors in more depth in the next chapter.

To enable these packages of aid to flow are grants, which are typically formulated around projects. These are produced in response to calls for proposals from donor agencies, or sometimes subcontracted out to management consultancy firms, that outline what specific kinds of change and approaches they will fund, as well as outline the possibilities that funding offers. The processes for these grants form a significant part of conditions and limitations for development projects. This set of hierarchies in aid funding means that most projects are the product of a complex set of relationships which are usually hierarchical, and within which demands are made in ways that cascade downwards. Examining it specifically is important to understanding the ways project management functions in practice and in relation to grants.

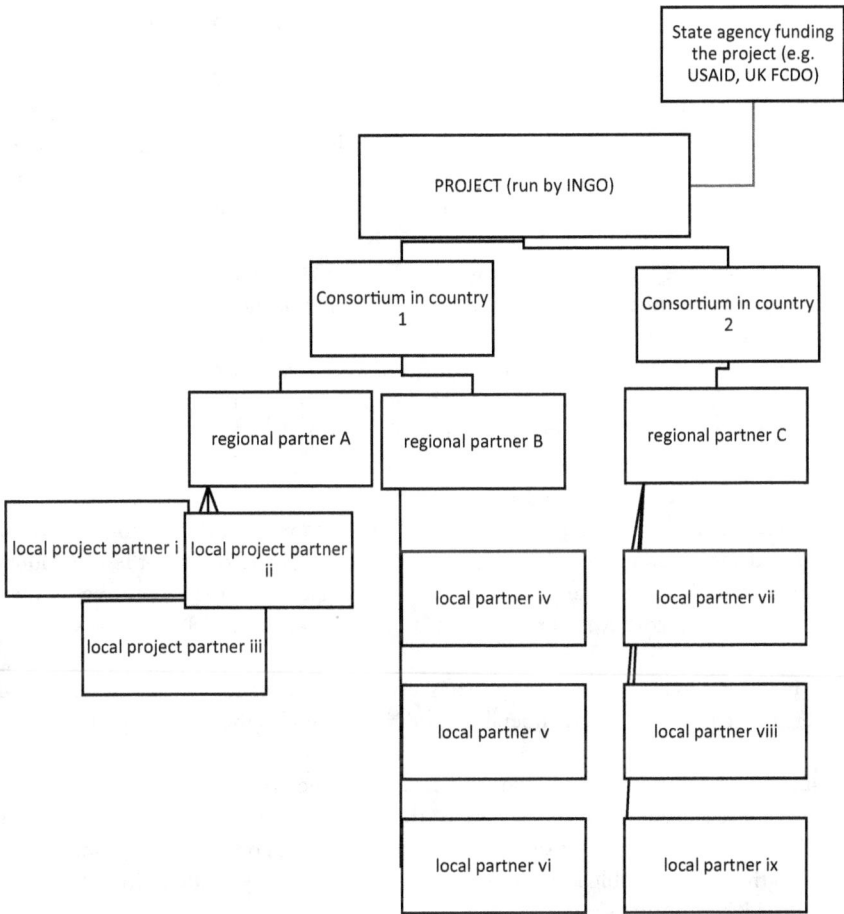

Figure 2.3 An illustration of a project in the aid chain
Source: The author

The diagram in Figure 2.3 shows an example whereby a set of local partners are receiving money from a regional partner, which in turn is receiving money from an organisation in another country, and this is taking money from a donor agency in a northern donor country. In this vertical slice of the aid chain, we see a series of links in a set of hierarchical relationships. At each level of these are relations of power, often involving the provision or withholding of funds. At each level of the chain, accountabilities flow upwards. Money trickles down, accompanied by reporting requirements, with complex systems for data as you near the top of the chain or hierarchy. To respond to these, data flows upwards, producing funding and reporting. The process of reporting on results places a significant onus on grant receivers.

These processes form the reporting infrastructure through which the power relationships of the aid chain are institutionalised. This chain enacts some of the more problematic effects of the contemporary focus on results, including the distorting effects they have on what aid workers do with their time and the manner in which indicators judge performance in ways which may inhibit learning. It is widely acknowledged that contemporary reporting systems involve a significant amount of paperwork, taking up considerable proportions of aid workers' time (Hindman and Fechter 2014; Scott 2022; Walsh 2016). Regular reporting against batteries of indicators for every stage of project implementation is time consuming, channelling energies towards monitoring pre-agreed indicators. This not only reduces the time and mental space in which development planners and thinkers can create and work on other issues, but it can also have distorting effects and offer perverse incentives. These show some of the impacts of audits on projects, whereby reporting does not just occupy time but also demands that work is shaped, in advance, by the knowledge that it will be inspected and thus shapes thinking. This distorting process is evident in indicators, for rather than reflecting work, indicators can easily become the targets, as per Goodheart's Law, which holds that when an indicator is used for control, it can be gamed or worked around (Muller 2018). So while these accountability systems are nominally there to improve aid effectiveness, they can distort, hinder learning (Scott 2016) and preclude honesty (Yanguas 2018), because so much is riding on meeting specific targets.

These processes suggest how projects become vehicles for spreading neoliberal governmentality, creating neoliberal sensibilities and enforcing the discipline of market logics. They enlist both agencies and workers in processes that demand both financial transparency and performative legibility. The emphasis on NPM rationalities has shifted attention from the *what* to the *how* within aid, such that concern is as much on efficacy and expertise in project management as on knowledge of context.

Two trends are notable in relation to this issue. One is the proliferation of projects within aid, the result of the parcelling of aid into a large number of smaller-value projects (Banks and Brockington 2020). The common language aid actors need to speak is not so much that of a deep humanitarian commitment, but one of project management. A second is the increase and diversity in the numbers of actors and agencies working on projects.

Who Runs and Works on Projects

Today, projects are delivered by a multiplicity of actors, large and small, corporate and not for profit, close to the grassroots and very far away from it, what some term the 'aid industrial complex'. From the 1990s onwards, NGOs around the world became recipients of new money as slimmed-down central governments looked to voluntary social institutions to provide services that neoliberal doxa deemed outside the remit of the state (Banks and Hulme 2012). NGOs began to compete in a market for both public attention and government funds, and around the world terms such as 'briefcase NGOs' rose to the fore as the market for projects grew. By the mid-2010s, this had led to complaints that NGOs had all but abandoned their 'long-term goals of social justice' in a sector that was very clearly 'narrowly focused on short-term results and value for money' (Banks et al. 2015: 708). As neoliberal logics entered the non-profit sector, so partnerships between the state and companies, or companies and charities, have all increased over recent years. These include the outsourcing of the management of state-funded work to private management consultancy firms, such as the accountancy firm Price Waterhouse Coopers in London which managed the DFID-funded Girls Education Challenge Fund (GEC Alliance n.d.[1]),

In the era of financialisation, extending the neoliberal logic of commodification into ever new areas and the means to "transform development into a new frontier for financial speculation" (Hart et al. 2021: 860), projects can also be purposively reframed as asset classes for investment (Mawdsley 2016). The impact for communities of this new strand of investment and set of actors is less clear. Other new sources of project funding include 'philanthrocapitalists' and large foundations such as the Open Society Foundation and the Bill and Melinda Gates Foundation, which disburse billions of dollars annually. Ironically many new donors have been enriched by, and are evidence of, capitalism's distortions and inequities, and are argued to act as extensions of neoliberal hegemony into development in unaccountable and opaque ways (Mediavilla and Garcia Arias 2019; McGoey 2012).

With the rise of project funding, projects also form a key organising principle of employment in the development sector. This has a number of notable impacts. One of these is that the project as a management tool proposes the division of the planned work into specific tasks and according to often siloed specialisms. This focuses people on specific sets of tasks, and by the same token, often enacts boundaries, which workers may not be invited to understand or move beyond. Indeed the stripping of professional autonomy has been noted as a key effect, if not also a goal, of results-based management systems in sectors as diverse as higher education and health (Shore and Wright 2015, 2018; Muller 2018). As per factory divisions of labour, the divisions of task-specific roles were in fact one of the key insights of early management science. A project's orchestrations means that within it, workers need not know or agree with the overarching goal to which different parts of the project are meant to contribute. That oversight is the purview of management, as is the way in which such a goal fits with other key objectives for a larger organisation or wider programme. This structural feature of the project is one of the salient features of what is noted to be one of the most successful projects, the Manhattan Project to build the atomic bomb. More than 100,000 engineers, scientists, technicians and others worked on individual parts of the project puzzle, but for multiple political and security reasons, only a very few knew about the final project objective.

Several other factors shape the ways in which workers function around grants. Linked to the fact that much funding in the sector is restricted to project grants with minimal funding for overheads, many aid workers are today employed on short-term contracts linked to grants. These short-term relations may be linked to a noted decreased in the prevalence of political or social motivations. Fechter notes the mixed motivations and intricate array in the moral economies in aid work that include motives which are financial, professional, personal as well as altruistic (2014: 141). In her analysis of aid workers in Nepal, Hindman notes that few mention the issues of poverty around them, and many do not see themselves as aid workers at all, but as technical experts who come in from one project to another to deliver a specific piece of work. Many are highly mobile, and so do not develop links to any place as they move between a series of short-term contracts (Hindman 2014: 183–186). This complements the depoliticising of NGOs, who because they often deploy generalist people with a lack of knowledge of context, helps organisations to produce little more than a "meek confirmation of western policy" (Jacoby 2005: 223).

Conclusions

Reviewing the way projects shape the work of aid suggests some of the disciplining mechanisms with which projects in the contemporary aid industry function. Short-termism shapes not only projects but also staff contracts, a brevity that has been observed to heighten a sense of disconnection amongst aid workers from the contexts in which they work. At the same time, reporting and audit mechanisms shape much of the content and day-to-day of aid work, as reporting on project progress and other kinds of upwards accountability are time consuming. The growing centrality of project management tools, such as the project cycle management approach outlined in the chapter, has been a key part of the history of development management, as approaches were brought in from commercial contexts to increase management control in the sector. Today each stage of project cycle management is accompanied by a range of tools that guide and to a significant extent determine the kinds of work that are done to shape and define projects.

The tools, however apparently innocuous and universal in their mechanistic allusion, in fact determine very significantly how problems are transformed from ones of deep poverty linked to historical inequities and global patterns of trade to ones amenable to a short-term intervention and a technical 'fix'. The disconnect from reality of many of the manuals and guidance documents is enabled by the way they are written, in a heavily generalised style intended to allow for translation into different realities. This is one part of the reasoning offered for the extensive gap between theory and reality. In the review of project cycle management, for example, the fact that the neat system of stages is unlikely to function that way in reality is also down to the realities of the aid chain and project time frames. The short-term contracted employees may well not be there to carry knowledge and learning between one project and another.

Moreover, the quantified means of auditing aid are linked to the aid chain, the hierarchy through which accountabilities are demanded. The logics in NPM that have had such an impact on the sector in the last twenty years are reflected in the techniques and the increasingly diverse new actors in the sector. Many of the new organisations and actors within aid are linked to private finance, as excess capital in western financial markets is being directed to financialised projects in developing economies, with more interest in returns than social objectives. Another aspect of the shift away from traditional bilateral donors is evident in the new class of philanthropists in the sector who have made extraordinary fortunes in the vastly unequal context of contemporary capitalism have also entered the sector, with their own agendas.

These shifts have been made possible by the neoliberal logics that underwrite development management today. Indeed, whatever shortcomings of NGOs and civil societies exist, is also the case that aid levels and their contingencies mean that there has never been anything like the level of support needed to redress the inequities of the global playing field. As global governance systems are increasingly tilted towards the interests of companies and markets rather than states and citizens, debate around how to address structural inequities is more urgent than ever. The fact that management may in fact conceal the ways in which it supports those inequalities was reviewed in relation to the ways management has entered the sector. In the next chapter, we consider what these look like at the start of a project, in the inception phase.

Note

1 See also https://girlseducationchallenge.org/.

References

Adam, B. 2003 When time is money: Contested rationalities of time in the theory and practice, *Theoria: A Journal of Social and Political Theory* (102) History and Liberty. (December), 94–125.

Alvesson, M. and W. Käremman 2004 Interfaces of control. Technocratic and socio-ideological control in a global management accounting firm, *Accounting, Organisations and Society*, 29, 423–444.

Alvesson, M. and Hugh Wilmott 2012 *Making sense of management: A critical introduction*, London: Sage.

Banks, Nicola and Dan Brockington 2020 Growth and change in Britain's development NGO sector (2009–2015), *Development in Practice*, 30(6), 706–721. DOI: 10.1080/09614524.2020.1801587.

Banks, N. and D. Hulme 2012 *The role of NGOs and civil society in development and poverty reduction*, BWPI Working Paper 171, Manchester: The Brooks World Poverty Institute. https://papers.ssrn.com/sol3/papers.cfm?abstract_id=2072157.

Banks, N., D. Hulme and M. Edwards 2015 NGOs, states, and donors revisited: Still too close for comfort? *World Development* 66, 707–718.

Baum, W. C. 1978 The world bank project cycle, *Finance & Development (pre-1986)*, 15(000004), 10.

Biggs, Stephen and Sally Smith 2003 Paradox of learning in project cycle management and the role of organizational culture, *World Development*, 31(10), 1743–1757.

Brown, Hannah and M. Green 2017 Demonstrating development: Meetings as management in Kenya's health sector, *Journal of the Royal Anthropological Institute (N.S.)*, 45–62.

Clist, Paul 2016 *Payment by results in development aid: All that glitters is not gold*, Norwich: University of East Anglia.

Cooke, Bill 2008 Participatory management as colonial administration, in S. Dar and B. Cooke, eds. *The new development management*, London: Zed Books.

Cukier, Kenneth and Viktor Mayer-Schönberger 2013 The dictatorship of data: Robert McNamara epitomizes the hyper-rational executive led stray by numbers, *MIT Technology Review*, Business Reports, May 31.

Dar, Sadhvi and Bill Cooke, eds 2008 *The new development management*, London: Zed Books.

Diefenbach Thomas 2009 New public management in public sector organizations: The dark sides of managerialistic 'enlightenment', *Public Administration*, 87(4), 892–909.

Duval, Anne-Marie, Yves Gendron and Christophe Roux-Dufort 2015 Exhibiting non-governmental organizations: Reifying the performance discourse through framing power, *Critical Perspectives on Accounting*, 29, 31–53.

Eyben, Rosalind, Irene Gujit, Chris Roche, Cathy Shutt and Brendan Whitty 2013 *The politics of evidence: Conference report*, The Big Push Forward. http://bigpushfor ward.com/wp-content/uploads/2014/06/BPF-PoE-conference-report.pdf.

Fechter 2014 Anybody at home? The inhabitants of Aidland, in M. Fechter and H. Hindman, eds. *Inside the everyday lives of development workers: The challenges and futures of Aidland*, London: Kumarian Press.

Fine, B. and K. S. Jomo, eds 2006 *The new development economics: After the Washington consensus*. London: Zed.

Fournier, Valerie and Chris Gray 2000 At the critical moment: Conditions and prospects for critical management studies, *Human Relations*, 53(1), 7–32.

Friberg Katarina 2015 Accounts along the aid chain: Administering a moral economy, *Journal of Global Ethics*, 11(2), 246–256. DOI: 10.1080/17449626.2015.1054563.

Fry Associates 1970 *Project evaluation and the project appraisal reporting system*, Vols 1 + 2, Washington, DC: Report for the United States Agency for International Development.

Gasper, D. S. 2000 *Logical frameworks potential and problems. Teaching material for ISS participatons*, Rotterdam: International Institute of Social Studies of Erasmus University. https://repub. eur.nl/pub/50949/.

Gosling, Louisa and Mike Edwards 2003 (1995) *Toolkits: A practical guide to planning, monitoring, evaluation and impact assessment*, London: Save the Children UK.

Hart, Jason, Jo-Anna Russon and Jessica Sklair 2021 The private sector in the development landscape: Partnerships, power, and questionable possibilities, *Development in Practice*, 31(7), 857–871. DOI: 10.1080/09614524.2021.1966172.

Hindman, H. 2014 The hollowing out of Aidland, in M. Fechter and H. Hindman, eds. *Inside the everyday lives of development workers: The challenges and futures of Aidland*, London: Kumarian Press.

Hindman, H. and A. M. Fechter 2014 Introduction, in *Inside the everyday lives of development workers: The challenges and futures of Aidland*, London: Kumarian Press.

Hirschman, Albert O. 1994 *Development Projects Observed*, Washington, DC: The Brookings Institution.

Hoggett, P. 1996 New modes of control in the public service, *Public Administration*, 74, 9–32. https://doi.org/10.1111/j.1467-9299.1996.tb00855.x.

Ika, Lavagnon and Damian Hodgson 2014 Learning from international development projects: Blending critical project studies and critical development studies, *International Journal of Project Management*, 32(7). DOI: 10.1016/j.ijproman.2014.01.004.

Jacoby, Tim 2005 Cultural determinism, Western hegemony and the efficacy of defective states, *Review of African Political Economy*, 104(5), 215–233.

Kerr, Ron 2008 International development and new public management: Projects and log-frames as discursive technologies of governance, in Sadhvi Dar and B. Cooke, eds. *The new development management*, London: Zed Books.

Klikauer, T. 2015 What is managerialism? *Critical Sociology*, 41(7–8), 1103–1119. https://doi. org/10.1177/0896920513501351.

Larsen, P. 2010 Strategic partners and strange bedfellows: Relationship building in the relief supply chain, in Gyöngyi Kovács and Karen Spens, eds. *Relief supply chain management for disasters: Humanitarian, aid and emergency logistics*, IGI Global.

Mawdsley Emma 2016 Development geography II: Financialization progress report, *Progress in Human Geography*, 1–11. DOI: 10.1177/0309132516678747.

Mediavilla, Juanjo and Jorge Garcia-Arias 2019 Philanthrocapitalism as a neoliberal (development agenda) artefact: Philanthropic discourse and hegemony in (financing for) international development, *Globalizations*, 16(6), 857–875. DOI: 10.1080/14747731. 2018.1560187.

McCourt, W. and H. J. Johnson 2012 The means – ends debate in development management: Introduction to the special issue, *Journal of International Development*, 24, 531–543.

McGoey, Linsey 2012 Philanthrocapitalism and its critics, *Poetics*, 40(2), 185–199. ISSN 0304–422X. https://doi.org/10.1016/j.poetic.2012.02.006.

Mosse, David 2005 *Cultivating development: An ethnography of aid policy and practice*, London: Pluto Press.

Muller, J. Z. 2018 *The tyranny of metrics*, Oxford: Princeton University Press.

Picciotto, R. and R. Weaving 1994 A new project cycle for the world bank? *Finance & Development*, 0031(004), A012.

PMI 2021 www.pmi.org/about.

Raab, D. 2021 UK official development assistance (ODA) allocations 2021 to 2022: Written ministerial statement – GOV.UK. www.gov.uk.

Rondinelli, Dennis 1983 Projects as instruments of development administration: A qualified defence and suggestions for improvement, *Public Administration and Development*, 3, 307–327.

Rosenzweig, Phil 2010 Robert S. McNamara and the evolution of modern management, *Harvard Business Review* (December), 87–93.

Sandler, Jen and Renita Thedvall 2017 Introduction: Exploring the boring: An introduction to meeting ethnography, in Jen Sander and Renita Thedvall, eds. *Meeting ethnography: Meetings as key technologies of contemporary governance, development, and resistance*, London: Routledge.

Shore, Chris and Susan Wright 2015 Governing by numbers: Audit culture, rankings and the new world order, *Social Anthropology*, 23(1), 22–28.

Shore, C. and S. Wright 2018 How the big 4 got big: Audit culture and the metamorphosis of international accountancy firms, *Critique of Anthropology*, 38(3), 303–324.

Shutt, Cathy 2015 The politics and practice of value for money, in Rosalind Eyben et al., eds. *The politics of evidence and results in international development: Playing the game to change the rules?* Rugby: Practical Action Publishing.

Scott, Caitlin 2016 Cultures of evaluation: Tales from the end of the line, *Journal of Development Effectiveness*, 8(4), 553–560. DOI: 10.1080/19439342.2016.1244701.

Scott, C. 2022 Audit as confession: The instrumentalisation of ethics for management control, *Critique of Anthropology*, 42(1), 20–37. https://doi.org/10.1177/0308275X221074834.

SIDA 2022 *SIDA's international work*. www.sida.se/en/sidas-international-work.

Thomas, Alan 2000 Development as practice in a liberal capitalist world, *Journal of International Development*, 12(1), 773–787.

UNDP 2009 *Handbook on planning, monitoring and evaluating for development results*, New York: UNDP.

Valters, Craig and Brendan Whitty 2017 *The politics of the results agenda at DFID 1997–2017*, Overseas Development Institute (ODI). https://odi.org/en/publications/the-politics-of-the-results-agenda-in-dfid-1997–2017/.

Wallace, T., L. Bornstein and J. Chapman 2007 *The aid chain: Coercion and commitment in development NGOs*, Rugby: Practical Action Publishing.

Walsh, Sinead 2016 Obstacles to NGOs' accountability to intended beneficiaries the case of ActionAid, *Development in Practice*, 26(6), 706–718.

Wilson, J. 2003 Gantt charts: A centenary appreciation. *European Journal of Operational Research*, 149(2), 430–437. doi.org/10.1016/S0377-2217(02)00769-5.

Yanguas, Pablo 2018 *Why we lie about aid: Development and the messy politics of change*, London: Zed Books.

3 Project Inceptions

In theory, a good project comes about as a response to a specific and carefully identified problem. Reliable data from a robust situation analysis are used to inform the design of an intervention that can offer real change and a lasting solution to problems. It will be developed with the use of a range of tools, including analysis of political and economic contexts and constraints, identification of relevant stakeholders, and based on input from the community or groups of beneficiaries. They will have participated in articulating a vision of what needs to change in their communities and lives for positive change to occur and be sustained. The project's approach will also take into account lessons learned from previous work in the field, building on a body of knowledge about effective and suitable work.

In *reality*, many projects put forward to funders offer a carefully calibrated compromise between what an agency wants to do and what a donor will fund. Projects may be initiated because an NGO sees an opportunity to gain more funding and expand its work, sometimes in order to hit targets, rather than in response to a clear vision of a need or a clear sense that what will be undertaken will necessarily be effective. Much of the design work will be done in a northern office, on a tight schedule, and with only some put from local teams. Despite apparently good intentions, many projects will fail to enquire what local people think and need, and will be designed in ways which are at odds with local social structures and dynamics. Projects may also be designed without due attention to learning in the sector and therefore replicate previous mistakes.

Introduction

This chapter considers the question of how projects come about and what tools are typically used in their initial development. As per the previous vignettes, despite the existence of well-recognised, effective approaches to project development, from using all relevant available data to ensuring lessons are learned from previous projects, many projects do not in fact benefit from or incorporate these lessons. The realities of the aid chain mean that long-distance project design is a strong feature across many development contexts, as is a corresponding failure to consult communities. The political economy of project design has meant that although the range of tools and processes that are commonly used for this have expanded significantly over recent

DOI: 10.4324/9780429427411-3

decades, that can also mean technical processes become divorced from the contexts to which they are meant to apply.

The chapter starts by exploring some of the typical circumstances through which projects are initiated, and considers what the early planning phases of a project should involve. It then moves on to consider a range of tools used in these phases. The tools discussed here are representative, if necessarily not exhaustive, of these, and demonstrate a range of epistemological and political trends within development management over the decades. One tool featured, the problem tree, is derived from the participatory approaches of the 1970s and 1980s that sought simple visual methods of involving communities in planning. The problem tree is both a tool and a metaphor that can be used to conceptualise the linkages between the root causes of a problem and its symptoms in a given context. Other tools for early scoping include broad situation analyses with identification of the kinds of data that can be useful to ascertaining the scale and depth of a problem. We also look at the role of political economy analyses, framed in varied ways by different agencies and approaches over the years, and responding to the realisation within the sector that claims to uphold the sovereignty of nation states, and avoid interference with internal politics, can lead to naïve approaches that do not take sufficient account of how power and interests align in relation to resource allocation. This rise of PEA and an awareness of politics is viewed as part of an 'almost revolution' (Carothers and de Gramont 2013) within aid, relating to increasing acknowledgement of the complexity of aid interventions, links with adaptive 'thinking and working politically' approaches to planning that we explore in the next chapter.

As we saw in the last chapter, a single project is often 'nested' within a larger structure of programmes, which in turn cleave to the demands of institutions, donors, funding trends and other factors very distant from the ground level need or problem. In turn, these issues can help produce a response which is ill-suited to local conditions. Considering the role of participation in shaping tools, the chapter looks at some of the trajectories of participation in planning in project design and management. If projects are commodities produced for a funding market, and designed accordingly (Krause 2014), they align more to the needs and frameworks of donors than to those of local stakeholders. The political economy of project formulation and institutional real politik means that while project design processes may produce a text, those texts need to be interpreted via a sociology of the document (Mosse 2005: 15), where actors are involved in using and negotiating tools and the meanings and possibilities those make and produce.

As critical perspectives on the effects of planning demonstrate, the will to improve can lead to fruitless paths. Planners too often imagine the contexts in which they work as a blank canvas, devoid of relevant history or culture. They also can compose analytical studies of a situation that frames problems only in terms of the elements that can be fixed as part of the process of rendering technical. This involves isolating the project terrain from wider historical, political and social forces, stripping that which is amenable for a technical intervention away from deeper and wider contexts. The project telos is to solve only that which it can, by converting problems into technical elements to which solutions can be applied. And while a situation analysis should consider questions of history and culture, there is a notable absence of tools for the analysis of these in most project planning approaches and manuals. The chapter looks at some of the reasons for this and reviews the conflicted relationship anthropologists have had with development over the decades. Factors which have shaped the visibility of culture in development include the assumption inherent in the development paradigm that modernity is to be aspired to above and beyond local cultural forms. These, in contrast, are all too frequently identified and blamed as a source of problems, and labelled either 'traditional', or worse, 'backwards', such as Lewis's 'culture of poverty' (1966) thinking, whereby economic and structural forces were ignored in favour of attempting to blame poverty on the poor themselves. Whilst such notions are largely dispelled and rarely explicitly stated in contemporary development, the reductionist thinking of contemporary neoliberalism can produce some ignorant judgements (Kapferer 2005) that through an emphasis on economic logic ultimately repeats prior mistakes of development.

It is a risk that comes with the plethora of tools that however progressive techno-normative approaches may aim to be, they have by their very inception integrated assumptions of rationalist planning, which very often focuses on small areas on which a project can have an effect. By rendering social issues into quantified data, and political challenges into types of analysis, tools are themselves instruments for the development of certain kinds of knowledge that are to be deployed in specific kinds of ways, rendering visible and amenable to intervention complex social and historical forces and processes. They can thus also be seen as instruments of governmentality asking aid workers to define and profile issues in specific ways, aligning them to professional perspectives, stabilising social dynamics for intervention planning. These processes start in the early stages of project design, so it is important to take account of how their use emerges in relation to the real processes whereby projects come about.

Project Origins: How Do Projects Come About?

The question of how projects come about involves understanding the way agencies, donors and communities interreact around funding. As outlined in relation to 'the aid chain' in Chapter 2, the origins of projects are often to be found in what will be funded. It might be logical to think that projects arise directly from need, but in practice, organisations have many different physical locations they work in, as well as relations with donors and communities that shape what they do and where. Some of the more common mechanisms and processes whereby new projects are generated and come into being include:

- **A situation of need arises in a location to which an organisation can respond**

  An organisation identifies a specific need and articulates a project to respond. It may be somewhere the organisation already works and has a presence or where they need to build new relationships and facilities. A project is then developed, which may be funded with unrestricted resources or from a new grant application to a new or existing donor. In the case of a UK-based water sector INGO, for example, new projects often emerge from the identification of locations in need of support within an existing country programme. Staff working there will become aware of and note the needs of communities who are not currently being reached, and start to scope a project that takes an existing or similar form of work done elsewhere to a new location.

- **At the request of communities within a country**
  In some well-established organisations, projects may arise in response to requests from a specific group of stakeholders who request assistance, to deal with a pressing situation that they feel the organisation can support. The organisation then might consider the requests and whether they can help, and if that is positive, then assess the situation in more detail to develop a project in response.

- **A shift or expansion of existing work**
  This might be when an organisation extends existing work into a new geographical area, such as when a health charity realises they have a cadre of expertise for define a new project. For example, after the 2014 Gaza conflict, a medical charity assembled overseas surgeons to be flown in to provide specialist surgery to treat as many affected children as possible within the time surgeons could be present.

- **In response to calls for proposals from donors**
  One of the most common ways in which NGOs create and define new projects is in response to a call for proposals. Many larger NGOs have fundraising teams who scour databases and receive notifications on when new grant funding is made available by bodies such as the EU. Alternatively, it might allow new areas of work in alignment to existing priorities or geographical presence, for example, when calls are issued by DFID or the EU for work on a specific theme in a specific country or region. In this case an existing programme may be re-packaged to fit new funding, or a new location or approach tried out.

- **Approached by a donor**
  Sometimes charities are approached by a donor directly, to undertake work on an area of interest they have. A human rights NGO in the UK recounts being approached by a UN body to undertake some work on a new sub-field of minority rights and statelessness, that could then form into a new set of work for funding.

- **Existing activities need packaging into a project form**
  A project can also allow for the continuation or expansion of existing work, with modifications to fit the specifics of the grant call. Small NGOs often struggle to get funding for charities they support abroad, and continuing funding means finding new grants. This means taking existing work and packaging it as projects to show what they will achieve in continuing to support this work. It can also be that existing work is repackaged into the form of a project with a results framework and associated rubric, to incorporate new goals, such as an agricultural initiative gaining advocacy objectives, to better suit the needs of funding arrangements.

- **Organisation needs to have a presence**
  Many higher-level projects are instigated for political reasons, as part of top-down planning that aims to bring a particular location or sector in line with improved technology. At the World Bank, for example, national governments liaise with relevant representatives to create new requests and initiate discussions around technical solutions to identified needs at a national level. These are the kinds of large-scale projects that have historically drawn most attention from academics (e.g. Ferguson 1994; Mosse 2005; Scott 1985).

Whilst necessarily not exhaustive, this range of generative mechanisms for projects suggests some of the complex interplay of forces as new projects come about. Political and financial considerations are essential components of the context in which most development projects take shape. The growth of new projects can thus be in response to calls from donors for new work, which means re-framing existing programmes to fit the latest 'buzzword' or concept that is in demand from policies of donor agencies. These policies are in turn shaped by the geopolitical and economic agendas of donor countries, which set the agenda for what they will and won't fund. In addition to modes and fashions that come and go in development, observers have noted that such work is often framed around categories that are deemed morally and politically suitable, such as orphans and vulnerable children in the AIDS pandemic (Green 2011). Where the goals of some NGOs are more radical, and aiming to transform power relations, it can be very frustrating to have to fit into the schemes and political agendas of the higher echelons of the aid chain. These funding realities demand that projects make clear accounts of the context into which they wish to have an impact, who they will engage with and influence, and how they interact with political agendas. These are some of the aspects of project design which engage with and make use of the many tools for project inception that are in common use in development, and which we consider next.

Tools of Analysis: Understanding Situations, Framing Problems and Defining Needs

In this section we look at a selection of the tools recommended for the pre-project design phase. These assessment tools help develop the contextual and background information for project design. These tools are but a brief selection from the wide repertoire of tools and approaches that may be used by NGOs or others to justify an intervention. They include:

- **Situation analysis**, a background account and justification or case for an intervention in a specific context
- **Stakeholder analysis**, identifying the key actors and participants who will be influence(d) and/or affected by an intervention

- **Political economy analysis**, that identifies and accounts for relationships between political actors and resources that are relevant to the intervention
- **Problem tree**, a visual tool with origins in participatory approaches to development used to explore root causes and symptoms of a specific problem

The following sections explain the kinds of data used in each tool, its role in planning and its history.

Situation Analysis: Explaining a Context and Justifying an Intervention

A situation analysis or similar is a broad concept which encompasses a variety of ways of setting out and understanding the context into which a justification for intervention is being made. A situation analysis as a phrase may refer either to the process of gathering of information and data and/or a report entitled as such. The kinds of documents they go into can vary, depending on what grant-making body they are appealing to and written for. The DFID 'business case' approach, based on a template from the UK Treasury, focuses on value for money and requires that a case be made which deploys relevant data to make "a sound case for the commitment of public funds" (DFID 2011: 1), before defining a specific project. Other agencies may use different systems to review data to justify interventions.

Situation analyses which seek to justify a case typically draw on a combination of primary data, as and when original research is feasible or needed, and secondary data, that is already in either the possession of an organisation or in the public domain. A combination of the two may be necessary, for example, using data from agencies such as the World Bank to help frame the macro-level economic situation and to create a rationale for intervention in a business case, whilst data for project designers and programme implementers is likely to need more nuance, if they are to develop an approach that responds to situation and needs.

Save the Children's *Toolkits*, for example, say that "[a] formal assessment is likely to be necessary" in the kinds of inception processes outlined in the prior section, including:

- Before starting a new programme
- When expanding an existing programme into a new area
- When starting work with a new partner
- When changing the direction of an existing programme so that new objectives and baseline are required (Gosling and Edwards 2003: 68–69)

Situation analyses can be conceived of in different ways and at different levels. At a macro level, a country-level (or even regional) analysis may seek to offer a summary of the situation in a specific country. At a deeper level, it might dive into sectoral analysis, looking at how, for example, education or access to water are experienced at the national or subnational level, according to the scope of the analysis being undertaken. In order to justify the intervention, the first part of a DFID business case model involves a strategic case, which should feature and

[s]ummarise relevant evidence demonstrating the need for an intervention. Provide or refer to appropriate qualitative and quantitative evidence, including social, political, climate change and environment, institutional and other evidence from the local context.

(DFID 2011: 8)

Because many of the key services and utilities needed to meet basic human rights and fulfil the SDGs are managed at a national level, it is usually relevant to start at the national level and work backwards to an understanding of the specifics. In many situations much of the data needed to develop a project may already be available, and this is also a function of what data a proposal needs (Figure 3.1). A country analysis, which many INGOs do regularly, looks at broad contexts, such as macro-economic trends, the political and policy environment, as well as key sectoral trends and issues. Many UN agencies produce key indicator data for countries that is relevant for development planning; the UN Statistics Division, for example, hosts a country data website,[1] while the UNDP's annual Human Development Report published key data on indicators for the Human Development Index, as well as regularly advancing data such as the Multi-Dimensional Poverty Index (MPI).[2] The World Bank provides data on key financial conditions, as well as on its own loans to a country.[3]

While useful for grasping relative conditions in relation to issues such as absolute poverty, life expectancy and educational attendance, it is worth bearing in mind that indicators only indicate, and do so particularly at a high level. They do not

Useful data	Sources
Statistics on poverty, inequality	National government agencies, geographically or sectorally relevant think tanks and research organisations, World Bank, UNDP
Statistical data on topics, e.g. education, health	UNICEF, UNESCO, UNDP, UNIS etc. involved in supporting governments in strengthening data collection
General sectoral data and analyses	Ministry, other sector actors with large-scale projects who are likely to have done comprehensive analyses at the outset of their work
Recent research or evaluative studies on relevant aspects of the topic	Universities, research institutes, individual researchers, development agencies, INGOs or local NGOs or CSOs; Cochrane Collaboration
Reports of independent agencies or coalitions working on a subject	Including alliances for monitoring, such as those working on Alternative Country Reports for Child Rights updates to the United Nations Human Right Commission

Figure 3.1 Data and sources

Source: The author

explain the reasons behind the number, particularly when aggregated to a global level. They necessarily generalise and provide many medians or averages that may not show variations within a country. This is important given that much poverty today exists within middle and higher income countries as well as the lower income ones, because of inequality. It is worth being aware of what disaggregated data is and isn't available: is data available disaggregated by gender, for example, or according to ethnicity? What might be hiding behind the statistics?

Ideally, such a report or analysis should also take into account social and cultural factors, including religious denominations and structures. Social trends as well as divisions are also important, in order to understand historically situated issues of inequality and difference. These may be related to class or caste, ethnicity, religion, or regional inequalities; although as discussed later in this chapter, there are few agreed-upon processes or tools for this.

Such a broad and sweeping national view needs to be sharply edited to help define programming priorities and possible fits. This process helps identify what the priority problems are in the country and gain an analysis of these. It may be that an organisation already has a specific group or issue it is focusing on, in which case the country-level data will help frame that focus and contextualise it in the wider national situation. There may already be a focus on the kinds of people an organisation aims to help. In an early Oxfam 'Field Directors Handbook', for example, guidance outlines the kinds of groups of people considered a priority – women, children, the disabled and ethnic groups – on the grounds that they are most vulnerable to poverty (Pratt and Boyden 1985).

In focusing on key sectoral issues, such as education, livelihoods or health – or combinations of these – data will be gathered from a range of secondary sources. This data might be used to help specifically quantify an issue or problem, such as data on scale, proportions affected, as well as numbers of potential beneficiaries, also sometimes termed an 'at-risk' population.

In planning the gathering of such data, a range of key indicators may predetermine what data is being looked for. Data for key quantitative indicators is often available online, from main actors and agencies that work in a sector. UNICEF, for example, has a Multiple Indicator Cluster System (MICS)[4] survey that collects data on a range of issues relating to children's wellbeing, health and education, an important starting point for any work with children requiring quantitative information. In some countries where, for example, there are ongoing crises such as health or climate emergencies or conflict, data may be harder to come by. Data needs to be *as up to date as possible*, and certainly not more than a few years old, as a major event such as Covid or climate disasters can quickly have a major impact on certain sectors of society. It's also worth thinking about the potential limitations of data, for example, about who is putting data forward and of why and how it was collected. This is especially the case with governments, but also agencies that have particular strengths or foci.

When analysing any issue, it's important to think about how a problem may be manifest at the surface, but with much deeper roots. Persistent poverty is rarely caused by one factor, but rather it is the product of multiple intersecting factors. This is summed up well in the concept of intersectionality (Crenshaw 1991), whereby different aspects of identity interact to form multiple vectors of inequality. Economic inequality also often links to social forms of discrimination or exclusion. Structural causes that relate to the nature of democracy, representation or other governance may perpetuate problems.

When understanding the interrelated and structural nature of problems, you will need more qualitative data that illuminates the statistics and gives more depth to the analysis you can make. Qualitative data can include sociological or anthropological analyses, political reviews, as well as more ground-level information of the views, experiences and perceptions of the groups of people you may be working with. For example, if quantitative data indicates that many girls drop out of school at a certain age, then qualitative data is needed to help understand *why* this is the case. In addition, it is important to understand how problems are *experienced*, by those involved in a situation, and what they feel the obstacles to their resolution are. Poverty is also often linked to discrimination, and understanding how that feels to children who are looked down on by their peers for having inadequate clothing at school, or in relation to women who are too humble to seek medical attention, understanding how that happens and what their views are is going to be essential to producing any change that is valuable to them.

Stakeholder Analysis

Stakeholder analysis is a commonly used tool for understanding who has interests in and around a project. A stakeholder is, in the simplest of terms, someone who has an interest or a 'stake' in a situation or context. An ODI tool provides the following succinct definition:

> A stakeholder is a person who has something to gain or lose through the outcomes of a planning process or project. In many circles these are called interest groups and they can have a powerful bearing on the outcomes of political processes.
>
> (ODI 2009: 1)

Identifying who these people are, their power and influence and what relationships and bearings they will have to a project is often thought about in relation to communications or advocacy and planning. It may be critical when planning partnerships and alliances around a project, or designing a media strategy and working on the targeting of influencers. You may use the chart to help design aspects of implementation, as well as monitoring, thinking through the various institutions and organisations you may impact.

There are typically a few steps to stakeholder analysis. A first is identifying who stakeholders are, then a second is to categorise or group them (or you may find it useful to use a grid of likely categories of stakeholders to help flesh that out). Then you identify their relationship to the project and likely interests and influence on it, on a grid. This matrix helps you think about the best way of approaching and managing such stakeholders, in terms of what communications and involvement they may want or need to have to the project.

Step 1: identification: You should be as thorough as possible in this step, to identify groups and individuals at local, regional, national and international levels who may have a direct interest in your work. In Figure 3.2, adapted from a health policy reform tool, various branches and levels of government are identified as relevant, as well as the ministry of finance, departments of government responsible for social security or welfare, and politicians. In civil society you may have unions or other labour interest groups, NGOs and community organisations (amongst others) who would have an interest in how changes are effected to health policy and provision.

Private-sector stakeholders	Public-sector stakeholders	Civil society stakeholders
Corporations Business groups and associations Banks, credit associations and other financial institutions Lobbying groups	National government ministers Elected representatives to national government Political parties and associations Civil servants at local and national government levels International bodies, e.g. UN agencies	Religious groups Educational institutions, schools and universities Social movements Trade unions Non-governmental organisations Traditional leaders

Figure 3.2 Categories of stakeholders

Source: The author

Step 2: Stakeholder analysis: As a second step, you need to analyse the kind of interests each group of stakeholders is going to have with your project. What will their view of it be? How much interest or influence or power will they have over it, and – most importantly – why? A classic approach is to create a table or chart, where for each category of stakeholder, a note is made of their importance, their influence and power, their interest in the project, and the possible positive impacts it may have on them. Take an example of improving water provision in an area. If asking how important the proposed change is to local groups, you might note that for farmers, it will be important for their productivity and could enhance this. For the governor of the area, s/he has a statutory duty to provide water and so could benefit from support to deliver this service.

Another column asks about influence and power. Farmers may represent a significant proportion of the local area population. They may also have the power to block an initiative if it is not in the interests of the majority. Importantly, the project might also affect farmers differently, depending upon the size of their land and/or what they produce. They are also important consumers, and in some locations, large farms take water from local populations; seeing distributional equity is important. In another two columns, you can ask about the positive or negative impacts a project could have, and the concerns stakeholders may have. Such identifications can help you tailor your communications, ensuring you answer questions of concern to such groups when you engage with them.

Step 3: Classic stakeholder assessment tool: A classic tool to shape thinking about this is a grid which has power on the vertical axis and interest across the horizontal axis, as per Figure 3.3. Mapping out various stakeholder groups according to this grid can help you define how much communication and other interactions you have with different groups, and how you are going to manage relations with them during your project.

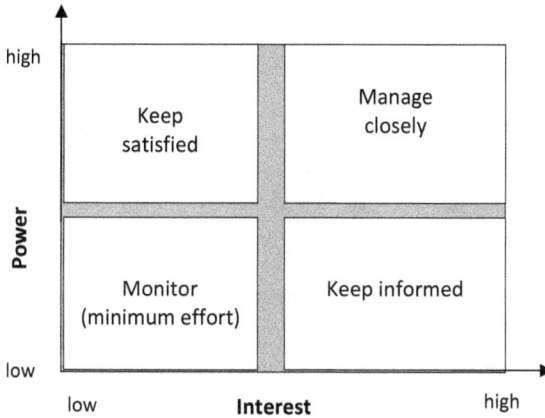

Figure 3.3 Stakeholder power/interest grid tool

Source: The author

In addition to thinking about these basic steps of stakeholder analysis, you can advance this process by thinking about different kinds of power that stakeholder groups hold, using analysis such as that of Gaventa's (2006) powercube model.[5] This conceptual model helps shape thinking about how power works in governance, relationships and organisations, and in ways that can help identify spaces and levels at which power functions. This can provide more nuance to your understanding of possible routes of influencing and resistance. Such approaches are complementary to thinking about power's directionalities, as per Oxfam's (2014/2021) guidance, which suggests looking at the vectors and dynamics through which power can work:

- *Power over*: the power of the strong over the weak, including the power to exclude others
- *Power to*: the capability to decide actions and carry them out: knowledge, skills, tools
- *Power with*: collective power, through organisation, solidarity and joint action
- *Power within*: personal self-confidence, often linked to culture, religion or other aspects of identity, which influences the thoughts and actions that appear legitimate or acceptable
- *Power for*: the power of a clear vision and sense of purpose
- *Power under*: passing on mistreatment to others through fear, humiliation, anger, resentment, superiority, arrogance

This approach became mandatory of programme design at Oxfam UK in 2014, but as Rowlands (2016) noted, it took some time to be translated into changes in programme design and management. Difficulties in institutionalising techniques for addressing power is a recurrent feature amongst such approaches, including that of PEA, which we turn to next. Such shifts have been enabled partly by growth in thinking about complexity and systems, which are explored in the next chapter, and linked to thinking about invisible forms of power, as manifest in cultural norms and values. Considerations of culture, however, remain conspicuous in their absence from most project design processes, which we explore as follows.

Political Economy Analysis (PEA)

Political economy analysis (PEA) refers to a branch or series of tools for analysing the ways in which political and economic dynamics might or can impact a project or other piece of work. Variants of PEA seek to analyse how power and wealth are distributed, and contested, across a given context. A good description of its goals is that PEA:

> aims to situate development interventions within an understanding of the prevailing political and economic processes in society – specifically, the incentives, relationships, distribution, and contestation of power between different groups and individuals.
>
> (McLoughlin 2014)

PEA came to the fore in development circles and practices in the wake of acknowledgments of the failures of many development efforts to produce desired changes through means which excluded analysis of political domains. In an influential text, Carothers and de Gramont (2013: 4–5) note that the failures which led to the rise of political analysis included misidentification of the causes of development problems where socio-political tensions had been overlooked; failures to understand institutional capacity; not acknowledging the ways development may threaten interests nor anticipate unintended consequences; and ignoring the political interests of citizens. The rise of PEA was broadly contemporary to the rise in concerns with governance in development policy circles. The Bretton Woods institutions had discovered shortcomings in the preceding decades of the so-called Washington Consensus, which involved major structural reforms to shrink the state via structural adjustment policies from the 1980s. However, shortcomings were identified not as lying with the contradictory premise that business with a small state sector could produce the welfare gains and create the infrastructure needed for development, but instead with questions of governance and institutional paradigms.

In practice, the rise of governance agendas gave a new bureaucratic space and salience to means of assessing PEA issues. A veritable flurry of PEA followed in later years and decades, with widespread acceptance of the importance of such tools and approaches (Hudson and Marquette 2015; Yanguas and Hulme 2014). Main OECD donors developed their own variants of PEA, which we look at in turn, emphasising different elements or levels in the guidance issued to applicants. In the UK from the late 1990s on, DFID commissioned a series of country studies which analysed the intersection of political systems, policy making and budgeting processes, with the World Bank drawing on these to develop their own variant, which was incorporated into the group's Governance and Anti Corruption Strategy (CGAS), to include diagnostic work on governance and corruption (Fritz 2017; Yanguas and Hulme 2014).

The question of sovereignty in PEA is not always addressed explicitly, but it remains a critical question given the World Bank's explicit prohibition, in its Articles of Association, from interfering in the political affairs of a member state (Yanguas and Hulme 2014: 7). As Carothers and de Gramont note, this was an important corrective to the long-standing premise that development was somehow apolitical. The view that development was (is) simply an exercise in humanitarian endeavour is surely one of the most debated in the sector, driving to the core of what motivates individuals and how civil society organisations can shape what appears to be a hegemonic enterprise of capitalist empire consolidation. In the context of western countries' invasions of Afghanistan and Iraq in 2003, new framings of fragile and failed states in relation to security concerns provided more grounds for interference where states were deemed fragile and thus posing a risk to the west (Duffield 2007).

Such issues notwithstanding, over successive iterations and deepening analysis, an interest in PEA has been combined with new tools of analysis such as complexity theory, which draws on environmental science to reflect on the myriad ways that stakeholder interests and social processes intertwine unpredictably. This has led to the development of wider approaches, such as thinking and working politically (TWP). While there are variants of this also (discussed in more depth in the next chapter), TWP approaches seek to expand the insights of PEA to a more flexible approach to planning. As a USAID note explains the distinction between the two,

> While TWP is a mindset and strategic orientation, PEA is a methodology developed to analyze the politics of how and why things happen, along with their implications for project activities.
>
> (USAID 2019)

At the World Bank, DFID and elsewhere, 'how-to notes' and similar were developed to guide their use. However, developing PEA into (yet another) technical area has arguably allowed it to remain somewhat outside the mainstream of agency practice, raising issues of the siloing of expertise and depth of institutionalisation (Yanguas and Hulme 2014). Despite an apparent preponderance of tools and capacity building, many challenges remain, as no matter how sophisticated the tools, they are no substitute for deep local knowledge and understanding (Hudson and Marquette 2015). We return to these questions later, once we have examined in more detail the technical issues involved.

Most variants on PEA are close to this definition from the OECD:

> Political economy analysis is concerned with the . . . **distribution of power and wealth between groups and individuals**, and the processes that create, sustain and transform these relationships over time.
>
> (2015; emphasis added)

PEA seeks to consider the implications of these distributions of power – often nested in political institutions and parties, but also materialised through social means such as caste or class differentiations – for development outcomes. What difference does social power make for political access and influence? How is that manifest? If, for example, you have done your stakeholder analysis as per the tool discussed earlier, and noted the relationships between cooperatives of small farmers, larger farmers and the ministry of agriculture, you might want to then consider who has more power and access, and look at the impacts of this in previous policy instances, or in the discussions had by farmers around their concerns for a project.

PEA attempts to get beneath formal structures, to identify and understand underlying interests and incentives that produce change (or don't). The consolidated impact of these power interests have been termed 'drivers of change', in the approach used by DFID. Here, the PEA is explained as getting "beneath the formal structures to reveal the underlying interests, incentives and institutions that enable or frustrate change" (DFID 2009).

A simple example shows how an analysis informed by PEA contrasts with a conventional analysis of problems in service delivery, where a conventional approach might see poor service delivery outcomes as the product of technical, financial or capacity weaknesses within a sector, a PEA analysis will look at some of the mechanisms and institutional dynamics behind these. These could include comparing how and why different sectors are prioritised in budgetary or planning processes, and who the winners and losers are from such decisions. Planning can then take these dynamics into account, looking to find suitable points of leverage or influence for a programme.

Case Study: 'The budget as theatre' approach in Malawi (from DFID 2009)

A 2004 study for DFID Malawi concluded that the country's formal budget process 'is a theatre that masks the real distribution and spending'. Its recommendations concerning the strengthening of actors outside the executive branch to increase demand for economic accountability were picked up in the new 2005–09 governance programme, 'Tikambirane' ('Let's Talk'). A subsequent change in the political landscape in Malawi – resulting in a minority government and strong opposition in Parliament – provided opportunities for Parliament to flex its muscles in challenging the Executive, and helped to create a receptive environment for this programme. The Tikambirane programme supported civil society to better scrutinise the budget and engage constructively with MPs (members of Parliament). It also supported the Parliamentary Accounts Committee to better carry out its oversight role. Training of journalists has been provided to improve coverage of economic governance issues. MPs were trained in budget monitoring, gender budgeting and budget analysis. Some of the impacts of the programme have been:

- More active civil society scrutinising the budget and holding Government to account
- More effective PAC scrutinising budget and calling line ministries to appear before hearings
- Increased pro-poor budget allocations following civil society engagement, for example in health and agriculture, and cuts for non-priority expenditures such as state residences
- Improved media reporting on economic governance – in particular, increased coverage on Front Pages, previously dominated by political events and gossip

The case study underscores how looking underneath formal political processes can reveal another set of dynamics at work; and ones which are arguably far more relevant than what is on paper, or institutionally prescribed. The example also highlights the role of the governance agenda and the idea of supporting civil society to hold government to account, as a mechanism for improving government performance and effectiveness, and also improving democratic institutions for the longer term. PEA analysis can help identify how and why different sectors are prioritised, and who the winners and losers of these processes are. With a deeper understanding of dynamics at work around policy and budgeting decisions, interventions can be designed to interact with these more effectively.

As mentioned previously, donors developed their own varieties of PEA analysis, stressing particular levels for analysis. These can be broadly grouped into three levels: a first country-level analysis of major political and governance issues; second, a thematic analysis that considers the key actors and political dynamics within sectors of the economy, such as natural resource management, that can then focus in on a more specific area, such as farming or water and sanitation; and a third level can look in detail at a single issue or policy area within this. There are also further variants of PEA which we do not consider here for issues of space, such as SIDA's Power Analysis.

DFID developed a Drivers of Change model to be used at the country level. This seeks to explore the wider historical, socio-economic and cultural environment. It looks at the political context and how this interacts with development agencies and processes. It attempts to consider immediate pressures that come from groups and interest areas, and who influences decision making, as well as the processes through which decisions are made. Its focus is unpacking the black box of political will, or lack thereof (Nash et al. 2006: 14). Useful for country planning and strategy, the process for a country-level study can take anywhere from a couple of weeks to two years; in most cases, specific pieces of work can draw on existing analysis and research like this that are already available within an organisation. These Drivers of Change questions start from a foundational level, scoping out the relationship of governance to territory, of political communities and also political processes. Medium-term factors include the embeddedness of the constitution, the institutionalisation of government and political mechanisms, with elites and minorities included in this medium-term set of institutional questions. This sharpens into a more present-day kind of analysis, that looks at capacity within government, as well as electoral cycles and accountability mechanisms (Nash et al. 2006: 15, drawing on Moore 2001).

The EC, meanwhile, adopted an approach which looked at sectoral levels directly, to analyse questions such as why reforms in a sector such as education might have stalled. In order to do this, it looks at dynamics such as constraints or incentives on civil servants, politicians and others, as well as identifying who the most influential actors are in a sector. The questions of 'who' are essential in any approach, then, and overall PEA has been noted to have its roots in institutional theory, that is, focusing on how institutions of the state and of governance are constituted and how they behave in practice. This focus stems in part from its origins, as noted at the start of this section, whereby formal processes and institutions are privileged for analysis.

A third key level of approach has been to start at the project level and consider how problems and issues arise here. The World Bank's Problem-Driven Governance and Political Economy (PGPE) framework, with a problem-driven focus, looks to understand problems and challenges at the project level (Poole 2011), and then maps the institutional and governance weaknesses which underpin these. To complement the PGPE is an Institutional and Governance Review (IGR) tool, with a focus on public institutions. The problem analysis starts with a definition – for example, a poor outcome, that runs counter to the goals of a policy or programme. It then asks about the institutions responsible for this area, identifying what laws, regulations and processes bring these into play. A relevant question may be about obstacles to this, such as corruption. At the next, third stage, we might ask why the dynamics are as they are and views about the status quo of politics according to stakeholders exploring social forces. The fourth step develops around plans for action, or how a project can be re-designed to ensure it can function effectively, given these known constraints and challenges. As with other PEA processes, exactly how you answer these questions, and what material and research you can draw on, depends in large part on the context in which a project is being designed.

The Problem Tree

The next tool we consider comes from a different set of social and political dynamics, but could offer a useful complement to the third project-level problem variant of PEA. The problem tree arises from the broad sweep of calls for bottom-up participation from the 1970s onwards and which came with the rise of participatory approaches to programme appraisal. The participatory rural appraisal (PRA) approach (e.g. Chambers 1983) and copied widely across development made space for the voices and views of those affected by the issue that development tries to solve in planning. To what extent, how, where and why this is effective is a broader question which we return to later. However, a raft of tools for planning stages were created, that aimed to hand the pen to local people. Methods which involve community members in articulating what is at issue for them, rather than what is identified by aid agency teams or foreign consultants. These include drawing maps, doing transect walks to understand the ways in which people experience their community spatially, and what places have what meanings to them, as well as timelines and more. A key one for the understanding of a problem is the problem tree.

The problem tree (Figure 3.4) is a simple tool that allows for a participatory discussion, analysis and illustration of the ways a problem is experienced in a community or other group, and is typically recommend for use with a focus group of six to eight people (e.g. Hovland 2005). It takes the surface manifestation of a problem, such as poverty at a household level, and looks through its causes, to find the deeper roots – hence, the tree analogy.

To carry out a problem tree activity and analysis, the steps and tools needed are fairly simple. The first step is to discuss and agree what problem is going to be analysed. This can go in the centre of a flipchart, or into a drawing sketched in dirt or sand with a stick, or on a whiteboard; the technical flexibility of this approach is one of its attractions. This problem core will become the trunk of the tree. In the prior example, a lack of economic opportunities in the village is identified as a problem. The discussion then moves to the roots of the problem: what is causing this issue?

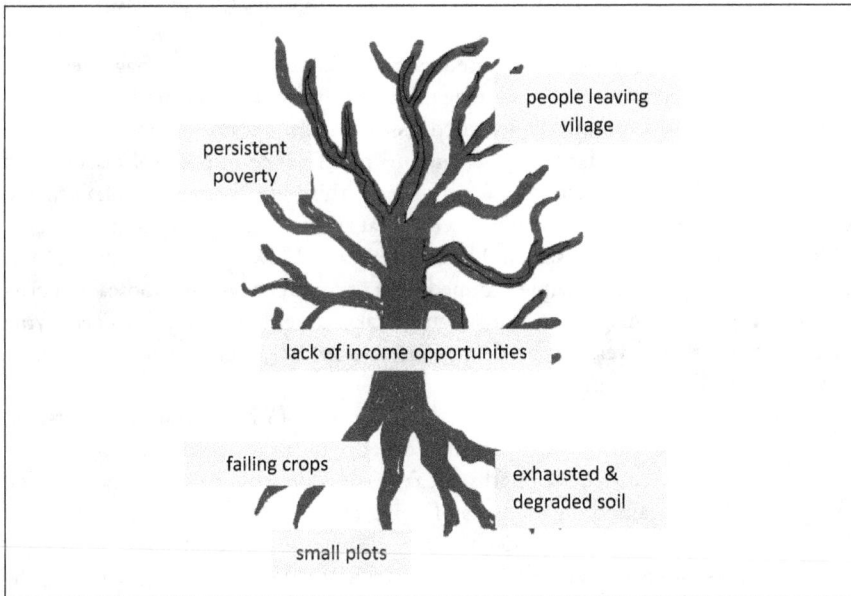

Figure 3.4 A problem tree

Source: The author

Several factors are often at work, and getting different people's views on them is also essential to understanding different dynamics at play. Causes of the problem could include lack of new opportunities for cash work, soil exhaustion, irregular rainfall and shrinking plot sizes as families grow and divide their land. At the top of the tree, discussion can be generated around the visible impacts of this problem, and denote these as the branches and leaves, where there is persistent poverty and people are leaving the village.

Problems at Conception: The Challenges of Using Tools

Although each of the kinds of tools outlined previously have been developed and refined by many aid thinkers and practitioners over decades, these can each come with their own drawbacks and limitations. In this section, we consider some of the challenges, both conceptual and practical, to their effective implementation. Some relate to the top-down nature of planning, whereas others have inherent problems of using concepts derived from other fields, such as commerce.

Critical Reflections on Stakeholder Approaches

The idea of stakeholder involvement might seem to have links with participation, but its roots are distant, deriving from ideas about how private ownership of companies fit to corporate structures in 1930s USA. Stakeholder theory came into use in policy circles from organisational management, focusing on concerns with who was leveraging power around policy-making processes (Brugha and Varvasovszky 2000: 240). In practice today, it is used as part of a language of management that cast people into certain roles, such that the community can then be referred to as 'stakeholders' because you have identified them as such, but not because they chose to be involved. Stakeholder language came to prominence in political discourse in the UK in the late 1990s as part of a vision for a 'third way' between capitalism and socialism (e.g. Giddens 1999). These ideological and political roots suggest the possible instrumentality of the stakeholder concept and how it can easily presume to give a unified logic to the people grouped under the category you choose. As a classic tool of project management, the language takes a benign approach to classifying people, rather than revealing the deeper interests which might be at work behind those classifications and uses.

Relationships with stakeholders are also conceived of in relation to threats and opportunities – for which organisations sometimes conduct what is known as a SWOT analysis, identifying strengths, weaknesses, opportunities and threats. Such analyses are often framed on the basis of being able to be open about who wields what power and influence over decisions in a given geopolitical space. This epistemological positivism may be suitable in stable and open societies where politics is not conceived of as dangerous or risky, but this is not always the case. In many contexts, including supposedly democratic ones, people may be fearful about articulating their views about power openly. Where developing an analysis requires further information gathering, differences in what can and cannot be said openly about power and politics may be pronounced, and awareness of this dynamic is important.

The Challenges of Institutionalising PEA

Understanding power and influence at local levels to define stakeholders has some continuities with the PEA approaches, which endeavour to establish this at often higher levels, such as national and subnational government. Despite the copious efforts referenced earlier, from a wide range of institutions including major donors to UN agencies, to engage with PEA and politically aware development, the consensus seems to be that PEA has not led to significant changes in how development is done that early proponents hoped it would.

To some, aid bureaucracies' internal organisational dynamics are largely responsible for the failure to institutionalise PEA. Bureaucratic structures, characterised by clear lines of accountability, risk aversion and a focus on results are antithetical to the adaptive management that TWP and PEA espouse (Yanguas and Hulme 2014). This, in their view, has combined with the siloing of areas of knowledge and practice that are typical of professional roles in agencies, such that PEA is seen as a technical area of expertise within the domain of governance specialists. This, is seen as a loss, because the goal of changing the way aid agencies think is far removed if PEA remains an occasional add-on activity done by specialists (Hudson and Marquette 2015). There is an irony here, however, around how on the one hand, PEA is currently framed as an area of expertise which comes with a range of how-to guides and specific technologies, and on the other hand wanting it to be adopted as a way of thinking about development. As with other tools which endeavour to bring more nuance into planning, a key challenge seems to be about the demands and clear-cut space made for this within planning.

PEA, with its 'how-to notes' at the World Bank (Poole 2011) and DFID (2009), has been developed with analytical and methodical steps for segmenting and organising pieces of knowledge. These analytical categories are also derived from western experiences of democratic states, such as corruption. PEA approaches draw on ideas of the links between politics, or the formal institutional arrangements and practice around these in relation to democratic or other government, and economics, the organisation of production systems, or wealth and prosperity. Terms such as *politics* originate in western writings, with politics having roots in the Greek in polity and economy οἰκονομία relating to housekeeping. These are rested on a set of assumptions about political economy where these words are joined into a distinct phrase with the advent of capitalism. As such, this is a specifically western view of the relationships and disciplines which distinguish these as separate analytical spheres, for the purposes of debating the most financially advantageous or morally preferable arrangement between markets and the state. The facts of its presence as a distinct analytical sphere in development may be seen as evidence of capitalism's hegemonic success, or of efforts to advance its intellectual tools elsewhere. The development of PEA has been through a vast body of debate in philosophy, economics and political theory, drawing on Weberian notions of the rational state and bureaucracy as the best form of managing resources, and with many PEA approaches drawing on Douglass North's (1990) 'new institutionalism' that focused on formal and informal institutions and their effects on trade and economic prosperity (Yanguas and Hulme 2014). The governance goals in the post Washington Consensus have focused on environments for business more than for people.

Apart from being technical, they are thus effectively normative standards, based on western experiences, rather than universal ones. So while the packaging of an analytical approach as a tool seems to underline its universality, the reality is that these are specific ideas and categories of thought, that entail an a priori tacit agreement on what kinds of corruption are important, establishing boundaries of whether political behaviour is acceptable, and so on. Yet, as anthropologists have long noted, concepts of politics and economics are hardly universal.

The technocratic approach that PEA can be seen to espouse, whereby political struggles can be turned into tickbox exercises, and institutional disputes can be stripped of their historical and social roots, can be seen as another expansion of the professionalisation of aid, with discrete areas of expertise and complex discourses that specify and protect realms of knowledge and exclude others. Tools are designed to be used easily, with the premise that these can be used to 'fix' the problems of development within technical framings that persist. The governance framing from which PE originated stems from an understanding of development in which politics has been kept at the margins, allowed to surface briefly like a submarine, but a periscope is not a substitute for full, open engagement.

The subtitle of Carothers and de Gramont's review of development's engagement with politics suggests a key point: this was an 'almost' revolution, but not the one hoped for by those who wished to see development fully engage with political dimensions and realities. While many agencies commissioned and demanded new approaches, these have had to work within the institutional parameters of the aid chain in which projects are designed and delivered, and those ultimately rest on accountability systems which are directed upwards to those wielding power and distributing funds. Whether these are multilaterals answerable to a range of nation states, or the development assistance branch of a Northern national government, the space for equal discussion and awareness of political constraints is within systems which are defined from the top. At the same time, there is a sense that a veil is thrown over the incontrovertibly political nature of development, and technocrats dare not identify the real character of their endeavours. Whether this is because of siloing and professionalisation, or the post-history notion of market capitalism's triumph (cf. Fukuyama 1992), whether a generation of aid workers struggle to envisage an alternative, is a topic for further research.

Participation and the Problems With Top-Down Planning

Issues around understanding project needs from the bottom up were the subject of calls from the 1970s onwards, and led to more participatory planning processes and tools, such as the problem tree. What are broadly termed 'participation' ideas entered development policies and programmes to challenge prevailing neocolonial top-down management systems, whereby aid was designed from afar. These ideas were inspired by the liberation and post-colonial independence movements across Africa, and anti-imperial and left-wing movements across Latin America. Amongst others writing about the nature of colonial oppression and need for liberation (e.g. Nkrumah 1963; Fanon 1961), these drew on the ideas of the Brazilian educationalist Paulo Freire, whose seminal *Pedagogy of the Oppressed* (1970) articulated ideas for reversals of power, a key means for liberation being understanding the conditions which enabled it. These views challenged dominant orders, arguing that people were oppressed by systems of power that subdued them via false consciousness of their conditions. Such hegemonies could be resisted through processes such as conscientisation, associated with Freire and Catholic movements of liberation theology, which sought to bring greater consciousness and knowledge to the people, particularly the rural poor (Cooke and Kothari 2001).

In development, Robert Chambers put these ideas to work in his groundbreaking *Rural Development: Putting the Last First* (1983), which argued for the need to involve locals in planning properly. In his critique, focusing on rural agricultural development, he argued that planning processes tended to overlook some of the most acute rural poverty, because it was beyond the quick site visits carried out as 'experts', briefly hopping in and out of Land Cruisers. He also argued that these approaches repeatedly and by design ignored local peoples' knowledge about their own problems and possible solutions. These influential arguments were developed into a series of participatory planning models for Participatory Rural Appraisal (PRA), providing an assortment of low-tech tools that could be adapted for use in a wide range of contexts. Combined with a professionalised approach, PRA was to enable NGO workers to 'hand over the stick' to villagers so that they could express their needs directly and via visual representations suitable for non-literate peoples.

This was followed by a flurry of work throughout the 1980s and into the 1990s around approaches that could help systematise this involvement (e.g. Nelson and Wright 1995; Blackburn and Holland 1998). This was in some ways an anti-project approach that was in favour of jettisoning rigid planning for experimental projects that could be planned and executed at local levels, and growing organically where they achieved a good fit – a point of comparison to the modes of project inception outlined at the start of the chapter.

Today, participation is something of an "act of faith in development" (Cleaver 2001: 36), an essential marker of organisations and commitment to trying to make development less top down and more relevant. Few critics of participation in development would take issue with the moral – or even logical – imperatives of involving local people, that those who might benefit are presumably best placed to understand what they need and how this should work. Even the World Bank, facing rising criticisms of desolating communities in the name of development, appointed social scientists (as did DFID) and demonstrated concern through publications such as *Putting People First* (Cernea 1985) and *Voices of the Poor* (2000).

However, the implementation of policies to involve communities in planning have met with varying degrees of success. Some aspects of this have to do with the ways in which projects are conceived, as set out in the first part of this chapter. Some NGOs, such as ActionAid, have made explicit attempts to ensure that participation is at the heart of what they do.

ActionAid and ALPS: a participation case study

In the late 1990s, the charity Action Aid made two large moves to shift power in the way it worked. One was to shift decision making away from their UK headquarters, by moving offices to regional hubs and a core one in South Africa. The other was to create a new system for planning and monitoring which had accountability and participation at its core. The Accountability Learning and Planning System, or ALPS, drew inspiration from Freirean notions of participation. The planning toolkit and guidance states clearly:

> ALPS requires that poor and excluded people take part directly in all processes of local programme appraisal, analysis, research planning, monitoring, implementation, research and reviews, including recruiting and appraising frontline staff. Poor and excluded people have a right to take part in decisions that affect them. (ActionAid 2006: 7)

Introduced in 2000 and rolled out across global programmes over the next few years, ALPS involved a major reworking of how projects were developed and conceived. These processes were to now include communities, using participatory methods to do planning with those whom programmes and projects would affect. A new focus on learning was part of this, to be achieved through dialogues and participatory review and reflection processes (ActionAid 2006; Gujit 2004; Walsh 2016).

Such a wholesale reorganisation of the way planning and learning were to be done was not without its challenges. As an organisation working across several continents, many countries and with thousands of partner organisations, to achieve such a radical transformation of planning practices was ambitious. In a review commissioned a few years in, some notable successes were found, including a broad understanding of the goals and need for participatory planning and efforts to collate learning through and with communities. Their conceptualising principles, core requirements and attitudes and behaviours of staff as complimentary factors or a 'stool with three legs' (Gujit 2004: iv), proved difficult in practice. This typifies obstacles that organisations grapple with when trying to roll out complex and ambiguous concepts across many institutional spaces. Translating a series of concepts and reconciling different demands and processes across time, space and languages is no small feat, as other organisations have experienced when rolling out rights-based approaches, for example. Analysis also suggests the tensions produced by trying to reconcile accountability to donors with that of accountability to communities.

Making planning processes participatory in practice was, even some years later, found to be somewhat harder than in theory, as a review by Walsh (2016) found. Participatory review and reflection processes around individual projects were key elements of the working definition of accountability within ALPS. These were intended to be fully transparent, participative, and to enable the transformation of power dynamics. However, for a number of reasons, the goal of community participation came up short in practice. Issues relating to ongoing and future programming were only discussed sometimes, rather than consistently, so were not the envisioned forum for consultation or transparency (ibid). It was also noted, in an example from Uganda, that the set-up for these meetings with communities sometimes replicated spatial and other hierarchies and inequalities of power. Accompanying this were facilitation styles that were often harsh and commanding, on one occasion a staff member berating villagers for their poor attendance, unaware that there was a funeral which many had gone to attend.

Amongst the challenges noted were the lack of staff time to adjust to the ALPS process, which came after a major shift to reduce numbers of staff and increased use of partners. However, there was also a lack of time for quality capacity building amongst partners, and insufficient time was allocated for ActionAid staff to participate in processes or partner support. Walsh found that many staff felt overworked on administration and doing accountabilities and 'preparing for the auditor'. As someone commented, "increasing donor insistence on the counting bednets style of accountability" left little time or room for reflection or context specificity and thus was incompatible with the goals of downward accountability. Another adviser was quoted:

it should have been the start of something. Now it's different, NGOs are imperialist, we set targets, filling dots. Results based management . . . now is not the time for innovation, participation, respect for local culture. (2016: 715)

This echoes strongly the broader argument made in this book about the constraining nature of contemporary planning and accountability processes on

NGOs and other actors. Such concern about the important kinds of work that can't be done because staff are too busy doing number crunching for account-ability processes shows how this also deprives staff of time to do the thinking and interaction with communities that gives development more credibility and chances of success. Indeed, amongst the other failings staff noted in the review was a lack of participation by communities during planning stages.

Other experiences show that it is not always size which is an encumbrance to producing more dynamic and inclusive processes. In my own research, the deputy director of a human rights NGO noted the organisational commitment to open-ness, but also the limitations around this commitment. The organisation went to significant lengths to try to ensure partners had consulted as widely as possible in project development, but in explaining whether members of the small Ik community in eastern Africa were consulted on a specific project, the deputy director pointed to the logistical and organisational constraints that they often worked within, so if:

> Your Ik member on the border of Uganda and Sudan has actually been asked anything . . .? I mean, we ask our partners to ask them. We ask our partners to make sure that they are representing the views of their community and the whole of their community. That's what we ask.

She also added:

> Could I put my hand on my heart and say 100% that either of those is true? I couldn't. . . . we're working with tiny organisations at the lowest level. So the Ik . . . community organisation didn't exist – there was a tree some people stood under periodically, so no office – they had nothing. So, you know, asking them to run full-on, you know, community consultation is not, is not realistic.

Practicalities and the nature of the ideas of planning, as well as the demands that a properly documented consultation process might involve, are amongst many opera-tional choices that have to be made. Good relationships and trust are important, but not every organisation even thinks of consulting with communities directly or sees it as an important matter.

However, there has been ample debate about the extent to which participatory processes have been effective at changing planning agendas towards the views of the poor, as well as much review over how best to do this, what Cooke and Kothari term 'constant methodological revisionism' (2001). In practice, it is very easy for partici-pation to become window dressing, or one of the many 'buzzwords' in development that periodically capture attention in the sector, which for a while seem revolutionary and promising, but ultimately change nothing very fundamental. Participation has been critiqued as easily instrumentalised, a co-optation for sustained control by management through processes that are only nominally inclusive. In this view, participation becomes just another form of control but which aims for those participating to internalise the means and norms that are approved of and selected for them by senior management (Cooke 2008: 117). Participation can thus be a means of extending management priorities. Related issues include which questions or issues are people locally given to discuss. What are the options and limitations of what is on the table? Ownership is not real if management has predetermined the processes and the goals (Cooke 2008).

Even PRA approaches have been noted to succumb to the hierarchies that pervade aid, between planners and those linked to funding, and those who are the objects of it. In PRA, it can be easy for the people running workshops to dominate local voices, who may not be used to asserting themselves. As Mohan notes, there can be a tendency for PRA approaches to "reinscribe relations of authority between outside facilitator and the grassroots" (2001: 153). Other parts of the project process may preclude effective participation. A key question is to what extent and where to integrate the views of locals into planning tools, such as the logframe. This managerialist tool, with its prescriptive grids and modes of thinking (discussed in detail in the next chapter), does not yield easily to alternative modes of thought.

Participation has been widely advocated in work with children, and specific efforts to make space for children's voices and views has been made in the last quarter of a century since the widespread ratification of the UN Convention on the Rights of the Child (UNCRC). In many societies, children continue to be seen as practically and financially dependent on adults, not just because of ideas about physical immaturity but their capacity to understand the world around them. However, in two key articles, 12 and 13, the UNCRC gives children the right to a say in any matter that affects them. In the 1990s, this generated a great deal of work trying to find the right kinds of spaces and fora for such participation, including bringing children to the UN in New York to speak on behalf of their peers.

But what impact does participation have in the problem analysis that informs projects? How much influence does what they say have? How much control over decision making is granted? Because the challenges for children's participation were so many, and the path to real participation seemed so steep, one means of conceptualising participation was as a ladder (Hart 1992). At the bottom of the ladder, children are brought in decoratively, or in a tokenistic fashion in which no serious account is taken of their views. Rising through the ladder's rungs are increasing levels of influence, both over their own actions and the decisions they can effect. At the top is shared decision making. The critical factor here is how much power adults or others who hold it are willing to yield, and a parallel can be drawn with any form of participation. What is the level at which input can have an effect? As Mosse (2001) notes, the effects of PRA and other participatory approaches are limited by institutional contexts in which they are implemented. The vertical systems of control which apply in more development hierarchies mean that there is plenty of opportunity for voices and input to be pushed down the ladder, however much care is taken in collecting local views. The more transformational views of participation have moved towards empowerment (Rowlands 1997), stemming from the idea that by participating and becoming research subjects, people can also become development actors. Empowerment has thus become an approach within planning, often framed as a specific goal or outcome of a programming approach, rather than a planning method per se.

It's also important to note that locals, or projects' intended beneficiaries, are rarely passive when it comes to a project in their locality. Presuming their willingness to participate, and overlooking the heterogeneity within communities, can lead to significant failures. Binary construction of us and them, or outsiders (developers) and locals, is rooted in a simplistic view of local communities. These views might be averted if development planning processes had a different means of apprehending local attitudes, needs, beliefs and other social and cultural factors. This leads us to consider the conspicuous absence of culture in development planning approaches.

Why Understanding Local Views Matters, and On the Absence of Tools for Assessing Culture in Development Planning Toolkits

One of the enduring reasons for project failure, and the yawning gaps between what is written on paper and what happens in practice in project life, is the absence of common approaches for thinking about and ensuring that the contexts of local people are taken into account in planning. Above we discussed the question of participation as a means to elicit the views of locals, as an attempt to reverse some of the top-down dynamics that characterised planning for much of the postwar period and meant that the views of those in offices in donor capital cities mattered more than those of the would-be beneficiaries. While participation has become something of an act of faith in development, and a cosy buzzword with which criticism of such dynamics can be deflected, it is by the same token something that is easily left out of the planning process. Therefore, there is no standardised or standard demand process for accounting for local culture, history and viewpoints in development planning.

That this should be the case is surprising given nearly fifty years of development planning tools and the abundance of examples where overlooking local thoughts and potential interactions with projects has sown the roots of failure. This has been the case in projects ranging from livelihoods and agriculture to nutrition to emergency food relief. One set of examples comes from aquaculture projects of the 1970s and 1980s that sought to encourage small-scale fishery, but that resulted in few ponds being built, rapid abandonment of those that were constructed, and services collapsing upon donor departure. As Crewe and Harrison's review of these projects shows, disproportionate attention went to natural science efforts and very little, if any, to the needs and motivations of communities. The net result of this was a tendency to attribute blame for failure to some aspect of culture amongst the locals (1998: 8).

In a very different context, explored in Chapter 6, evaluation of a multimillion-dollar nutrition project in Bangladesh shows that this had failed to take account of who in a household had decision-making power over what children ate, with significant consequences. Planners made gender-based assumptions about domestic work and simply assumed that it must be the mother, ignoring local realities of kinship. Or take the case of food relief in South Sudan, which was delivered in ignorance of the role of kinship systems in the distribution of food resources, until an anthropologist was contracted to explain, show the error of western assumptions and restate the importance of talking to locals (Harragin and Changath Chol 1998). While the problem tree can be used to find out what people think, it only tackles a superficial level of knowledge, and it does not get at the question of why people think the way they do. Such a question might be the purview of a consideration of culture.

But culture is usually conspicuous in its absence from development planning. It is most often simply not thought about, leading to the kinds of problems outlined earlier. This is a kind of sin of omission that is the product of development's myopia about its own historical, social, technical and therefore cultural origins, and through which stereotypes and assumptions about gender, hierarchies, kinship and many other aspects of social life can prevail. Programme cycle management guidance and tools, for example, rarely make explicit references to culture, as discussed at the start of the chapter. Instead, as commentators have noted, development processes regularly charge ahead without any regard for the history of a place or people whatsoever. As Duffield notes,

> To experience a surplus population as devoid of culture and history is entirely functional for aid agencies in the business of creating new forms of social organisations and identity: a blank page is all the better to write on.
>
> (2007: 96)

In a typical view, development and the modernity which produces it are not seen as cultural; after all, technology is rational and scientific, not cultural, so development sees itself as technical and extending the benefits of technology. Interactions with science and technology are thus also assumed to be universal. Where this proves not to be the case, a second typical strand of development's interaction with culture opens up, and that is to blame poverty on local 'tradition'. This was the case in the aquaculture project Crewe and Harrison explored, whereby the failure of these projects in communities was attributed to "aspects of their 'culture' that were resistant to innovation" (1998: 8). This was aligned with the view that 'they' – whoever the targets of development interventions are that do not behave as predicted – "have cultural barriers, whereas 'Westerners' are guided by modern rationality" (ibid: 133).

Culture is too easily conceived of in terms of identity politics, consumer 'lifestyles' or narrowly as the performing arts, but not acknowledged as linked to or embedded in the economic models of modernity that development exports. While a full treatment of the reasons and means by which Western societies treat culture is beyond the scope of this book, development practices' alliance with modernity and rationality often comes with an implicit framing of it as superior to whatever is local. Part of this hinges on the central role of rationality in relation not just to science but also to economic thinking, and in particularly neoliberal commodification discussed at the start of the book. This is a reflection of the extent to which rational choice theory dominates in economics, for example, and the role of ideas about economic man here, where an individual is seen as a rational benefit-calculating individual with no moral obligations, only maximising his (sic) wellbeing. Where people do not choose to maximise profit, because they imbue objects with other values which a poorly trained economist cannot comprehend, they are thus labelled as irrational.

This exportation of modernity is linked to the implicit quasi-evolutionary paradigm of economic and social development buried deep in development thinking (Hobart 1993). Within this is an unquestioned assumption that the peculiar trajectory of western development, "where self-sufficient farmers became peasants and emerged 300 years later as wage labourers in post-industrial capitalism, should be replicated elsewhere" (Moore 2015: 807). This ignores not only the archaeological record (Graeber and Wenbrow 2021) but acts as a convenient gloss over colonial regimes of exploitation that gave the wealth upon which European industrialisation and social development were possible (Escobar 1995; Galeano 1971; Hickel 2017). Indeed, the ascription of state failure to cultural patterns has been a feature of the contemporary depiction of failed states, extending long-standing imperialist European notions of cultural hierarchy (Jacoby 2005). Ignorance of political and economic history is thus deeply linked to implicit issues of racism in the sector. Recent efforts to bring greater realism of the histories of exploitation and racist thinking to development (e.g. Wilson 2012; Pailey 2019) attest to its historical myopia. In practical realms, development planning processes rarely function with a clear historical awareness of the precise trajectories through which this has evolved, as explored in Chapter 2.

Anthropologists, for whom cultural life and the social relations through which this is woven are central to their modes of analysis, tend to see culture as a symbolic field that is both dynamic and contested, and for whom reification of static views are unhelpful (Kuper 1999). The idea of packaging it as a concrete thing to be isolated for examination is difficult, if not implausible. This has been the source of heated internal debates within the discipline in relation to engaging with development. For some, development has been identified as a neocolonial enterprise that needs to be avoided and critiqued rather than engaged in. This view links the historical complicity of development with colonialism, and the fact that many development planners and agencies were built on the foundations of colonial administrations (Eyben 2014). At their most virulent, such views have posited development as anthropology's 'evil twin' (Ferguson 1997). However, such radical critiques may be said to involve a kind of ideological deconstructionism (Oliver de Sardan 2005), that ignores the many challenges and contradictions within development, as well as what Li (2007) terms the will to progress. Anthropological dismissal of any activism based on their studies also reifies the position of academic knowledge, and often ignores the often extractive, usually unequal and sometimes post-colonial contexts through which this knowledge is generated. Others have argued for an engaged anthropology and the moral standpoint that anthropologists can take as activists, via a re-appraisal of praxis (Gow 2002; Scheper-Hughes 1992; Farmer 1996).

Some of the more productive engagements with development underline what an anthropological lens can offer, looking at how development misunderstands peoples' relationships with their natural and social worlds. Anthropological analyses of the notion of childhood offers a number of examples where anthropological understandings of social and cultural context can have significant implications for project interventions. One is around the efforts to end child marriage and female genital mutilation, both issues which have been the subjects of large elimination campaigns in recent years (e.g. Girls Not Brides). While the abolition of each has widespread support, understanding how and why they are practiced within certain communities is important to avoid unintended consequences. Boyden et al. (2012) note that there needs to be consideration of the risks of being excluded from the social support networks that marriage ceremonies can serve to both create and underpin. Looking at the ways child marriage was practiced in different parts of Ethiopia, they observed how the logic of this cultural practice related to the need for protection from other kinds of risk, such as that of hunger. This shaped community motivations and understandings, but practices also varied among communities, underlining the need for nuanced and specific local knowledge. Making practices illegal without understanding the role they play in survival strategies can put children at risk of other new forms of harm.

Anthropologists have also challenged development to think more deeply about the categories they use, from street children to early child marriage, and what those categories are related to. In the following chapters we will see further examples of cases where anthropological insights offered important correctives to dominant framings of child labour as slavery and the spread of Ebola. Clearly, no matter which area, from child marriage to emergency food distribution, understanding how locals will receive and interact with a project is an essential part of good design.

Conclusion

Many technical tools and analytical processes are drawn upon in the development of new projects, as reviewed in this chapter. Projects are conceived of and come into being in myriad ways, such that no single formula or process can be described as typical in the sector. The sector today draws on vast amounts of data from development agencies, think tanks, academia and more, to help identify problem areas. Broad and deep gathering of quantitative data about economic trends and a range of widely used indicators of areas of human development, such as education and health, provide insights for a sound analysis of context. Tools such as PEA and stakeholder analysis are designed to ensure that project design is as well-grounded as possible in local political dynamics and realities. Such techno-normative improvements on the most rigid processes have led to changes and arguably improvements in the way some aid is done. Approaches such as participation have been brought into planning to ensure that such quantitatively informed understandings are complemented by perspectives directly from the community, and ideally, even involve the community in planning, so that whatever project plans are developed are grounded in local knowledge. However, the experiences of trying to do participation show that while development planning can be amenable to some flexibility, there are significant challenges to implementing this broadly. Participation and the kinds of political values it speaks to may not be universally understood by all the organisations working with an aid chain, and may also be difficult to reconcile with institutional accountabilities and the reporting requirements made of contemporary projects.

As noted in relation to culture, development has some typical blind spots, around its own historicity, the implicit evolutionary paradigms whereby technological modernity is shorn of the historical and colonial contexts which produced it, and is presented as some kind of model for all global futures. We have also seen an absence of a role for anthropological knowledge in most preplanning research contexts. Instead, the kinds of knowledge required by project design and business cases can often be reductive and fail to grasp the nuances and historical nature of problems as understood by a local community. This underlines the temporal nature of the project and coincides with the risk-averse nature of agencies to create a fairly specific kind of identification of situations and contexts into which short-term interventions are justifiable. Were the nature of political problems to be analysed through a Marxian lens, for example, exposing the role of class and other structural vectors of inequality, a different set of solutions might be posed. Instead, these tools show us some of the ways in which the technical framing of aid are a result of the ways in which tools take a complex reality and measure it according to predetermined categories and kinds of analyses, that are amenable to the demands made by donors.

While participatory approaches called for bottom-up and locally led planning, a continuous theme in these tools are the challenges of making these a reality in the often-top-down manner in which projects are formulated for grant purposes. In the wider context of the gap between theory and practice, key challenges remain around the power that administrative systems exert over the ways in which tools are used, as we saw with PEA. These chains of power are apparent when we consider key planning tools in the next chapter.

Notes

1 https://unstats.un.org/UNSDWebsite/
2 Human Development Reports | United Nations Development Programme (undp.org) https://hdr.undp.org/
3 Countries | Data (worldbank.org) https://data.worldbank.org/
4 Home - UNICEF MICS https://mics.unicef.org/
5 www.powercube.net

References

ActionAid 2006 *ALPS accountability, learning and planning system*, London: ActionAid.
Blackburn, Jeremy and Jeremy Holland, eds 1998 *Who changes? Institutionalising participation in development*, Rugby: Practical Action Publishing.
Boyden, Jo, Alula Pankurst and Yisak Tafere 2012 Child protection and harmful traditional practices: Female early marriage and genital modification in Ethiopia, *Development in Practice*, 22(4), 510–522.

Brugha, Ruairi and Zsuzsa Varvasovszky 2000 Stakeholder Analysis: a Review, *Health Policy and Planning*, 15(3), 239–246.

Carothers, Thomas and Diane de Gramont 2013 *Development aid confronts politics: The almost revolution*, Brussels: The Carnegie Endowment for Peace.

Cernea, Michael, ed 1985 *Putting people first: Sociological variables in rural development*, Published for the World Bank, Oxford: Oxford University Press.

Chambers, Robert 1983 *Rural development: Putting the last first*, Harlow: Longman Scientific and Technical.

Chambers, R. 1994 Participatory rural appraisal (PRA): Analysis of experience, *World Development*, 22(9), 1253–1268.

Chambers, R. 1997 *Whose reality counts: Putting the first last*, Rugby: Intermediate Technology Publications.

Cleaver, Frances 2001 Institutions, agency and the limitations of participatory approaches to development, in B. Cooke and U. Kothari, eds. *Participation: The new tyranny?* London: Zed Books.

Cooke, B. 2008 Participatory management as colonial administration, in Sadhvi Dar and B. Cooke, eds. *The new development management*, London: Zed Books.

Cooke, B. and U. Kothari 2001 The case for participation as tyranny: Participation: The new tyranny? In B. Cooke and U. Kothari, eds. *Participation: The new tyranny?* London: Zed Books.

Crenshaw, Kimberlé 1991 Women of color at the center: Selections from the third national conference on women of color and the law: Mapping the margins: Intersectionality, identity politics, and violence against women of color, *Stanford Law Review*, 43(6), 1241–1279.

Crewe, Emma and Elizabeth Harrison 1998 *Whose development?* London: Zed Books.

DFID 2009 *How to note: Political economy analysis.* www.gsdrc.org/docs/open/po58.pdf.

DFID 2011 *How to note: Writing a business case.* https://www.ids.ac.uk/download.php?file=files/dmfile/DFID_HowtoNote_BusinessCase_Aug2011.pdf.

Duffield, Mark 2007 *Development, security and unending war: Governing the world of peoples*, Cambridge: Polity Press.

Escobar, Arturo 1995 *Encountering development: The making and unmaking of the third world*, Princeton: Princeton University Press.

Eyben, Rosalind 2014 *International aid and the making of a better world*, London: Routledge.

Fanon, Franz 2007 (1961) *Wretched of the earth*, New York: Grove Atlantic.

Farmer, Paul 1996 On suffering and structural violence: A view from below, *Daedalus*, 125(1), 261–283. www.jstor.org/stable/20027362.

Ferguson, James 1994 *The anti-politics machine: "Development," depoliticization, and bureaucratic power in Lesotho*, Minneapolis: University of Minnesota Press.

Ferguson, James 1997 Anthropology and its evil twin, in F. Cooper and R. Packard, eds. *International development and the social sciences: Essays on the history and politics of knowledge*, 1st edition, Oakland: University of California Press.

Freire, Paolo 1970 *Pedagogy of the Oppressed.* New York: Seabury Press.

Fritz 2017 Doing development differently: Understanding the landscape and implications of new approaches to governance and public-sector reforms, in Renate Kirsch, Elke Siehl and Albrecht Stockmayer, eds. *Transformation, politics and implementation book subtitle: Smart implementation in governance programs*, Baden Baden: Nomos Verlagsgesellschaft mbH.

Fukuyama, Frances 1992 *The End of History and the Last Man*, New York: The Free Press.

Galeano, Eduardo 1996 (1971) *Open veins of Latin America: Five centuries of the pillage of a continent*, trans C. Belfrage, New York: Monthly Review Press.

Gaventa, John 2006 Finding the spaces for change: A power analysis, *IDS Bulletin*, 37, 1–33.

Giddens, Anthony 1999 *The third way: The renewal of social democracy*, Cambridge: Polity Press.

Gosling, Louisa and M. Edwards 2003 *Toolkits: A practical guide to planning, monitoring evaluation and impact assessment*, 2nd edition, London: Save the Children.

Graeber, David and David Wenbrow 2021 *The dawn of everything: A new history of humanity*, London: Allen Lane.

Green, Maia 2011 Framing and escaping: Contrasting aspects of knowledge work in international development and anthropology, in T. Yarrow and S. Venkatesan, eds. *Differentiating development: Beyond an anthropology of critique*, Oxford: Berghahn Books.

Gow, David 2002 Anthropology and development: Evil Twin or moral narrative? *Human Organization*, 61(4), 299–313. www.jstor.org/stable/44127571.

Gujit, Irene 2004 *Taking stock II: A review of ALPS*, ActionAid International.

Harragin, Simon and Chol Changath 1998 *The Southern Sudan vulnerability study*, Nairobi: Save the Children Fund (UK) South Sudan Programme.

Hart, R. A. 1992 *Children's participation: From tokenism to citizenship*, Florence, Italy: United Nations Children's Fund International Child Development Centre.

Hickel, Jason 2017 *The divide: A brief guide to global inequality and its solutions*, London: William Heinemann.

Hobart, Mark 1993 Introduction: The growth of ignorance? in M. Hobart, ed. *An anthropological critique of development*, Routledge.

Hovland, Ingie 2005 *Successful communication a toolkit for researchers and civil society organisations*, London: RAPID Toolkit ODI. https://cdn.odi.org/media/documents/192.pdf Accessed 21 September 2022.

Hudson, David and Heather Marquette 2015 Mind the gaps: What's missing in political economy analysis and why it matters, in Whaites Alan, Eduardo Gonzalez, Sara Fyson and Graham Teske, eds. *A governance practitioner's notebook: Alternative ideas and approaches*, Paris: OECD. www.oecd.org/dac/accountable-effective-institutions/Governance%20Notebook.pdf.

Jacoby, Tim 2005 Cultural determinism, Western hegemony and the efficacy of defective states, *Review of African Political Economy*, 104(5), 215–233.

Kapferer, Bruce 2005 Introduction: The social construction of reductionist thought and practice, in B. Kapferer ed. *The retreat of the social: The rise and rise of reductionism*, Oxford: Berghahn Books.

Krause, Monika 2014 *The good project: Humanitarian relief NGOs and the fragmentation of reason*, London: University of Chicago.

Kuper, Adam 1999 *Culture: The anthropologists' account*, London: Harvard University Press.

Lewis, O. 1966 The culture of poverty, *Scientific American*, 215, 19–25. https://doi.org/10.1038/scientificamerican1066-19.

Li, Tania Murrray 2007 *The will to improve*, London: Duke University Press.

Mcloughlin, Claire 2014 *Political economy analysis: Topic guide*, 2nd edition, Birmingham: GSDRC, University of Birmingham.

Mohan, Giles 2001 Beyond participation: Strategies for deeper empowerment, in B. Cooke and U. Kothari, eds. *Participation: The new tyranny?* London: Zed Books.

Moore, Henrietta 2015 Global prosperity and sustainable development goals, *Journal of International Development*, 27, 801–815.

Mosse, D. 2001 'People's knowledge', participation and Patronage: Operations and representations in rural development, in B. Cooke and U. Kothari, eds. *Participation: The new tyranny?* London: Zed Books.

Mosse, D. 2005 *Cultivating development: An ethnography of aid policy and practice*, London: Pluto Press.

Narrayan, Deepa, R. Chambers, M. Shah and P. Pestesch 2000 *Voices of the poor: Crying out for change*, Published for the World Bank, Oxford: Oxford University Press.

Nash, Robert, Alan Hudson and Cecilia Luttrell 2006 *Mapping political context: A toolkit for CSOs*, London: ODI.

Nelson, Nici and Sue Wright 1995 *Power and participatory development: Theory and practice*, Rugby: Practical Action Publishing.

Nkrumah, Kwame 1963 *Speech to inaugural meeting of organisation of African states*, Addis Ababa Ethiopia. https://face2faceafrica.com/article/read-kwame-nkrumahs-iconic-1963-speech-on-african-unity.

North, D. C. 1990 *Institutions, institutional change and economic performance*, Cambridge: Cambridge University Press.

Oliver de Sardan, Jean-Pierre 2005 *Anthropology and development: Understanding contemporary social change*, London: Zed Books.

Oxfam 2014/2021 *Quick guide to power analysis*. https://policy-practice.oxfam.org/resources/quick-guide-to-power-analysis-313950/ Accessed 22 August 2022.

Pailey, Robtel Neajai 2019 De-centring the 'white gaze' of development, *Development and Change*, 51(3), 729–745.

Poole, Alice 2011 *How-to notes political economy assessments at sector and project levels*, World Bank Public Sector and Governance Group (PRMPS). www.gsdrc.org/docs/open/pe1.pdf Accessed 5 October 2021.

Pratt, Brian and Jo Boyden, eds 1985 *The field directors handbook: An Oxfam manual for development workers*, Oxford: Oxford University Press.

Rowlands, Jo 1997 *Questioning empowerment. Working women in Honduras*, Dublin: Oxfam.

Rowlands Jo 2016 Power in practice: Bringing understandings and analysis of power into development action in Oxfam, *IDS Bulletin*, 47(5).

Scheper-Hughes, Nancy 1992 *Death without weeping: The violence of everyday life in Brazil*, Oakland: University of California Press.

Scott, James 1985 *Weapons of the weak: Everyday forms of peasant resistance*, Hew Haven and London: Yale University Press.

USAID 2019 *Discussion note: Thinking and working politically and strengthening political economy analysis in USAID biodiversity programming*. www.wilsoncenter.org/sites/default/files/media/uploads/documents/Discussion%20Note%20Thinking%20and%20Working%20Politically%20and%20Strengthening%20Political%20Economy%20Analysis%20in%20USAID%20Biodiversity%20Programming_2019.pdf.

Walsh, Sinead 2016 Obstacles to NGOs' accountability to intended beneficiaries: The case of ActionAid, *Development in Practice*, 26(6), 706–718. DOI: 10.1080/09614524.2016.1200537.

Wilson, Kalpana 2012 *Race, racism and development: Interrogating history, discourse and practice*, London: Bloomsbury Academic & Professional.

Yanguas, Pablo and David Hulme 2014 *Can aid bureaucracies think politically? The administrative challenges of political economy analysis (PEA) in DFID and the world bank*, 20 May 2014, ESID Working Paper No 33. https://ssrn.com/abstract=2439237 or http://dx.doi.org/10.2139/ssrn.2439237.

4 Project Planning

From Logframes to Adaptive Management

In theory, a good project plan sets out what a project will achieve. Having conducted a thorough situation analysis, established who the target beneficiaries are, included an up-to-date PEA at the sectoral level, and incorporated feedback from participatory sessions with various segments of the community, a project team will have a good idea of what they want to accomplish. They then need to consider carefully what approach is best suited to achieving their goals and plan the project in detail. This is often set out in a logframe or results framework, that summarises the key elements of the project in an easy-to-follow grid or sequence that is used widely across the sector. These frameworks set out the key activities and resources that will deliver the project intervention, as well as explain what products this involves, be that cash transfers, educational materials or empowerment workshops. A theory of change diagram will explain how these changes unfold, and what effects these inputs and activities will produce. A results framework will outline the indicators of project delivery and achievement that will be used to manage and measure performance, to ensure and assess project efficacy.

In practice, many projects do not turn out as set out in the neatly edited project results framework that were finally signed off and then approved by a donor. On the ground, the project team struggles to make sense of the logframe that was designed with the neat categories of beneficiary that the donor required, rather than reflecting the diversity of the community as described in emails from the local team. Local colleagues may also disagree with the outcomes and consider them unachievable, and question the logic of cause and effect suggested between the delivery of certain activities and the realisation of intended changes. The staff tasked with undertaking certain strands of work may encounter delays and disinterest from local communities and officials, and struggle with partner NGOs who want to change the indicators set out for monitoring because they think they are impractical. Some activities will take place as planned, but the impacts will be harder to achieve than the logframe optimistically set out.

Introduction

In this chapter, we consider the theory and tools through which development projects are planned, once the initial scoping phase outlined in the previous chapter is complete. The tools we explore, including the logframe and theory of change–based

DOI: 10.4324/9780429427411-4

planning approaches, demonstrate some of the challenges and changes in develop-ment planning and management in the last half-century. These changes reflect both the problems that have arisen with tools rooted in techno- managerial approaches and the ways in which techno-normative approaches have tried to make practice more effective. These changes have taken place at the same time as the increased spread and standardisation of tools such as logframes have imposed new demands on planners in line with the results agenda's focus on efficacy and efficiency. Plan-ning systems now involve a wide range of demands and ever-evolving tools which require that projects articulate goals, objectives and activities in specific ways which are amenable to tracking and other forms of audit. Audit systems emanate from these articulations of specific goals, and become tools of governmentality which are hard to avoid within the reporting requirements which the logframe and other results frameworks enable.

We start the exploration of key planning tools with the logframe. Long a corner-stone of techno-managerial planning, in more recent years the logframe has been critiqued for its imposition of rigid and predetermined categories for project inputs and effects. In the wake of such critiques have come theories of action and change, which seek to unpack in finer detail the assumptions of cause and effect mecha-nisms that exist between inputs and outputs, assumptions which remain implicit and untested in the logframe model. Techno-normative advocates of theories of change tend to also favour adaptive planning and management strategies. In their view these offer better approximations of the complex and often quickly changing environments in which projects and other development interventions unfold. In other words, they seek to address some of the drawbacks of the traditional logframe model and its presuppositions.

As in other chapters of this book, the tools and processes are explored in relation to the challenges that development practitioners experience in putting models into practice. If it is something of an axiom that what is written on paper rarely translates directly into practice, this is particularly true of the tools explored in this chapter. Over the decades, there have been robust debates over how to improve planning. Since the 1960s concerns have been voiced over the problems of using the planning approaches in corporate America put to work in development, where contexts were much more variable, and where different sorts of interest groups and issues play out (Hirschman 1994). Goals of participatory management or project design have, how-ever, been hard to reconcile with what is still in many ways a donor-led sector, in which a competitive and demanding funding environment can leave agencies little scope for creativity. In recent years, adaptive management techniques promoted by techno-normative practitioners to enable creativity have also endeavoured to address some of the power imbalance inherent in logframe tools.

The Logics of Planning

It is often said, and sometimes apocryphally attributed to American polymath and 'founding father' Benjamin Franklin, that failing to plan is planning to fail. If you don't have a clear roadmap or another kind of plan of where you want to go and how you are going to get there, it is at least true that it is going to be extremely difficult to get any funding for a project. However, the scientific planning methods that came to the fore in the 1970s, such as the logframe, were soon tested by challenges that included inadequate data, weak or spurious logic, and environments that did not render themselves easily knowable to the quick scientific knowledge and analysis that development administrators required. Indeed, the history of development planning is riddled with attempts to grasp the many and varied complex elements that need to be taken into account when trying to construct a neat project proposal. If these represent an attempt to reckon with scientific logic, and make project planning as technically effective as possible, a second kind of logic that projects must contend with is political. Over half a century ago, Hirschman (1994) outlined how a "hiding hand" was often at work in World Bank projects. This hand, playing ironically on the idea of Adam Smith's invisible hand of the markets, screened from view the multiple possible difficulties and potential sources of less predictable threats to large infrastructure projects. Through the hiding hand metaphor he argued that projects are presented as possible solutions to problems not because there was bravery in undertaking challenges, but because the "task looks easier and more manageable than it will turn out to be" (1994: 13).

Projects also need to look as if they are consistent with a technological advantage of transferability, and that they are in keeping with the 'best practice' or – even better – are producing a new model for that type of problem. Concerned with efficiency, and assuming the possibilities of scientific regularity that characterise development's technocratic approach, best practice models are designed to facilitate the economies of scale that many agencies look to achieve, as evidence of their expertise. Hirschman's noting of this issue was prescient, as we explore in contemporary challenges that surround trying to make this model a reality in the vastly varied locations where development attempts replication.

Hirschman's well-hidden challenges and technical mastery are important elements of a project's apparent proficiency. The pressure on aid agencies to put forward projects that are both ambitious and (apparently) efficient has only increased, as have the means through which project performance is kept under surveillance, as we look at in Chapter 5. They are part of the wider context in which projects are 'a bid for political support' and demonstrate how project design is

> the art . . . of making a convincing argument and developing a causal model (relating inputs, outputs and impacts) oriented upwards to justify the allocation of resources by validating higher policy goals.
>
> (Mosse 2005: 15)

This view emphasises the social obligations at play in constructing a projection of reality, a possibility for a plan and its execution, that are eminently feasible. They thus become fundable, and it is these creative processes of arrangement and the organisations of certain kinds of facts into a coherent whole, that Mosse sees as an art.

Design and planning must reckon with competing sets of demands. On the one hand, a proposal needs to be a clear articulation of a relevant solution to a pressing problem, and on the other, it needs to be reasonably realistic if colleagues or partners are going to have much chance of delivering it. But design challenges also must grapple with the design tools that the development industry has asserted are necessary for the contemporary project. Throughout the chapter we explore some of the challenges that demands and realities present.

Core Elements of Project Planning

In planning a project, various steps and elements need to be identified. To start a project, a vision of what can be achieved is essential (Figure 4.1). A core and primary one is to identify the **vision or goals** and **objectives** to be achieved. This effectively articulates what the intervention will be and what the desired change will achieve or deliver. The goal is often considered something beyond the direct scope or sphere of influence of the project, but something the project wishes to contribute to – so a project for girls' education may have a vision of all girls having a good-quality education so that they can become income earners as well as mothers in adult life. Meanwhile the objective should be something that can be achieved and delivered by the project, such as improved educational attainment by a specific cohort of young women in a particular location.

Once the goals and objectives are clarified, the second step is to formulate the **strategies** needed to achieve the outcomes. This is often discussed in relation to approaches, sometimes best practices, or more recently 'best fit', acknowledging the varied contexts into which an approach must engage, and the arrogance of a singular presumed best model. The work of a project often needs to be broken down into a number of strands of work that complement each other to help achieve the overall objective. Each of these strands of work may have its own specific sub-objective: for example, working with civil society to build a working group to do advocacy and lobbying of government, and another aimed at service support or delivery at the local or regional level. Once identified, these various strands of work necessary to achieve the objective are mapped out sequentially in a project delivery framework such as a logframe or results framework.

This can be accompanied by a Gantt chart or workplan, that identifies what specific activities will be done and in which sequence, in a manner that allows assignment of human and other resources, which may be linked back to a cost on the results framework for each strand of work. This allows a full identification of the financial resources required to achieve these objectives. These are typically

---

Planning is **"the process of setting goals, developing strategies, outlining the implementation arrangements and allocating resources to achieve those goals"** (UNDP 2009).

Figure 4.1 What is planning?

Source: UNDP 2009

encapsulated in a budget proposal identifying the exact financial resources necessary for each distinct activity and subcomponents.

Alongside the development of the main strands of work come the plans for **monitoring** progress towards a project's objectives, by setting indicators and targets or milestones for the completion of the project, as well as overall outcome indicators that will be used to help establish whether or not the objective(s) were achieved and then **evaluating impact** at the end of the project life cycle. We start this process by looking at the planning tool that so often frames and communicates these core aspects of planning, the logframe.

The Logframe

The logframe – or one of the many variants of it – is now a cornerstone of planning in aid, and sits at the heart of most planning systems and presentations. The term *logframe* refers to a visual matrix or grid that sets out the key elements of a programme in a table often consisting of four columns and four rows. The grid that is one of its key benefits allows anyone looking at a project proposal or framework to quickly understand the key elements of what is being done and to what ends. However, logframes are also known as the logical framework analysis, or LFA.

The analysis is "a way of testing the *logic* of a plan of action by analysing it in terms of means and ends" (Gosling and Edwards 2003: 222; emphasis in original). The logframe matrix helps to "clarify how the planned activities will help to achieve the objectives" and to "be explicit about the implications of carrying out the planned activities in terms of resources, assumptions and risks" (ibid).

The logframe was first developed for USAID by Fry Associates in 1970, in a wave of advances to increase rigour in planning across development agencies, as a way of bringing the most scientific forms of management to their work. In so doing, there were echoes of planning systems used across commercial and military systems (Ika and Hodgson 2014), and its apparent rigour and scientific approach gave it significant appeal across donor agencies. This model soon gave way to a second generation of logframes that spread widely through the 1990s as a range of variants were adopted across Europe's NORAD, DANIDA, the EU and the UN system (Gasper 2000; Fushimi 2018). One review of the logframe approach found it was "easy to ask if an organisation uses the LFA, but their understanding of what it means varies greatly" (Bakewell and Garbutt 2005). During this period of growing use of the logframe, agencies also experimented with the language used to express different components and levels. This led one community-spirited planner to create what was termed 'the Rosetta Stone of logframes' (Rugh 2005) designed to help those baffled by the profusion of varied terms (Figure 4.2).

The varied language in use at the time of this tool's creation has, in the decades since, stabilised significantly, and with this become more standardised. This is true not just of the language being used as logframes' use proliferated, but also how they are used.

Today, many organisations have shifted to terminology and frameworks that emphasise results, putting the emphasis more firmly on the final outcomes. At the same time, the growth of the use of computer software has enabled much greater flexibility in their use, leading some to term logframes made with computer packages a 'third generation' (Sartorius 1996, in Gasper 2000) variant. We are arguably now using a fourth generation of logframes, those that involve a focus on results as much as on logic, as I explore further.

At the core of the logframe's scientific appeal is its referencing of an underlying logic, on which it is apparently constructed. The 'logical' framework proposes that all the elements in the matrix have a logical and consequential relationship with each other, that is to say that if one thing happens, the next can be assumed to follow, in an observable and obvious chain of causality. This logical underpinning is necessarily based on certain assumptions about how change will happen. This casual chain starts at the bottom of the left-hand column of a basic logframe, with effects rising upwards from inputs through activities to produce outputs, which in turn effect outcomes.

This chain starts with resources, which flow upwards to produce activities. These activities, which might include running training sessions, generate outputs, or the tangible products of the project, such as acquisition of new knowledge. This output in turn generates the outcomes or the primary changes the project is looking for. Finally, these outcomes help realise the overall goal to which the project contributes.

As per Figure 4.3, the typical logframe contains the following elements:

- **Goal** (also 'purpose' or 'aims', sometimes 'vision'): What do you want to change? This is usually in relation to a more long-term vision, for example, to improve education and futures for children. It is typically beyond the time frame of the project to achieve this, but identifies the wider social good or vision to which the project wants to contribute.
- **Outcome(s) or objectives**: What will the project itself achieve? This should be a statement of the immediate development outcome that the project will deliver, and which contributes to the goal; for example, achieving higher enrolment and completion rates and better attainment levels in children's education in a specific area.
- **Outputs**: This is where the logframe becomes concrete and explains what will be substantively produced or done. This includes what materials and events will be created, for example, training to improve teaching quality for teachers, as well as the development of quality assurance systems for teaching delivery to be used by local government to help ensure that standards are upheld.
- **Activities**: These are what will actually be done day to day, year to year, by the project in pursuit of those higher objectives. They might include contracting the lease of a new building, the delivery of forty-five training sessions, or the publication and distribution of manuals and textbooks.
- **Inputs/Resources**: Logframes also often contain the first or starting element, the resources which are going to help shape all these processes. These include the financial or material, as well as human, resources. Logframe formats (and donors' requirements of them) vary in exactly what they stipulate, but typically a combination of either inputs or activities and sometimes resources, or a budgetary figure attached to a line of work, are required.

COMPARISONS BETWEEN TERMINOLOGIES OF DIFFERENT DONOR AGENCIES for RESULTS/LOGICAL FRAMEWORKS

Compiled by Jim Rugh for CARE International and InterAction's Evaluation Interest Group

	Ultimate impact	End outcomes	Intermediate outcomes	Outputs	Interventions	
Needs-based	*Higher consequence*	*Specific problem*	*Cause*	*Solution*	*Process*	*Inputs*
CARE terminology[1]	**Programme impact**	**Project impact**	**Effects**	**Outputs**	**Activities**	**Inputs**
CARE logframe	Programme goal	Project final goal	Intermediate objectives	Outputs	Activities	Inputs
PC/LogFrame[2]		Goal	Purpose	Outputs	Activities	
USAID Results Framework[3]	Strategic objective	Intermediate results		Outputs	Activities	Inputs
USAID Logframe[4]		Final goal	Strategic goal/ objective	Intermediate results	Activities	202E
DANIDA + DfID[5]	Goal		Purpose	Outputs	Activities	
CIDA[6] + GTZ[7]	Overall goal		Project purpose	Results/outputs	Activities	Inputs
European Union[8]	Overall objective	Project purpose	Results	Activities		
FAO[9] + UNDP[10] + NORAD[11]	Development objective		Immediate objectives	Outputs	Activities	Inputs
UNHCR[12]	Sector objective	Goal	Project objective	Outputs	Activities	Input/resources
World Bank	Long-term objectives		Short-term objectives	Outputs	Activities	Inputs
AusAID[13]	Scheme goal		Major development objectives	Outputs	Activities	Inputs

This table has been referred to as the Rosetta Stone of logical frameworks.

1 CARE Impact Guidelines, October 1999.
2 PC/Logframe (tm) 1988–1992 TEAM technologies, Inc.
3 Results Oriented Assistance Sourcebook, USAID, 1998.
4 The Logical Framework Approach to Portfolio Design, Review and Evaluation in A.I.D.: Genesis, Impact, Problems and Opportunities. CDIE, 1987.
5 A Guide to Appraisal, Design, Monitoring, Management and Impact Assessment of Health & Population Projects, ODA [now DFID], October 1995.
6 Guide for the Use of the Logical Framework Approach in the Management and Evaluation of CIDA's International Projects. Evaluation Division.
7 ZOPP in Steps. 1989.
8 Project Cycle Management: Integrated Approach and Logical Framework, Commission of the European Communities Evaluation Unit Methods and Instruments for Project Cycle Management, No. 1, February 1993.
9 Project Appraisal and the Use of Project Document Formats for FAO Technical Cooperation Projects. Pre–Course Activity: Revision of Project Formulation and Assigned Reading. Staff Development Group, Personnel Division, August 1992.
10 UNDP Policy and Program Manual.
11 The Logical Framework Approach (LFA). Handbook for Objectives–oriented Project Planning.
12 Project Planning in UNHCR: A Practical Guide on the Use of Objectives, Outputs and Indicators for UNHCR Staff and Implementing Partners. Second Edition. March 2002.
13 AusAID NGO Package of Information, 1998.

Figure 4.2 The 'Rosetta Stone of logframes'

Source: Rugh 2005

Note: Some of these sources are not clear on distinction between columns 2 and 3 (Ultimate Impact and Project Goal).

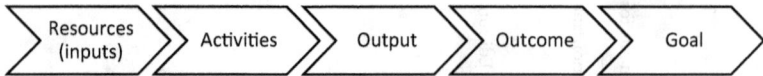

Figure 4.3 The logical flow of the components of a logframe

Source: The author

In the visual representations of the logframe, the changes flow upwards. Inputs and activities flow upwards towards the outputs, which are expected to causally contribute to the achievement of the outcome. These four elements constitute the left-hand side column of a logframe, while on the right a logframe typically asks for the risks and assumptions about those risks made in the development of the logframe. The basic outline of a logframe is shown in Figure 4.4.

	Project description	Objectively verifiable indicators of achievement (OVI)	Sources and means of verification	Assumptions
Goal				
Outcome				
Output				
Activities				

Figure 4.4 A basic logframe format

Source: The author

In the central two columns are spaces for the indicators and means of their verification. The second column from the left holds the objectively verifiable indicators of achievement or OVIs, that shows how the project's progress and what is being achieved will be measured. These indicators can be both qualitative and quantitative, as well as developed as proxies. Next to this is the third column, which identifies the means of verification or MOV for those OVIs. This must effectively include a list of the specific kinds of data which will be collected for the indicators and where it will come from. This data and indicators should enable project managers to demonstrate clearly what has been done and delivered. This is discussed in more depth in the next chapter on monitoring and in Chapter 6 on evaluation.

Against this neat chain of causality rests the assumptions column, on the far right. This column outlines and lists those possible risks which might affect the unfolding of the project. These relate to factors outside the ambit of control of the project, such as the political will necessary for the project to go forward or stability in climatic conditions. In this column, those risks are turned into assumptions which must hold for the statements to remain true and the presumed chain of causality to be effective. While full project descriptions often have sections on risk analysis to complement these short statements, the risk and assumptions column has a key role in supporting the logic underneath the frame. The way the causal chain rises and unfolds through the frame is often set out as:

- **IF** these activities are undertaken **AND** the assumptions hold true, **THEN** the intended outputs will be created.
- **IF** these outputs are delivered **AND** the assumptions hold true, **THEN** the outcomes will be achieved.
- **IF** the outcomes are achieved **AND** the assumptions hold true, **THEN** the intervention will have contributed to the goal.

Clearly, there is a lot riding on those statements of 'if' and 'and'. To explore this further, take an example from vaccination projects (Figure 4.5, adapted from DFID 2011).

Inputs of vaccines and related equipment such as syringes ('consumables', first box on the left) are delivered by and to implementing agents through an efficient logistics process of cold-chain freighting to clinics and other locations where children are to be vaccinated. This immunisation should mean they are then less susceptible to major childhood diseases, such as polio or measles. Diseases can have severe lasting health impacts, as well as be costly to both families and health systems, so a vaccination programme should produce a healthier population in the longer term. As such, vaccinations deliver both a positive outcome and contribute to longer-term development goals, such as to the overall reduction of poverty – here represented as poverty reduction, MDG4.

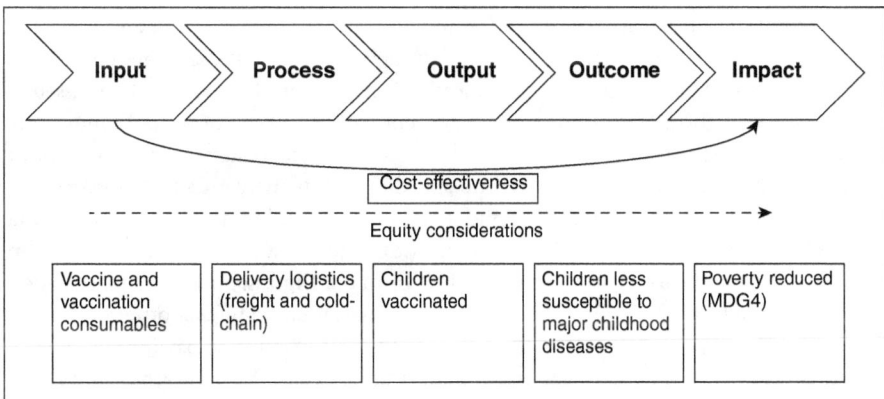

Figure 4.5 A results chain for a vaccination programme

Source: DFID 2011: 4

While no one would dispute that vaccinating children is a valuable objective for a variety of reasons, or that vaccines are an essential part of that, many elements of the chain are more complex than can be represented in a diagram. Two weak links stand out here. Firstly, the link between the activities or as labelled here, process, whereby the vaccines have to reach children. Having vaccines available at a public health post, probably with a campaign to raise awareness and a monitoring system to prompt mothers (as they are often held responsible by public systems for such welfare issues) to bring children to be vaccinated is not the same as 100% of those children being immunised. Some may not make it to the post on the appointed dates, because they could not travel. Children might also be ill, in which case vaccines cannot be administered. Vaccination campaigns are also subject to suspicion, rumour and misunderstanding, sometimes the targets of politically motivated campaigns to undermine them. Providing vaccines alone thus does not guarantee that children will get them.

Secondly, immunisation does not guarantee health, or prosperity, so the longer-term link can be weak, even if ostensibly reasonable or desirable. This is because logframes do not provide a space in which to take into account the wide range of other factors that impact on health such as malnutrition, climate change and disease. To test and prove a casual link beyond reasonable doubt is, as we will explore, a goal of evaluation at the end of a project cycle (Chapter 6), and such proof with certainty poses methodological challenges.

To illustrate these ideas in practice, Figure 4.6 shows an example of a completed logframe for a simple education project. The project aims to raise the proportion of children proceeding to high (or secondary) school in an unspecified location, with a target beneficiary population of children in Grades 5–6. The goal is thus stated as a 10% increase in the number of pupils going on to this from primary school within three years, a typical project duration. The indicator for this goal is the percentage. The aim or target is 10%, and the project's performance will be measured against whatever percentage increase it manages to achieve. This will be verified using data gathered from primary and high school enrolments. Here, no specific risks or assumptions are made.

At the next level, across the second row is the outcome statement and associated information. This is to improve reading proficiency amongst the target children by 20%. This will be measured by an indicator of reading proficiency levels, assessed by tests with a national proficiency measurement tool every six months. As indicators, these are clear and relevant to the process. In the next column is the assumption around the link between the outcome and the goal, namely, that improved reading proficiency produces improved confidence that helps children stay in school. While this sounds plausible, implicitly the assumption is that low reading proficiency more than any other factor is preventing children from continuing on to secondary education. While this may be the case for many children, it could be that other things stop children from continuing their education, such as an inability to pay for fees or associated costs of education such as books and uniforms, as well as opportunity costs such as lost income from not working while they are at school. A good contextual analysis in the main body of a project proposal should explain why this particular set of issues has been identified as the most relevant for intervention, and how any

	Project summary	Indicators	Means of verification	Risks/assumtions
Goal	A 10% increase in the number of Grades 5–6 primary students continuing on to high school within 3 years	Percentage of Grades 5–6 primary students continuing on to high school	Comparison of primary and high school enrolment records	N/A
Outcome	Improve reading proficiency among children in Grades 5–6 within 3 years	Reading proficiency among children in Grades 5–6	Six monthly reading proficiency tests using the national assessment tool	Improved reading proficiency provides self confidence required to stay in school
Outputs	1. 500 Grade 5–6 students with low reading proficiency complete a reading summer camp	Number of students completing a reading summer camp	Summer camp attendance records	Children apply what they learnt in the summer camp
	2. 500 parents of children in Grades 5–6 with low reading proficiency help their children read at home	Number of parents helping their children to read at home	Survey of parents conducted at the end of each summer camp	Children are interested in reading with their parents
Activities	1. Run five reading summer camps, each with 100 Grades 5–6 students who have low reading proficiency	Number of summer camps run	Summer camp records	Parents of children with low reading proficiency are interested in them attending the camps
	2. Distribute 500 "Reading at Home" kits to parents of children attending summer camps	Number of kits distributed	Kit distribution records	Parents are interested and able to use the kits at home

Figure 4.6 Logframe for a reading project

Source: Tools4Dev

other factors may be managed, as discussed in the previous chapter. This underlines the importance of a good situation analysis.

In the lower half of the logframe, more detail is given of how this proposed change will be achieved. The key set of outputs here are around the completion of summer camp by students, and parents helping children read at home. In each case 500 sets of children and parents are being targeted, and their involvement measured through indicators based on children's summer camp attendance records and a survey of parents of the children done at the end of the camp sessions. Here, the key assumptions are that children apply what they learn in camp and that children are interested in reading with their parents. Sometimes this will be achieved or at least attempted by ensuring that books children and parents are given access to are particularly creative and well-designed, so that they related to a wide range of children's interests, or with books that are specifically designed to support reading ability, perhaps even a combination of both. The activities through which these outcomes will be delivered are running a series of five reading camps with 100 children in each, selected on the basis of their low proficiency in reading. For the parental strand of the work, the main intervention is the distribution of reading-at-home kits. Both sets of activities can be measured through fairly simple records kept at the camps and of the distribution of kits. As schools and similar educational institutions track attendance on a daily basis or even at multiple points during the day, using smart technologies, and the delivery of boxes of reading kits to homes can be tracked, these are fairly straightforward sources and types of monitoring data to collect.

Looking at the logframe example in Figure 4.6, we see some of the reasons why it is in widespread use and beloved by managers and donors (Bakewell and Garbutt 2005). Firstly, it is a useful communication tool (UK AidDirect n.d.). It lays out the key things anyone might want to know about a project clearly and neatly, in a standardised format that gives those who have to review many such projects a quick and ready manner of apprehending the key facts. In a matter of minutes (or less), one can quickly scan and see the approach, indicators and goals. Secondly, it is supported by presumed logic, as in the process of creating it, a logframe is meant to demand that the creator(s) think about whether or not the levels do flow and follow logically, and realistically, from one to another.

Fourth-Generation Results Frameworks

As the logframe has evolved, it has responded to growing demands made of the sector and the increased focus on the results. Many organisations now refer to their requirements in terms of results frameworks (RF) rather than logframes, which integrate a wider range of indicators and target information into a spreadsheet. If the logframe has evolved through three generations (Gasper 2000), we could term this RF the fourth generation of the logframe, one which more effectively weds the principles of the logframe to the results agenda. These typically are more prescriptive in terms of the levels or kinds of indicators they require to be identified, and often include elements of costings, linked to value-for-money calculations.

An example of the RF used by the DFID, DEFRA and other branches of the UK government for aid management is shown in Figure 4.7. The first row to be completed under the descriptor headings are statements of overall impact aim and a box for the overall impact indicator. Moving to the right, this is followed by baseline and target milestones for progress. The provision of a space for a baseline makes this a mandatory element, rather than something which can be omitted, and the requirement to provide milestones also demands thinking about the rate at which aspects of the progress will be achieved. Underneath this are rows for costings, so that overall headline budget figures and staffing input requirements are instantly visible. This culminates in a proportional estimate of the budget being demands of the donor, alongside identification of who other donors are.

The section beneath this is one of multiple outcome sections which can be completed for a project. Contributing towards the overall goal, each outcome then has to be accompanied by similar, multiple indicators for baseline and milestone and target progress. Sources of the verification of these are, instead of being a column in the classic third-generation logframe, now given in a row beneath these varied indicators, suggesting they can be gained from the same stable source throughout the project life cycle.

Gantt Charts and Work Planning

To accompany this detailed results framework, a system is needed for outlining the delivery and implementation. Indeed, as outlined in Chapter 2, this is one of the core functions of contemporary project theory and also one of its limitations (cf. Morris 2013). In development contexts, a range of tools is used for this project delivery mapping, from complex project management software such as PRINCE I and 2[1] to simpler project Gantt charts or workplans. Because of the wide availability of variants, it is common to simply require some kind of workplan, as per the UNDP, for example, which stipulates the need for some form of what it terms a 'workplan' in a core planning manual (2009: 113–114). However, one of the advantages of a Gantt-style chart is the attachment of specific pieces of work to a time frame, within one visual field. Gantt's chart is a visual tool that allows for plotting the delivery of specific pieces of work across time. It shows each strand of work, with a start and end date noted, and can be developed to show dependencies between strands of work. Gantt charts can be created in most common software systems including those for spreadsheets, with predesigned templates readily available.

The development of a Gantt chart is effectively based on the strands of work identified in the logframe, and connected to the approach being used, identifying each activity that is needed to complete that line of work. This means thinking about who will be responsible for the commissioning or delivery of each piece of work, identifying when it will take place, noting if this is on a repeating pattern such as monthly intervals, and across what periods of time. When these pieces of work have all been identified, it's also a starting point for developing a budget. This may all sound fairly straightforward, unless of course you are aware that things do not always go according to a neatly made plan.

IMPACT	Impact Indicator 1.1	Planned →		Baseline	Milestone 1	Milestone 2	Target
INPUTS (£)				Source			DEFRA SHARE (%)
				Final evaluation			
				Govt (£)	Other (£)	Total (£)	
INPUTS (HR)	(FTEs)						
OUTCOME 1	Outcome Indicator 1.1			Baseline	Milestone 1	Milestone 2	Target
		Planned →		Source			
	Outcome Indicator 1.2			Baseline	Milestone 1	Milestone 2	Target
		Planned →		Source			
	Outcome Indicator 1.3			Baseline	Milestone 1	Milestone 2	Target
		Planned →		Source			

Figure 4.7 Example of a fourth-generation results framework

Source: UK Aid Direct n.d.

The Problems With the Logframe

Despite the logframe's visual neatness – although also because of this – a couple of decades of widening use was enough for the format to be fairly roundly critiqued (see, for example, Gasper 1997; Earle 2002; Wallace et al. 2007). As noted at the start of this chapter, a key premise of planning is that correct and necessary knowledge is available and used in order to pre-plan an intervention, information which the logframe then summarises. The logframe thus has embedded in it "the belief that fundamental change happens because of carefully planned and coordinated action" (Burns and Worsley 2015: 5), embodying a rationalist vision of planning in which things happen according to plans because these can be scientifically orchestrated. Many of the critiques that apply to project planning overall are associated with the logframe. This is partly because of their historical evolution together, with the logframe in use for a significant part of the last fifty years of development. In a sense all the logframe did was crystallise the key elements of a plan into a grid for assessment. The ways in which it was used – by distant 'experts' in a western capital deciding what was needed by people whose opinions were never asked – were very much aligned with those earlier phases of development planning.

The logframe is also steeped in the language and logic of rationality. This holds that if *a* happens, then *b* can be predicted. This may work reasonably well for car manufacturing – if you put certain parts on an assembly line in a specific order, and control quite closely those who are doing the assembly, be they robots or workers, a car will come out the end. This logic looks much less suitable for social change and is one of the reasons many organisations and actors consider the logframe a frustrating tool to have to use. Its rigidity has been a commonplace criticism of the logframe, because too much is predetermined in advance, and then set into the four-by-four square as if in stone, or little gaol-like quadrants. This rigidity is one of the many reasons critics have felt it to be unsuitable for development contexts, and there are myriad examples of where the intransigencies of the 'lockframe', as Gasper (2000) calls it, in reference to the manner in which statements pin down thinking at an early stage in planning. The definitions of outcomes at this stage can become a highly contentious issue.

Secondly, and perhaps more critically, it invites – indeed, demands – the assumption of a simplistic cause-and-effect relationship between inputs and outputs, and between outputs and outcomes. Gasper (2000) also calls the relationships between these levels jamming, as trying to link activities to societal goals, for example between outcomes and goals, lifts the ambit of the project into non-project areas, or as he puts it:

> in a few strides the project design showed us the way from standard means to uplifting developmental ends. But this usually snaps the links to mundane activities: too many levels became jammed.
>
> (ibid: 11)

Such jammed links are neither clear nor logical. It also lacks 'because' statements in the grid (Teskey 2021).

This also links to problems around assumptions that are meant to create the link between the levels. There is only space to spell out some elements, but often there are quite profound – and faulty – assumptions written into programmes. These could be about the uptake of an initiative, or the extent to which it is considered relevant by local people, as well as about the overall extent to which specific changes can be sustained over time to support the achievement of longer-term objectives. Underneath the neat rows lie more than the assumptions summarised in the column on the right. In many projects, activities are nested amidst a wide range of social and cultural factors and variables that a context analysis needs to have assessed for a project to be effective, but which the logframe does not call for – and which as we saw in Chapter 3, there is little guidance for either. In relation to the reading proficiency example discussed earlier, these could include why there is low proficiency in some parts of the population rather than others; it may be for example that not all parents can read, which would challenge one set of assumptions that underpinned the effectiveness of half the project. So in the four-by-four grid, only *some* of the assumptions about how a programme is to operate are made explicit, and they do not necessarily go into much depth. What might be the most important column is left to the end, as focusing too hard on the key 'show pieces' such as the goals and outcomes of a project in the left-hand column, means the assumptions are relegated to last place in thinking, and by which point people are often tired. But in this last column are an essential set of issues whose cumulative impact is highly significant (Gasper 2000: 13–14). Indeed, here the industrial heritage of management tools is worth referencing again, because if an assumptions column was devised for engineering and management in the US, where there is typically significant control over the immediate environment in and around factories and production supply chains, contingencies would be minimal. The same cannot be said of the development context. Operating contexts are quite different and often unstable, meaning the logframe continues to produce a false sense of security and certainty in the development world.

A third set of problems relates to the idea that the focus of the logframe is on the donor. Because logframes are often developed for the purposes of gaining funding, the logic they are based on is reasoning which is intelligible to a donor, rather than the kind of thinking that might exist or make sense locally. Despite often calling for local teams to be involved in their development, project finalisation often involves a small group of people who have to make decisions quickly and who are also tied to internal management hierarchies. These factors determine what goes in a logframe and mean it easily becomes a classic instrument of top-down management and control rather than participatory and emancipatory planning. In my own research with practitioners, many of these challenges were echoed. As one experienced consultant put it, whatever the problems of the logframe, it was still in use in no small part "because it's the most comfortable way for a bureaucrat to give the illusion that he knows what's going on without leaving his air-conditioned office."[2]

This focus on the donor also tends to mean that the logframe is used in a relatively restricted way, and that boxes aren't updated once a donor has agreed to them. If changes are needed, they may be difficult to agree on or implement, factors which can frustrate learning and preclude adaptive management, as we will discuss in the following chapter. Whilst project managers vary on this, and some say they do update logframes, this can be dependent on the kind of donor, as well as on the relationship the grantee has with the donor.

Critiques of the logframe in practice tend to consider the project's recipient end, as an essential perspective to explore the reality of these issues. In a review of practice amongst NGOs in several countries, for example, researchers found that most NGO staff involved with actually delivering projects "did not refer to the logframes once funding was agreed and implementation begun" (Wallace et al. 2007: 96). Although many found it a generally useful way of framing a piece of work, most found it difficult to translate into practice at the local level, with one saying that here it "fails dismally" (ibid: 97).

Attempts to bring participation into planning within a logframe have been attempted, notably with the ZAPP framework at the German development agency GTZ in the 1990s. This required participatory processes at various stages of planning, but though its stipulations about the nature and content of participatory approaches became rather prescriptive, echoing some of the critiques of participation discussed earlier in the book, and seemed to underline its relation to a planning culture that prioritised technical expertise and funders rather than allowing for a shift to bottom up ideas (Gasper 2000). Indeed, attempting to open the logframe to culture is to ignore ways it will curtail or preclude the elaboration of anything sufficient to represent such complexities (Earle 2002). Ultimately the LFA is often only in place because of power imbalances, as "it responds to needs of certain levels of management in the development hierarchy" (ibid: 8).

A fourth set of issues arises around learning, and when the logframe is put into use. Because the logframe has only taken some issues into account, in a confident manner with little space for identifying or noting unintended consequences, rigid adherence offers very little space for lessons or learning, if assumptions turn out to be incorrect. The kind of planning that follows from a logframe can mean that lessons from problems are 'swept under the carpet' rather than learned from (Figure 4.8). This is not to say that this is always the case, and some respondents in my research noted they used the logframe creatively, with donors that were flexible around it.

Figure 4.8 Sweeping unexpected change under the logframe carpet

Source: Silva Ferretti

While monitoring indicators and their means of verification are provided for, there is no space in which the process can be diverted if the process proves problematic, as per the critique of the lockframe variety. As a summary statement, the rigidity is also a demand for achievement rather than reflection or learning. The inputs of money and time are spent on activities including meetings, which in turn produce outputs, including 'lots of logic models' that give way to outcomes of no improvement. But nowhere does the logframe ask for reflections, or of what should happen if things that aren't predicted to happen occur. These could have a significant impact on a project and be a useful source of learning for the future. The logframe's very layout suggests they won't be necessary.

Theories of Change

Partially as a response to some of these critiques of the logframe, a more recent addition to the toolkit of planners is the theory of change. The theory of change is meant to articulate a theoretically coherent argument for why a project can be expected to achieve its change objectives, spelling out how it is that changes in behaviour, productivity or other aspects are to be effected and delivered. If a major critique of the logframe was its rigidity, and the buried and implicit logical connection between certain inputs, outputs and changes, then the theory of change demands that this be brought to the surface and made explicit. A good diagram illustrating the changes and the more fluid possible shape of a theory of change is in Figure 4.9.

The theory of change is meant to illustrate the ideal pathway of a project's change, but also allow variations on this. If the logframe outlines a series of change steps that relate to an implicit causal chain of events, then the theory of change spells out the steps and causal sequences. This qualification arises from the enormous number of assumptions that development planning is typically based on. Making the precise connections visible also allows movement and change in the direction of planning. If the logframe locked planning into a series of steps, the theory of change approach, and diagram, are meant to allow for changes to that model if the assumptions do not hold true, and to create alternative pathways for change. Developing a theory of change thus requires articulation of what all those implicit steps are. For example: Will children read the books their parents are given in the kits? How much do they enjoy summer camp and improve their reading there? What if attendance is low and the approach needs to be changed to a two-week-long camp instead of one, or if parents also need to be brought in to learn to read? A theory of change–based planning model should allow space for these to be tackled as they arise and acknowledged as unforeseen elements of planning.

In answering these questions more specifically, a theory of change can then be nested or situated in a more complex reality. As mentioned earlier, the logframe originated in the planning context of industrial production in the post-war US, where conditions were largely fairly stable. Production processes, supply chains, the policy environment and the availability of disciplined labour were largely given. But a challenge for development is that it operates in contexts that could not be

Logical Framework

Shows just the pathway that your program deals with – neat and tidy

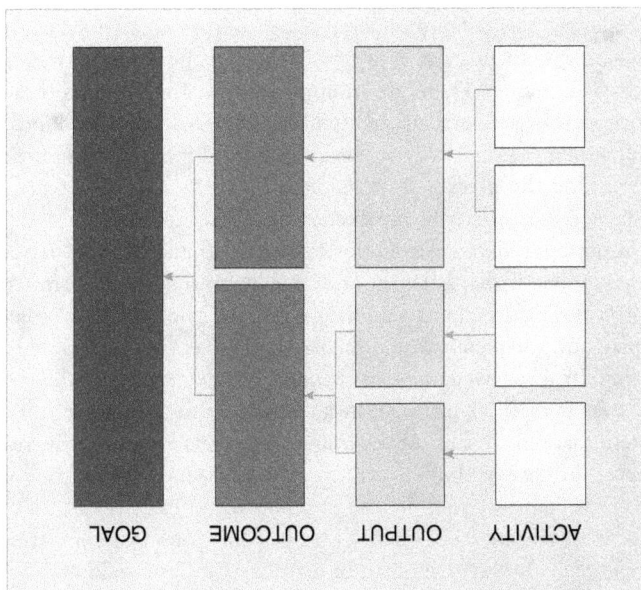

GOAL

OUTCOME

OUTPUT

ACTIVITY

Theory of Change

Shows the big picture with all possible pathways – messy and complex

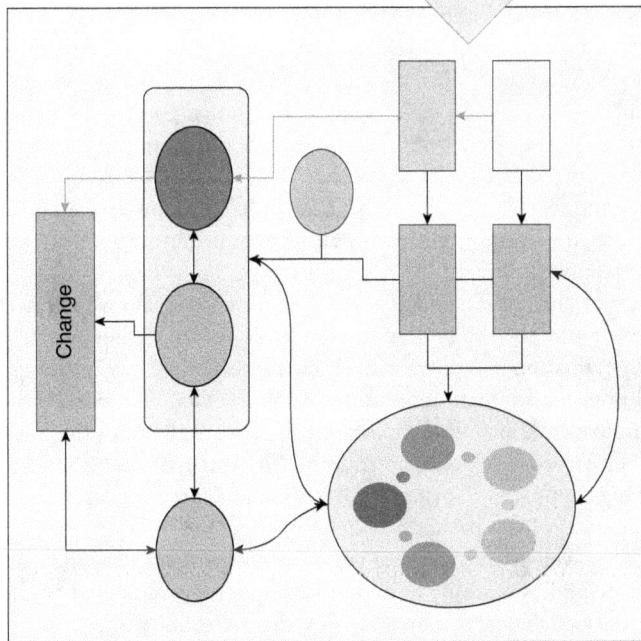

Change

Figure 4.9 Logframe versus theory of change-based approaches

Source: Tools4Dev

much more different from factories, and an advantages of theories of change is that they are more suitable for use in more diverse and unpredictable contexts, one of the prime challenges that more traditional planning systems have faced. As a result, many donors now demand that a theory of change be presented alongside and in addition to a logframe. There are multiple potential advantages to a theory of change. As noted, they are particularly useful and relevant when the kinds of change that are being aimed for have a lower level of predictability than simple linear planning. By unpacking the presumed connection between any one of the levels of a logframe or project, it can clarify expectations and assumptions.

Another important difference from the standard logframe, with its two columns of indicators and sources, is that a theory of change pathway invites more active monitoring of a project. Because there is uncertainty about how exactly a project logic or theory will play out, the pathways and theories are subject to regular review through that monitoring. In acknowledging that change is unpredictable, the theory of change can be used as part of a "dynamic, critical thinking process" (Vogel 2012), with a planning system that reflects this. At the more comprehensive end of the scale, visions of how a theory of change should work as part of a whole approach are described in James (2011) as "an on-going process of reflection to explore change and how it happens – and what that means for the part we play in a particular context, sector and/or group of people". Multiple versions of a theory can be developed as the project progresses. Keeping track of these, on paper or digitally, provides a record of the evolution of the thinking and responsive management as the project evolves. It thus facilitates and promotes learning from work as it goes on, feeding back into new developments.

Another significant and important shift that the theory of change promotes is to approaches that respond to local realities, rather than imposing predetermined 'best practice' models from outside. If the logframe is heavily associated with the blueprint approach of planning, whereby a given model is assumed good and suitable, then the theory of change moves away from this and upends the assumption that what works in one place will necessarily work in another. This is often referred to as a shift from a best practice model to a best fit. Given how little attention is often given to context and culture in planning, this seems an important innovation, or evolution, in development planning thought.

The theory of change model has also come about in relation to concerns about aid effectiveness and the wider results agenda. As noted earlier in the book, the concern with evaluation and proving the effectiveness of aid interventions has led to a panoply of impact assessment innovations, from the establishment of whole monitoring and evaluation units within aid agencies (as considered in the next chapter), to the development of new evaluation approaches (discussed in Chapter 6). Using a theory of change approach in planning allows for a new set of possibilities for evaluating a programme. This is particularly helpful where the links between outputs and outcomes are less well established, and where a simple statistical analysis of effectiveness is not as helpful as a means of understanding why certain changes do or don't happen. A theory of change can thus enhance the evaluability of a project, providing a set of ideas that can be tested and analysed in relation to a project. An evaluation can consider what theory of change was behind a project, how it was adapted, why and according to what monitoring data, and then see what may or may not be useful lessons for other contexts.

A strong theory of change process has a few key principles (Valters 2015). Firstly, it should be about process, rather than a product that can sit on a shelf, as logframes tend to do. There is little point in drawing a theory of change and then not updating it when data is received that demonstrates its flaws. Secondly, a theory of change should be about learning, that is structured into a project purpose, and whereby adaptation is envisioned as a critical element. Valters notes that it can be useful to see a theory of change 'more as a compass, than a map', absorbing the messiness of the route along the way, and responding to this.

As with the logframe, there is wide variety in how theories of change are used and understood. Theories of change can and are used at various levels, from project to programme to organisational goals, and it is important to distinguish between these and ensure the right level is being focused on. Guidelines for theories of change from the Dutch NGO Hivos distinguish between a theory of change and a theory of action, which forms small component parts of this. This suggests the ways a project section can link to higher levels, in what they term a 'project hourglass' (Van Es et al. 2015: 37–39). At the project level, a theory of change is primarily a theory of action, as in a theory that relates to specific action, whereas at high levels, theories of change may not be so elaborate (ibid: 39). At the project level, a theory of change needs to elaborate on the assumptions that link outputs to immediate or early outcomes. These feed into intermediate outcomes and then ultimate objectives, but are also subject to the impacts of assumptions, valid or otherwise, along the way.

At its most elaborate and coherent, as suggested in Figure 4.10, a theory of change is about a process, that encapsulates not just a new way of visualising the

Figure 4.10 Theory of action and theory of change
Source: Silva Ferretti

ways a development process unfolds, but also be created via a broad and participatory process that is then kept 'live' with regular updating and review. So where the logframe was about producing a rigid and boxed idea of what a project would contain and achieve, defined and confirmed by a set of managers before a project had even started, a theory of change approach should allow such rigidity to give way to a dynamic and reflective process, which can adapt to varying reality in ways that make projects more effective, and involving a wider set of people in reviewing the data and the flow of the project.

Visualising a Theory of Change

As per the prior discussion on the different ways in which the idea is used, a theory of change can refer to a set of ideas, a process, as well as a diagrammatic representation of those. This last point is because for communication purposes, theories of change are very often diagrammed, providing a visual representation of the theory process. This can be a bit of a map, and the level of detail to which they go can vary. They can be more complex and show the back-and-forth dynamics that should be associated with the kinds of adaptive management that a theory of change facilitates and enables. In the language of complexity, these are sometimes referred to as 'feedback loops', which draw from one possible pathway to another with feedback data on progress.

Figure 4.11 shows an extract from a detailed theory of change diagram from work on children's rights. The work is diagrammed around supplementary reporting materials on a country-level progress in relation to the UNCRC, and the period reporting that countries are required to do to the Human Rights Council progress in realising children's rights. It illustrates pathways for assessing steps in developing advocacy work around supplementary reporting to human rights bodies. Because many civil society organisations do not necessarily agree with a country's own report on whether it is doing enough to deliver on rights for children, alternative reporting by and via coalitions of child-focused NGOs and CSOs is an effective means to hold governments to account for what they are, or aren't, doing. These reports are useful for advocacy and so an important target of children's rights advocates' attention.

The chart in Figure 4.11 starts at the bottom with an established need to do supplementary reporting. The central strand of work then progresses around the building of that alliance. Work to build and establish a functioning alliance can be complex, relying on bringing together multiple organisations, each with their own agendas, in the hope of uniting behind one common goal, all within a fixed time period. The flow diagram is designed to show the issues and questions that need to be asked or addressed at every stage. In the illustration, a diamond shape is used to indicate a critical juncture or decision point, which affects the flow of work to the next activity. So a first diamond juncture is the existence of a coalition, the answer yes or no leading to different next steps and sets of work. At the next stage, the fact a coalition exists cannot be assumed to mean that it is strong and capable of undertaking the activities that are envisaged. This leads again to two divergent

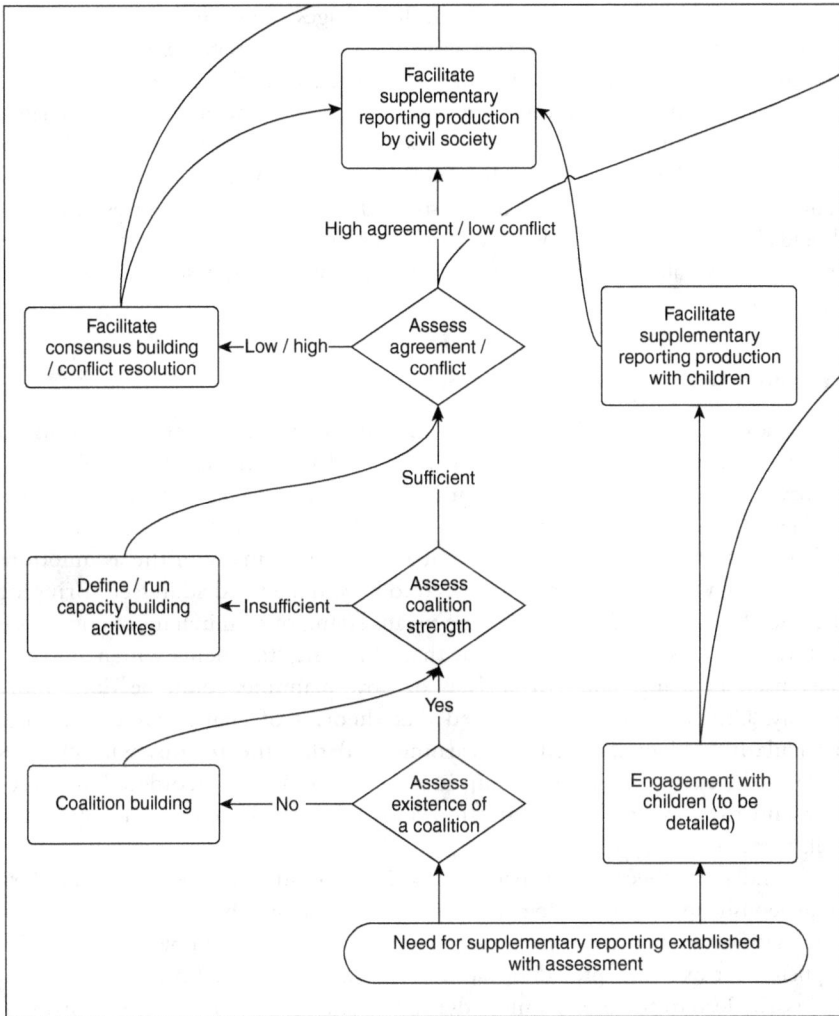

Figure 4.11 Diagram of theory of change for a children's rights project
Source: Silva Ferretti

paths, directly to the next question or via new work to develop and strengthen the coalition. Following this a new set of issues need to be tackled, around whether there is sufficient agreement or consensus on what the coalition should do, for it to move forwards.

Clearly the kinds of questions that need to be asked about every activity or set of activities for them to lead effectively to the next level of work – be that expressed as immediate or intermediate outcomes, or outputs – depends on what work is being done, and what assumptions about the linkages and chains of causation need to be examined. Distinct elements of a theory of change are often represented along one pathway, potentially aligned to one sub-objective, so that a series of pathways converge to produce a final outcome or change. A good-quality theory of change includes causal pathways that are mapped well in a diagram, with sufficient detail so as to be comprehensive and including intermediate outcomes. It should be accompanied by a good narrative and be consist with the logframe. Theories of change should also be accompanied by a monitoring system that is alive and feeds back data and knowledge about how a project is proceeding in real time, so it can be used to change tack as needed.

Problems With Theories of Change

These are attractive and compelling principles; however, several contingent factors need to be born in mind. Live and adaptive management in a good theory of change planning approach hinges upon management that is suitably enabled. One of the challenges that arises when getting people to think with a theory of change approach for the first time is that many of the assumptions they are used to working with will need to be surfaced and addressed. Bringing them to the surface of a project's logic means laying out a much more complex – and dynamic – series of causal paths than the basic statements which are typically used in a logframe. In analysis of how planning could be done more flexibly, Christian Aid (2022) noted that theories of change were often not particularly well configured for learning, and that the reasons why changes were made, such as revising assumptions, often didn't get recorded. Their recommendation was to make reflection and strategy moments more open and collaborative (ibid: 31).

Secondly, the theory of change can also be as broad in its meaning and as heterogeneously applied as the logframe. It can, for example, be used in quite a simplistic fashion to illustrate what an organisation plans to do and how it thinks it will happen – for example, providing vaccines and improving child health. It does not necessarily lead to the use of a more dynamic planning process. Some organisations have a theory of change for their work overall. These may be based on a grand theory of social change rooted in long-term historical analysis. Theories of change also usually stop at programmatic levels, and will still have to rely on assumptions or common-sense understandings for other aspects and levels. In practice, one can find a theory of change title applied to relatively short statements about how change is expected to happen that rest on as many assumptions as the old-fashioned logframe: 'if we develop training for teachers, then there will be better learning outcomes for students', for example.

A third issue is that while for many, one of the a core value of the theory of change is the principle that it can be locally led, as opposed to defined from afar, putting this into practice can still be difficult. Donors, need to be ready for such approaches and potentially fluid outcomes, and management, need to have the time and inclination to see lesson learning as positive rather than evidence of professional failure.

One of the challenges with both of these points is the pressure produced by results-based management or the 'results agenda' (Eyben et al. 2015). This focus on what is achieved draws attention, and thus time, away from process and to outcomes. Donors need to be ready to hear that the work they have funded has not gone according to plan. Lastly, to provide the sort of alternative to a logframe's static mode of what should happen, the theory of change should be updated as evidence comes in of how a project, or is happening. Does the original theory of change made within the project plans actually get updated, and these lessons of how it has evolved learnt?

Complexity, Systems Theory and Adaptive Management

A central intellectual approach that has accompanied the shift to a theory of change model is complexity and systems thinking. As noted previously, one of the challenges associated with planning is working out how the project is going to interact with what is beyond the control or spheres of influence. The chart in Figure 4.12 maps out these things which are under the control of an organisation, such as managing resources, directing donor money and conducting its own assessments.

However, agency or project control diminishes as soon as those products or services reach the clients, or beneficiaries; for example, once food aid is delivered or civil participation groups established, it is to a large extent in the hands of communities what happens next. Of course, there is an idea of what should happen next, but as we saw at the start of this chapter in the guide of the hiding hand, sometimes the unknown factors are minimised as a project sets out its stall and plans. A robust theory of change can help the project and explain expectations, but it may never be able to envision all of the kinds of risks which a situation may produce.

Apprehending the vast range of issues which interact with development interventions has led to the use of complexity theory. Explorations of complexity theory–informed approaches since the early 2000s emerged as a response to this, acknowledging that assumptions of input-output-outcome relationships as linear processes were profoundly mismatched to the complex social and political environments in which most aid efforts

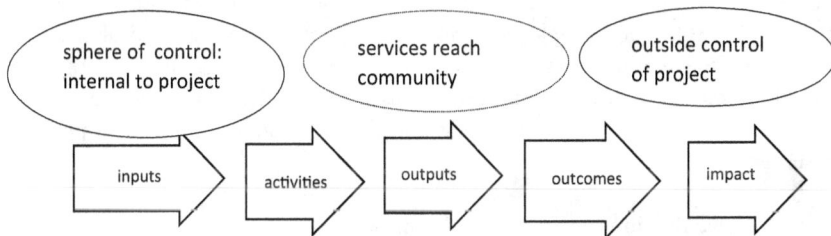

Figure 4.12 Decreasing spheres of control over project

Source: The author

occur. Derived from systems thinking and environmental contexts, complexity-based approaches recognise that change may not be linear, and that there may be high levels of uncertainty about elements of a context (Barder and Ramalingam 2012; Honig 2018; Hummelbrunner and Jones 2013). A good example of the contrasting contexts in which a complexity-aware approach is important is advocacy within civil society, if contrasted to the delivery of vaccinations. Where giving out vaccinations entails the organisation of a supply chain and of the recipients of the injections to specific times and places, mobilising civil society to demand more accountability is likely to be a more chaotic, messy process that will be affected by the other interests of members, as well as over a much longer time frame. So instead of assuming that things are likely to work and play out in a predicted order, planning acknowledges the dynamic and nonlinear fashion of change and is designed for adaptation.

Complexity science is often noted to be a bundle of ideas and theories, drawing from chaos theory, cybernetics and complex adaptive systems, around ideas of the dynamics of non-linear processes rather than a neat package of principles. Systems and complexity theory pay attention to the multiple interacting parts of a system and interactions between systems. Amongst the best-known examples of complexity science is the butterfly effect, described by Lorenz in relation to how small and almost imperceptible changes such as a butterfly flapping its wings can lead to larger effects later, such as storms over New York (Ramalingam et al. 2008: 4–5). Because development contexts involve multiple interacting parts – such as subtle effects of social structure, unpredictable political processes and interconnections with global economic changes – trying to predetermine how an intervention that interacts with all these effects can be challenging, at best. A further benefit of a complexity-embracing approach is the question of attribution. Much of the focus on results produces tension that inspires agencies and projects to look at themselves as agents or causal factors in change, and to try to show donors that their project did deliver the results that were promised at the outset. However, attributing change to one single element in a complex system is more difficult, for example, in shifting civil society to be more demanding of accountable governance. One project may play a role, but not be the single factor to which causality can be attributed.

Most planning systems rely on a good degree of ex ante knowledge, which can produce a simple planning context in which there is a high degree of certainty over the goals of a project, as well as how best to achieve outcomes. At the other end of the scale, complex situations arise when there's a good deal of uncertainty and disagreement about what the best solution to a problem is, and that may include elements of the diagnosis or root causes of a problem (Hummelbrunner and Jones 2013). An Oxfam guide to the implications of systems thinking for planning observes:

> We believe that in most of our work, our knowledge about how change will take place is limited, and that in reality all we can ever provide is a broad hypothesis of how change may happen. We can use systems analysis to generate hypotheses about how change happens. We then need to find ways to test

these hypotheses. This means that programmes need to take an experimental approach. We need to try out things on a small scale, learn from them and adapt and expand when appropriate. Programme development should thus be based on a series of learning cycles that are facilitated by rapid feedback.

(Bowman et al. 2015: 15)

One system – and these are often categorised in some of the familiar conceptual domains of western social science – might involve politics or governance systems. Within any political sphere are multiple actors and institutions that influence each other and are in turn also influenced from outside that system. Complexity recognises that these are not simple or linear relationships, and instead recognises that complex operating environments can necessitate operational and management changes, that pose challenges to the logic of an intervention. What has become known as 'adaptive management' recognises this, and the need for flexibility and adaptation.

Many of the issues that complexity thinking give rise to echo, and are indeed inspired by, the issues raised in politically sensitive programming as discussed in Chapter Three. As political analysis came to increasingly inform the approaches agencies have taken to project development, a range of practice groups have arisen. These include doing development differently and thinking and working politically, each with a community of practice for sharing ideas and lessons, but not without some debate from practitioners about exactly what each of these mean.[3]

In the adaptive management envisioned by Doing Development Differently agenda, this might be achieved by setting short-term goals, as part of wider processes, which are mapped but not defined a priori. The Doing Development Differently (DDD) agenda emerged in 2014 and has been widely shared as a series of principles to incorporate both politically informed approaches and more dynamic planning. Key features of the DDD agenda can be contrasted to conventional practice in a number of specific ways, as per Table 4.1.

Table 4.1 Comparing conventional practice with the Doing Development Differently Agenda

Conventional development practice	Doing development differently
Donor-controlled (even though it might be publicly stated to be locally owned)	Locally controlled and owned
Rational planning	Romantic creative ideas
Results-oriented	Process-oriented
Solution-based	Problem-based
Predetermined design and results	Retrospective review of results
One big step to get those results	Many small, easy-to-achieve steps
Politically not so smart	Politically smart
One-off learning at the end	Iterative learning – organisational capacity assessments
Seeing development as a project separated from social and political processes and complexity	Seeing development as a complex social process

Where traditional development has been driven by donor agendas, with rational planning tools (such as the logframe) and oriented towards results, the DDD vision rejects the use of predetermined models and replaces them with problem- and process-based projects.

The following case study of the SAVI programme in Nigeria highlights some of the ways in which features of the DDD agenda were incorporated.

Case Study: The State Accountability and Voice Initiative (SAVI) in Nigeria

The SAVI programme, funded by DFID, aimed to support governance reform, widely acknowledged as a complex or 'wicked' problem.

One of the key approaches the programme aimed to nurture was 'demand-side' governance, that worked by enhancing the capacity of the 'public' (including NGOs and CSOs) to exert pressure on higher levels of government, referred to as the supply side. SAVI's aim was to facilitate issue-based partnerships between three 'demand-side' stakeholders – the media, civil society and actors in the state house of assembly, and not to make grants in the traditional form.

SAVI incorporated some key features learned from prior negative experiences. It did not call for proposals, or put a lot of money on the table, because this had been shown to attract some of the wrong kinds of 'briefcase NGOs', with the wrong incentives and 'capability mimicking'. At a management level, it did not require formal reporting of results, but instead used a flexible results framework with retrospective reporting of results.

Finally, it did not involve ex-patriate staff on the front line, had a minimal public profile and did mostly behind-the-scenes work. A key factor in its successes were the relationships built between partners and local organisations.

Source: Booth and Chambers 2014

A number of different characteristics feature across these newer approaches. A first is a reaction against externally determined agendas or practices. Instead, both the nature of the problem to be addressed and at least some of the solutions come from the local actors. This has continuity with and may draw inspiration from the logic of bottom-up, participatory approaches whereby the local takes primacy, instead of the universalised premises of common approaches and models that aid agencies may attempt to impose.

A second is the level of knowledge and understanding which exists before intervention, or humility and realism about capacity to understand context. Both complexity theory and the necessity of adaptation, which it logically necessitates, stress the unknowable nature of change pathways, when there are multiple systems interacting. There is also an acknowledgment in adaptive practice that the knowledge needed to make a project effective may not be available before the project's inception, so adaptive approaches may have extended inception and design phases, with more time to develop understandings and test ideas locally. To what extent the limitations of preplanning contextual knowledge are acknowledged may depend on internal working culture of an organisation.

A third is that solutions emerge and may be tested through multiple pilots, rather than being imposed or predetermined in a plan associated with the logframe. This puts both the emergent properties of complex dynamic systems and adaptive management styles at the centre of project implementation. There is no longer a script set out by the rubric of the logframe, but propositions, meetings and dialogue. An example of work from an NGO which illustrates these three points comes from World Vision's transformation approach, that involves significant upfront community engagement prior to specific programmes or grants. This work is funded from unrestricted sources, and grant funding can subsequently be used for projects that are identified through that process, thus enabling a longer-term relationship with communities (Algoso 2017).

In many ways, these approaches provide a series of correctives that have arguably long been necessary for the development machine. At a more systematic level, and endeavouring to engage the donor agendas in the run-up to the SDG formulations in 2015, Wild et al. (2015) argued that these dynamic, adaptive and politically sensitive properties are also essential at donor levels. They argued that a wholesale shift is needed in the way aid works because the gaps between the aims of development, as manifest in the MDGs, and the way benefits of development are accruing to wealthier sections of developing countries rather than the poorest. The core of this problem is the idea that "domestic politics and policy processes are by far the most important drivers of development outcomes and improvements in service delivery" (2015: 8), yet these are difficult to influence. Work on governance reform such as that of Andrews et al. (2012) argues that policy processes often fail because of isomorphic mimicry, whereby processes of reform look suitable, and mimic or echo those being sought, but substantively are unchanged and do not deliver changes in practice. He argues that the problem of uneven outcomes can be approached through a problem-driven and politically smart approach that takes account of the way political systems interact with other things to produce such variations.

An example of this approach is the market for transfers in healthcare workers in Nepal (Wild et al. 2015: 27–28). A challenge here was that healthcare workers were disproportionately concentrated in the Kathmandu Valley because of the better working conditions, such that people tend to shun the jobs in outlying areas that are remote and difficult to live in and cut off from family and other social networks. So healthcare workers have used clientelistic relationships with political parties and pay these to be transferred back to Kathmandu. The authors argue that this shows the need not only for more transparency of political financing, but also note the need to make health postings in rural areas more attractive to workers through increased salaries but also other means, such as perhaps scholarships. Merely supporting either rural healthcare or political processes to change would be too simplistic, but understanding the interactions between political and health systems, as well as economic and social dynamics, allows for a more nuanced view of the specific challenges in delivering healthcare to the poorest and more rural areas.

Changing Planning: Links in the Chain?

Despite progress with approaches such as DDD ideas and principles, which have diffused amongst practitioners and become part of a lexicon of a more reflective approach, this hasn't translated into widespread change in the ways things are done by donors. On the contrary, the demanding fourth-generation results framework, for example, ties the project implementer to a strict timetable and budget, and gives greater scope and visibility of the elements that a donor is tying the project to, such as delivering inputs and change according to a system where the value for money of each outcome can be assessed. The work of project planning can act as a restraining force, as RBM forces the attention of measurable outputs. RBM's focus on ensuring quantifiable and other forms of auditable results have disciplining effects. Indeed, the sense of control and security and risk avoidance that the logframe entails for donors is seen by some to connect to wider problems of the sector, including the lengthening chains within the aid hierarchies, as summarised in the quote below:

> Many of our donors are suffering from 'logframitis'. They want us to package the long-term and systemic change we are passionate about into neat little fundable projects that fit their programme and timelines. They work through complex chains of 'fundermediaries' who channel ever-smaller chunks of money with ever-larger relative reporting requirements. Many in civil society are good at playing this game but many of the most innovative, most ambitious initiatives rarely involve project proposals.
>
> (Sriskadaraja 2015)

These can make project designers risk averse, as they think to the future and conduct self-auditing processes to ensure that they will be able to meet future audit demands. The significant spread of standardised tools in the last twenty years has also produced some practitioners who are so conditioned and disciplined by the logframe, that even when offered the chance to propose alternatives, they cannot think of what these might be.[4] As per the quote then, the logframe is about more than tools; it summarises a whole way of thinking about development that is projectised, that is so concerned with neat beginnings and ends that the larger goals of development are occluded from view.

A critical issue is that planning descends from a project's objectives, as clarified in the core concepts of outcomes and goals at the start. Objectives and parameters of action for a project can therefore be contentious areas. One informant, the director of a small project, talked about negotiating and then re-writing the objective seventeen times with the donor, just for a one-year grant. They tussled over how the work that she felt was realistic could contribute to the higher-level policy change that the foundation manager needed to align it with at his end. Project objectives need to align with what is feasible in the aid chain and what can be achieved within the neat packages of time that projects involve. Indeed, some donors now have predetermined objectives and outcomes complete with corresponding indicators outlined in advance in their funding calls. Projects must then seek to fulfil this specific objective through approaches of their choice, but which must deliver to those predetermined outcomes, which are not open to negotiating but articulate the very specific goals of the agency. Larger systematic work is often precluded, for many reasons.

Trafficking Myths and the Projectised Interventions

One example that showcases these issues is around child trafficking work in Benin. In the early 2000s, Benin was designated as an apparent 'epicentre' of child trafficking, after a boat with 250 children onboard was stopped heading around the coast to Nigeria. The ensuing outcry that the children were being trafficked to work in mines led to the creation of a host of new policies and project interventions, including sensitisation campaigns aimed at convincing parents that children should be home rather than in risky work. However, these interventions were at odds with the views of people in the communities where the children had come from, who did not think children were being trafficked but were going to work. Local beliefs held that child work was a cultural norm and learning process, a necessary part of growing up. Children were expected to take on small tasks aligned to their growing physical and mental abilities, so that as a village elder noted that by 12 "you can begin to work like a man" (Howard 2012). The importance and expectation for young people to contribute to supporting family and community was summarised in the phrase: "it is better to have dust on your feet than dust on your bottom".

Villagers had also seen migration as part of a necessary livelihood strategy, in the face of losses in the country's cotton industry on which locals had depended. The industry had suffered reduced prices due to subsidised US supplies, but such root causes were not explored in relation to the children's situations. In fact, organisations in the country said they could not tackle structural issues beyond its borders even if they wanted to. As one government representative said:

> The foreigners here in Benin know that their policies cause poverty and trafficking. Many of them even want to change it, but they can't. Politicians aren't going to change these policies just because a few kids are trafficked. In their reports they just say "poverty is the cause". They say the poor national use and distribution of resources is a problem. It is organisational hypocrisy, we know it's bad, everyone knows, but what can we do? It's very difficult to change the macro-structure.
>
> (ibid: 470)

This example underlines the macro-sphere away from which projects are formulated and what is circumscribed by political realities in terms of interventions. The framing of the problem as one of faulty childhoods diverted attention away from root causes and towards what could be tackled, echoing issues of depoliticisation outlined earlier in the book.

Moreover, few aid actors had bothered to ascertain the views of people in the villages where the young people came from, in a manner which underlies the importance of not taking project objectives for granted, and of asking people directly what they think the problems are. As Howard recounts,

> When I asked one group of men how they themselves defined the work that teenage boys do in the mines, I received a genuinely emotional round of applause as 'the first person from outside to have ever come here and posed us this question.'

> (2012: 464)

Many development projects are formulated in similarly constrained spaces, defined by what can and cannot be tackled or addressed according to the parameters which govern aid funding and issues. Ensuring that conversations are had that scrutinise how these parameters have come to be, and whether they are suitable, is important, as is an awareness of the political environment into which a project is being pitched.

Conclusions

The tools of planning reviewed in this chapter demonstrate the many efforts both techno-managerial and techno-normative approaches have made to improve the planning of development projects. The location of planning processes in relation to the aid chain, with many decisions often made near the top of aid hierarchies, can mean that efforts are poorly attuned to the needs of those they are designed to benefit. Logframes, for example, usefully summarise the key elements of a project in ways that make them a key communication tool, at least for some located at the upper levels of the aid chain, quite possibly sitting in an air-conditioned office. On the other hand, nesting these key statements into a four-by-four grid can also be seen as highly restrictive, and be very distant from the realities of beneficiary communities.

The discipline the logframe entails, of reducing the whole purpose and means of a piece of work into short statements, can be trying for project designers, grappling to fit complex social realities and processes into small boxes. Tools such as the logframe may serve to give the illusion of control desired by managers and necessitated by the accountability mechanisms at work within publicly funded institutions, but despite such drawbacks it has had an extraordinary durability, and so remains a key feature of much project planning. This is in no small part because it is linked to projectisation of aid, whereby small pieces of work can be agreed on according to technical managerial rationales, specific budgets, timeframes and outcomes.

Theories of change and complexity-aware design put forward by the techno-normative reformists are two approaches that aim to overcome the weaknesses of the logical framework, providing more space for the messiness of interactions with contexts that may be poorly understood by those at upper ends of the aid chain. As a result they allow local staff, government and communities more influence over project trajectories, at least in theory.

However, as ever, a number of challenges persist. The move from the logframe to theories of change has taken place within a period when shifts in the global political economy and domestic donor politics mean that the sector has been subject to ever-tighter regulation and surveillance under the auspices of results-based management (e.g. see Valters and Whitty 2017). RBM systems, focused on indicators and targets, linked to costed budgets, have precluded space for discussing learning and problems in many contexts. RBM and problem sharing are diametrically opposed tendencies. RBM and audit systems have been part of a reification of the economic and reductionist thinking that continues to displace the social. While these are not mutually exclusive, and much of the debate about local action is about effectiveness, adaptive management is difficult to square with persistently upwards accountability systems that dominate aid and shape how agencies relate to each other (Gutheil 2020).

In replacing one advanced planning system with another, higher levels of institutional power are retained, with the resource to shape and effect aid remaining in specific, northern hands. The complex scientific language of complexity theory derives from goals of mastery and knowledge, to discuss issues of statecraft function (e.g. Andrews et al. 2012), that pursue ever more complex agendas while not acknowledging the wider global environment in which dysfunction is a likely outcome of the historical processes western states have subjected them to. Indeed, instead, the aid process and the project with its disciplining forms can be another way in which development processes enmesh actors and agencies in rigid norms and forms. How these function in relation to monitoring is explored in the next chapter.

Notes

1 PRINCE software is project management software, in versions 1 and 2, that was first developed in the late 1980s for the UK government by the Central Computer and Telecommunications Agency (CCTA), a government support agency. PRINCE2 is now a commonly used software tool for project management in industry and state sectors.
2 Interview, October 2017
3 See https://oxfamapps.org/fp2p/what-were-missing-by-not-getting-our-twp-alphabet-straight/
4 Cathy Shutt, personal communication

References

Algoso, Dave 2017 *How INGOs are doing development differently*, Position Paper, WVI. Milton Keynes: World Vision International, www.wvi.org/sites/default/files/How%20INGOs%20are%20DDD.pdf Accessed 17 March 2023.
Andrews, M., L. Pritchett and M. Woolcock 2012 *Escaping capability traps through problem-driven iterative adaptation (PDIA)*, Working Paper 299, London: Centre for Global Development, June.
Bakewell, O. and A. Garbutt 2005 The *use and abuse of the logical framework approach*: A *review of international development* NGOs' *experiences*, Swedish International Development Cooperation Agency. http://www.sida.se/shared/jsp/download.jsp?f=LFA-review.pdf&a=21025.
Barder, O. and B. Ramalingam 2012 *Complexity, adaptation, and results*, London: Center for Global Development.
Booth, David and Victoria Chambers 2014 *The SAVI programme in Nigeria, toward politically smart locally led development*, London: ODI.

Bowman, Kimberly, John Chettleborough, Helen Jeans, Jo Rowlands and James Whitehead 2015 *Systems thinking: An introduction for Oxfam programme staff,* Oxford, UK: Oxfam.

Burns, D. and S. Worsley 2015 *Navigating complexity in international development: Facilitating sustainable change at scale,* Rugby: Practical Action Publishing.

DFID 2011 *Guidance on using the revised logical framework -how to note,* Doing Development Differently, January. http://doingdevelopmentdifferently.com/.

Earle, Lucy 2002 Introduction, in L Earle ed *Creativity and Constraint: grassroots monitoring and evaluation,* Oxford: INTRAC.

Eyben, Rosalind, Irene Gujit, Chris Roche and Cathy Shutt eds 2015 *The Politics of Evidence and Results in International Development: playing the game to change the rules?* Rugby: Practical Action Publishing.

Fushimi, Katsutoshi 2018 The puzzle of the universal utilization of the logical framework approach: An explanation using the sociological new institutional perspective, *JICA Research Review* (14) (December).

Gasper, D. 1997 *Logical frameworks: A critical assessment managerial theory, pluralistic practice,* The Hague: Institute of Social Studies. http://repub.eur.nl/res/pub/19007/wp264.pdf.

Gasper, D. 2000 *Logical frameworks potential and problems,* Teaching Materials for ISS Participants. http://hdl.handle.net/1765/50949.

Gosling, Louisa and M. Edwards 2003 *Toolkits: A practical guide to planning, monitoring evaluation and impact assessment,* 2nd edition, London: Save the Children.

Gutheil, L. 2020 Why adaptive management will not save us: Exploring management directives' interaction with practice, *Public Administration and Development,* 40(2), 129–140.

Hirschman, Albert O. 1994 *Development projects observed,* Washington, DC: The Brookings Institution.

Honig, Dan 2018 *Navigation by judgment: Why and when top-down management of foreign aid doesn't work,* Oxford: Oxford University Press.

Howard, Neil 2012 Protecting children from trafficking in Benin: In need of politics and participation, *Development in Practice,* 22(4), 460–472. DOI: 10.1080/09614524.2012.673557.

Hummelbrunner, R. and H. Jones 2013 *A guide for planning and strategy development in the face of complexity.* Background Note, March, London: ODI.

Ika, Lavagnon and Damian Hodgson 2014 Learning from international development projects: Blending critical project studies and critical development studies, *International Journal of Project Management,* 32(7). DOI: 10.1016/j.ijproman.2014.01.004.

James, Cathy 2011 *Theory of change review a report commissioned by Comic Relief.* www.actknowledge.org/resources/documents/James_ToC.pdf.

Morris, Peter 2013 *Reconstructing Project Management,* Chichester: John Wiley & Sons.

Mosse, D. 2005 *Cultivating development: An ethnography of aid policy and practice,* London: Pluto Press.

Ramalingam, Ben, Harry Jones, Toussaint Reba and John Young 2008 *Exploring the science of complexity: Ideas and implications for development and humanitarian efforts,* Working Paper 285, London: ODI.

Rugh, Jim 2005 Comparisons between terminologies of different donor agencies for results/logical frameworks, *Compiled for CARE International and InterAction's Evaluation Interest Group* http://awidme.pbworks.com/w/page/36051640/The%20Rosetta%20Stone%20of%20Logical%20Frameworks Accessed 20 March 2023.

Sriskadaraja, Danny 2015 Message from the secretary general, in *Civicus state of civil society report 2015.* Johannesburg: Civicus Alliance.

Teskey, Graham 2021 In praise of . . . logframes, *Blog Post on From Poverty to Power*. https://oxfamapps.org/fp2p/in-praise-of-logframes/#comments-wrapper UK AidDirect n.d.

UK Aid Direct nd Logframe Template, https://www.ukaiddirect.org/guidance/impact/ accessed 17.03.2023

UNDP 2009 *Handbook on planning, monitoring and evaluating for development results, other languages*, New York: UNDP.

Valters, Craig 2015 *Theories of change – time for a radical approach to learning in development*, London: ODI. https://odi.org/en/publications/theories-of-change-time-for-a-radical-approach-to-learning-in-development/ Accessed 23 March 2023.

Valters, Craig and Brendan Whitty 2017 *The politics of the results agenda at DFID 1997–2017*, Overseas Development Institute (ODI). https://odi.org/en/publications/the-politics-of-the-results-agenda-in-dfid-1997–2017/.

Van Es, Marjan, Irene Guijt and Isabel Vogel 2015 *Theory of change thinking in practice – a stepwise approach*, Amsterdam: HIVOS.

Vogel, Isabel 2012 *Review of the use of 'theory of change' in international development*, London: DFID.

Wallace, T., L. Bornstein and J. Chapman 2007 *The aid chain: Coercion and commitment in development NGOs*, Rugby: Practical Action Pub.

Wild, L., D. Booth, C. Cummings, M. Foresti and J. Wales 2015 *Adapting development: Making services work for the poor*, London: ODI.

5 Monitoring

Indicators, Adaptation and Learning

In theory, monitoring is a key part of project cycle management, ensuring that a project is performing according to plan. If things are not on track, monitoring data allows a team to make adjustments to implementation plans and schedules, enabling adaptation. Monitoring should involve collecting data on the indicators identified in the project's logframe or results framework at regular predetermined intervals. The means of verification and methodology for these indicators should have been agreed on with all parties beforehand; for example, the school or clinic where a project is being delivered is tasked with ensuring that when students or patients attend, their presence is clearly recorded, with data allowing identification of gender, age and other relevant characteristics. In a manual system, that data may be collected by workers from the responsible agency, at quarterly intervals, or technology permitting, may be sent via an app directly to a database. Monitoring staff in a monitoring, evaluation and learning (MEL) team then collate this with data from other locations and pass it on to the relevant coordinating offices, which then pass it to grant or project managers, who in turn recommend adjustments to keep delivery on track before writing up a report and passing it to the donor as per the agreement. In a donor office, staff can look at the data and be reassured that the money granted to the project is delivering the intended services to the right beneficiaries, and that project staff are learning to adjust delivery to make it as efficient and effective as possible.

In reality, monitoring is one of the most technical parts of project management. It is often an operational or administrative function carried out by staff who work in MEL teams, which are often separate from project implementation and strategy teams. Monitoring is easily reduced to formulaic processes, and with more data filed than are actually used, given the typical volume and complexity of indicators required for successful grant funding. Monitoring is also often burdensome, occupying a large proportion of staff time. It often involves collecting data on a vast array of indicators from a diverse range of partners, who may have neither the interest nor the technical capacity to do this to the standard demanded by donors. Such obstacles notwithstanding, monitoring data has to then be cleaned, collated and organised into large bundles, and sent to donors in detailed reports. After all this work, the data and reports may be put on a shelf in the project office (real or virtual) instead

DOI: 10.4324/9780429427411-5

of being actioned, despite shifts to adaptive approaches to project management and ideas about learning from monitoring data. Another common problem is that teams do not have the time to make detailed records of what changes they make to project implementation as a result of data, meaning learning opportunities are missed. If the data is really bad, they may get hidden, as institutional and individual reputations can also be put at risk by a poorly performing project. Staff may also feel that these processes are a kind of audit, to check on their performance as much as on project delivery, and know they are accountable if things are found to have gone awry. Monitoring may thus be less about learning what has gone well or poorly than project cycle management theory holds to be the case, and instead felt to be a time-consuming burden based on reporting to donors.

Introduction

In this chapter, we look closely at both the theory and the reality of project monitoring, and where and why these divergences occur. We consider what is meant by monitoring, what kinds of activities are involved, and at different tools used, including various kinds of indicators. We also look at some of the challenges in implementing these approaches and using these tools, including how monitoring can amount to a form of surveillance that encumbers rather than facilitates learning.

As explored in the previous chapter in relation to adaptive management, monitoring is central to good project design and management. The process of developing a monitoring and evaluation (M&E) framework, and then designing a monitoring system, involves translating the problem statement and objectives into indicators that can be measured. It is about understanding both the process of delivering the project and the kinds of changes that are occurring as a result along the way.

As outlined in relation to the core planning tools such as logframes or results frameworks, indicators and the information used for their monitoring need to be spelt out in these and in advance. The process of identifying the right indicators also involves taking the theory of change and asking two questions. One is 'how will we know we are here?' at important points such as milestones or critical junctures when the theory of change might deviate from the first draft or iteration. The second is 'so what?', asking whether or not the project is making the kinds of difference predicted and whether specific assumptions still hold. Are people getting involved with the project? Have processes of consultation and participation yielded the right insights? Are there parts of the community who aren't being reached, because of some previously unperceived dynamic? A good monitoring system should be able to pick up on key aspects of a project's unfolding and produce data for both reporting and reflection, on the validity of assumptions and redirection as needed.

The tasks of M&E or monitoring evaluation and learning (MEL) have become increasingly technical and demanding in the last twenty or so years, and involve expertise in designing complex sets of indicators, managing data quality, doing capacity building or training on data collection, as well as data cleaning and aggregation. This has led to the establishment of discrete technical skill sets and professional M&E teams with diverse functions within them, teams or functions which are often separate from those doing day-to-day project management. Depending on the size and scale of the project, this can range from a single person working part time on project data to having a sizeable team of people employed for the area of work. This can mean that M&E functions are isolated and siloed, and seen as unrelated to project learning, or even to basic implementation, which is a risk that consciously adaptive projects try to minimise.

This functional separation is both a symptom and a cause of some of the challenges experienced in producing good learning in management systems. One of the risks associated with contemporary metric-focused project management is the process whereby an indicator becomes a goal and is turned into a target, or Goodheart's Law. Demands and challenges on the ground may sit at odds with the demands from distant donors, who expect the project to deliver in a systematic way as per the logframe. Monitoring systems can also be a source of significant frustration on the ground, collecting data that is felt to be meaningless and diverting attention and time from other issues which are not subject to data surveillance, but which matter more locally. Indicators can easily become some of the most restrictive elements of contemporary project management. The governmentality effects of these are to enmesh actors in complex systems of audit and surveillance, and exemplify some of the distorting effects of the power dynamics of the aid chain.

Monitoring and Indicators

As a technical area, the definitions of and for different kinds of indicators re an important starting point of the field. OECD (2002) definitions are widely used across the sector, offering a fairly consistently useful view of what these terms mean:

> 'Monitoring' is the ongoing, systematic collection of information to assess progress towards the achievement of objectives, outcomes and impacts. It can signal potential weaknesses in programme design, allowing adjustments to be made. It is vital for checking any changes (positive or negative) to the target group that may be resulting from programme activities. It is usually an internal management activity conducted by the implementing agency.

At a very basic level, monitoring a project is an extension or formalisation of things we do every day to check on the world around us. A mechanical analogy can be found in the range of monitoring gauges on a modern car dashboard. Whether containing a series of mechanical dials or a range of digital displays, a car dashboard contains information about key elements of an automobile's functions. These typically include a fuel gauge, to tell you if you have enough petrol or electric charge to get to your destination; a speedometer giving you your travel speed towards your destination; and warning lights for alerts if there are critical mechanical malfunctions such as a lack of oil, an overheated engine or a flat tyre. With attention to these and suitable remedial actions as necessary, you can safely reach your destination.

A few key characteristics help us envision what monitoring for development projects involves and what it doesn't. The first is that monitoring is most often an *internal* area of work, that relates directly to stated project activities and objectives. It is typically carried out by staff involved directly in a project, and often involves staff of partner organisations. As noted previously, it involves identifying, collecting and analysing key aspects of project delivery and performance, and tracking them through the life span of the project. This means, amongst other things, checking that project activities are being delivered. By contrast, evaluation, which we will consider fully in the next chapter, typically looks at what a project achieves over the full trajectory of implementation and more evaluative judgments. Because of the risks of bias, or principal agent complicity, evaluation is often done by external experts, using a range of methodologies.

This means that much classic monitoring often relates to indicators, or specific ways of measuring whether a certain kind of change is happening as the project progresses, as per gauges on the car dashboard. These can be anything from a child's growth, monitored at regular health checks, to a change in a household income as the result of a livelihoods intervention.

Indicators

A range of types and levels of indicators are used in planning, as seen in the discussion of the logframe in the previous chapter. Here we consider in more depth which kinds of indicators are relevant when.

Input and output indicators are the most basic sorts of indicators, and they often count implementation of activities such as the supply and delivery of basic goods or the holding of individual training events. Inputs or activities are the resources including people involved in the effort or event. Outputs are the number of people trained. Of course, simply providing a workshop does not mean that anybody will necessarily absorb everything that is being said. Just ask a teacher how much effort is required for full absorption of new material by a classroom of wriggling six-year-olds or a lecture hall of sleepy university students. Pedagogical assumptions about what progress is likely must therefore be verified by checking what has happened as a result of the training: has children's proficiency in distinguishing a verb from a noun improved? Have the students understood the importance of understanding local perspectives and the potential role of anthropological knowledge for project design? This question of effect takes us to the next level of indicator, the outcome indicator. At this level we are checking what happens as a result of the inputs or outputs. What if the input is a water well? You would want to be sure the well was being used – and not just in the week after the installation but months and years later. This shifts discussion into time, and as noted at the outset, projects are often defined by their short-term nature, which may well preclude the conduction of such long-term monitoring, but which is crucial to understanding development projects' impact.

Monitoring indicators typically relate to the lower levels of the logframe discussed in the previous chapter, where inputs activities and outputs are listed. These are often referred to as process or progress indicators, that can be complemented by questions about the quality of the things being delivered. The diagram in Figure 5.1 illustrates the kinds of questions you ask about inputs and outputs.

Indicators for this level of project implementation often centre on schedules, budgets, personnel, quantity and timing. Are people doing the right job and well, in relation to the inputs? And are the outputs leading to what was expected? Each layer of the logic chain needs to be checked for progress, and that delivery and changes are both going according to plan.

Impact is the long-term change that is seen to result from an intervention. If a well is built, does the incidence of waterborne disease diminish? If care standards in line with the UN Convention on the Rights of the Child are introduced, and explained to care workers through workshops, are they then able to ensure that care providers are abiding by those standards? How would we know if this took effect fully? There is potential for bias in many contexts, so it is often wise to check directly with those you hope will be positively affected by a change. So you have to ask the children, in conditions that are safe, amongst other things, to comment on relevant issues during evaluations. It is at this higher level of outcome, or impact, where significant tension mounts. Over recent decades, the sector has produced an enormous cornucopia of terminologies for indicators and other content in results frameworks, as noted in the 'Rosetta stone of logframes' (Rugh 2005) in the previous chapter. However since then, the results agenda has tended to focus attention on outcomes, which tend to be quantified, as the most relevant level of change to observe. This shift in attention to the direct outcomes of a project has been at the expense of a focus on the longer-term kinds of impact (Scott 2016).

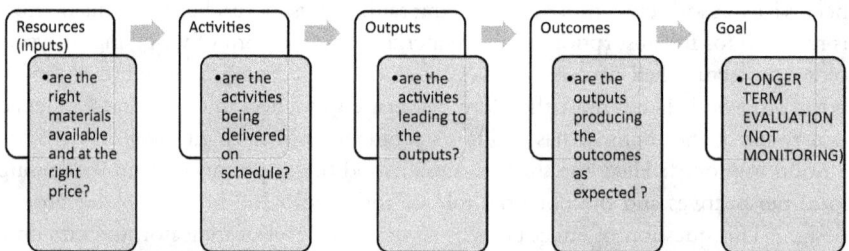

Figure 5.1 Monitoring diagram showing the relation of monitoring questions to levels of the logframe

Source: The author, adapted from IFRC 2011

The political implications of indicators mean these can be sensitive topics, because they are used to measure success or failure. In my research, many of those I spoke to about project management held indicators in a special kind of regard for these reasons. They are highly technical, and getting them right is difficult, but also very important. One interviewee who worked for a post-conflict NGO talked about how they acted as a 'perverse incentive' if they were the wrong kinds of indicators. Donors often want proportions or absolute numbers of progress in delivering inputs or changes, but when negotiating a new post-conflict political settlement, such measures are quite clumsy and often unsuitable. Finding the right kinds of flexible indicators and alternatives to inappropriate measures required persuading people both within the agency and the donor community that the work was better measured by other means.

One of the reasons for inappropriate indicators and units of analysis is the derivation of these terms from management mapping of corporate processes, as the categories to which they refer have been abstracted from vastly different contexts. Translating the meanings into development-appropriate measures and units of analysis has been a key aim of much 'capacity building' or 'disciplining' over recent decades. When do you use the word input or output? What is an outcome of an output? Is this an appropriate indicator? Questions like these, often posed in capacity-building events, reflect the challenges of learning the discipline and M&E lexicon.

A second reason for deviations between the theory and practice relate to the debates around the ultimate results of an intervention. Political pressures and the results mean agencies need to be able to show good, clear and measurable results for the projects they design. Some don't get paid until they can show evidence of results. This has led some to shy away from words such as impact, and get creative in how they apply the logframe hierarchy, which of course has implications for monitoring. Overambitious plans can result in outcomes that are challenging for insiders to measure without support from monitoring and evaluation specialists.

Assembling Indicators

Indicators for these various layers are developed alongside the core elements of the logframe and then form a central part of a monitoring and evaluation system. In many cases, these may be quantitative, such as counting numbers of people attending trainings or clinics, looking at budgets to verify expenditure and matching it to delivery of activities.

As indicators are assembled, they require the identification of key details, stemming from their definition and means of verification (or MOV in the third logframe column). Each indicator tends to rely on specific information and data collection, for example, via a survey of registration data at a childbirth facility, and it is easy to imagine how managing the data for a large cluster of project indicators soon becomes a significant task.

At the Start: Baselines

A key part of measuring any journey, or social change, is knowing where you have started from. Baselines are an essential feature of many M&E design and systems, although they may be developed later in the case of adaptive programmes. Baselines explain and establish the situation at the start of a project, such as latrines per number of people, or proportion (%) of farmers using credit mechanisms. By knowing that it is only 20% at the start, a target of 50% by the end of the three-year project helps to clarify a reasonable distance to achieve within three years, and also helps establish what suitable change might look like in the course of the project.

Baselines can be established for a wide range of data, and in theory much of the data should be part of the process of situation analysis done before the start, as described in Chapter 3. However, data is not necessarily always available at the right level of detail in these steps, and projects are often undertaken without adequate baselines.

Underway: Progress Indicators

Another key concept for indicators is that they measure progress, very much like milestones on roadways, that often show how far you have come and how far you still have to go. Progress indicators are ways of measuring (indicating) progress and achievement. They may help show important moments in the advance of a project, where things like the formation of a coalition, or the signing of an agreement, or the establishment of a new clinic, have occurred. Milestones can be set in relation to predetermined targets, and as we consider next, may be particularly useful in relation to a theory of change. If your baseline for the project shows 10% participation in activities around agricultural improvement, you may have a target of increasing that to 20% after one year and 30% after two years. These could be the basis for reasonable progress indicators.

More qualitative indicators and data can also be collected, and to make these as meaningful as possible, participatory monitoring may be suitable. This could involve people from affected communities helping define their own progress and quality indicators, helping to discuss and verify output levels that are suitable for the context, and incorporating local satisfaction with the outputs and process.

At the End: Outcomes

In many thematic areas of development, substantial debate and coalescing of objectives has led to the identification of ideal or typical indicators of outcome for programming in that field. From governance to healthcare, agricultural livelihoods to WASH (water, sanitation and hygiene), over recent years professionals working in the sector have developed and made public lists of indicators that are considered useful for particular sectors. Following are some examples.

On empowerment changes, one guidance document sets out five domains of change in empowerment projects and a set of indicators that might be useful for them, as per the following examples (from Bond 2012: 10):

- Number and percentage of marginalised people represented on public decision-making bodies

Typically for many areas, an overall absolute number of people and a proportion of the relevant population are given here as key denominators of the indicators. This can be made more specific by adding detail about who the changes will involve and where they will take place.

- Number and percentage of *women* represented in *local government bodies*

An important characteristic of indicators as you set out to measure them is having definitions for the **numerator and denominator**. An example on participation in elections might have an indicator of achieving a specific number and proportion of marginalised people who voted in the last local or national election. Here, the numerator is the actual number of people from marginalised groups (which for the sake of argument we will assume are carefully targeted by the intervention) that vote in a specific election. The denominator is then the whole of that community eligible to vote such that it can be expressed as the number that vote as a proportion of all those eligible to vote.

A common criteria for indicators such as these and those seen in many project logframes and statements is that they be 'SMART'. Giving both a number and a percentage, they are specific, but other features are also important. SMART is a common standard for indicators, which suggests that these be:

- **S**pecific – so that it is clear what exactly is being measured and well defined
- **M**easurable – effectively quantifiable, given a value of some kind, either for ranking, percentage or total.
- **A**chievable – so that it shows good reach and effect
- **R**elevant – closely linked to the context where it is being applied
- **T**ime-bound – taking place within a specific time period, e.g. six months or by a certain date, often the end of project

These criteria are particularly important in the case of outcome indicators since they are about establishing a major marker of the project's achievements. So for the example, it might mean framing the proportion of active voting within a specific time period of elections, say the three years of the project. It would need to be measurable, so you would need some way of getting fairly exact details of participation in voting from the community, perhaps through anonymous reporting via an app, and compare that to the total as available from an electoral register for the community.

Overall, the research required for the means of verification and the data required for indicators, especially as you assembled a battery of them on a results framework, can be complex, and managing them usually involves making a summary table of all that needs to be counted and collected. This data then forms the core elements of an indicator table such as the one in Figure 5.2 (USAID 2017: 2).[1]

Next to each indicator, the table lists the type, the data source, the frequency with which that data will be collected and the unit of measure for that. The final four columns keep track of the base and endline or outcome targets and dates for these.[2] Such specificity is essential if indicators are to be meaningful; and it is in this level of detail that means the M&E sections of aid organisations are often hard pressed to produce the kinds of data the sector's management systems require. Overall, the process of identifying indicators that is part of filling out an indicator table like the one in Figure 5.2 helps to determine the *scope* of the M&E system, which we turn to shortly.

When data is difficult to come by, the range of data gathered may suffer from limitations. A key part of the quality of the monitoring relates to the question of what you monitor in the unfolding of a project. Monitoring the right things is important, as it is for monitoring to go beyond simple (or simplistic) indicators of project activity. If a project is to learn about its effectiveness while there is still time to address problems, monitoring data should show not only whether or not activities happened, but also shed light on who it is reaching. Ensuring there is data on beneficiaries, including which people the project activities are reaching, needs to be done by enabling the disaggregation of monitoring data by socio-economic status, gender, age, ethnicity and location amongst others. This data helps ensure distributional equity in project design. Unfortunately, this kind of monitoring is less common, and such community-linked participatory methods are often not factored into logframes, or that HQ (and the donor) don't need this level of detail, or that the skills are not available.

M&E Systems

All the various data on indicators outlined in the diagram need to feed into an M&E system for a project. As per the table in Figure 5.2, by the time a project is designed, it is likely to require the use and regular analysis of a large suite of indicators, all of which need to be tracked at regular points in time. Some donor funding calls come with predetermined outcome indicators. The tasks associated with organising the data collection and management for a project usually falls under the auspices of an M&E system, and in most cases, specific staff and partner responsibilities are also developed in and around this. An effective M&E system starts from understanding and agreeing to the scope and purposes of such a system, with careful analysis on how monitoring data will be used. Developing M&E systems also requires attending to practical questions such as ensuring staff have time and appropriate skills for the requisite data collection (Kusters et al. 2017: 166–170).

Indicator Summary Table Template *(Example)*

Development Objective 3: Health Status of Target Populations Improved

Intermediate Result 3.4: Improved maternal and child health in East Tambou

Sub-Intermediate Result 3.4.1: Improved child birth outcomes in the southern region of East Tambou

Indicator	Type	Data Source	Frequency	Unit of Measure	PPR	Baseline		Endline		
						Date	Value	Date	Target	
Example . . .										
3.4.1.(a) Neonatal mortality rate (number of deaths of infants during the first 28 days of life per 1.000 live births) in child birth facilities in the southern region of East Tambou	Performance/ Custom	Survey of child birth facility vital registration data by the MCH–Tambou Project	Quarterly	Number per 1,000	Y	01/2016	55.3	09/2021	40.0	

Figure 5.2 Detailed indicator table

Source: USAID 2017

A few key characteristics are typical of a good M&E system. An M&E system:

- Exists to document and store information from various data collection systems
- Ensures that monitoring requirements are fulfilled
- Supports analysis and feedback into the strategic management of a project. Monitoring data and analysis should inform single-loop learning and decisions to tactically adapt or at the least improve development projects and enable double-loop learning.
- Enables managers to verify what actually took place. Checks also need to be made on outputs, be they the workshops, clinic sessions or other products or services being produced. Finally, the outcomes and associated changes also need to be tracked.

In many cases, the M&E (or MEL or MEAL – adding the 'A' for accountability) system will be linked to and expected to feed into wider organisational systems for monitoring and data collection, such as indicator collection systems on core programme indicators that an organisation wishes to track. A single project may be one of many in a constellation of projects that are part of an international programme or portfolio of work, all of which are required to report against one or more common indicators.

But M&E systems also need to reflect principles such as being rights-based or participatory; getting information directly from important stakeholders can be essential to verifying assumptions about them, as illustrated in Figure 5.3, as well as understanding the project's impacts. M&E systems need to meet requirements of utility and provide practical information to meet the needs of a range of intended users.

Figure 5.3 The importance of reflecting on assumptions when monitoring

Source: Silva Ferretti

Practicality is also important, and an M&E system needs to be designed with a view to feasibility – be realistic, prudent and frugal. M&E can involve collecting sensitive data, so all systems need to comply with both legal standards for data protection and ethically with regard to those involved in and affected by development projects. Such system components complement those that rely on other organisational systems, such as HR and financial management systems, that consider and track inputs such as money, material and human resources. Questions on who and how to do M&E also usually mean having technical capacity for M&E, and as identified elsewhere in this book, this specialist technical area has seen tremendous growth in recent decades. Such individuals may be part of a project team, or they may be situated within an M&E unit that employs specific staff. The resources dedicated to M&E are debateable, and depending on how they are structured can vary. While a rule of thumb used to be that donors expect something in the region of 10% of overall project budget and resources should be devoted to M&E, this has become expanded as well as more ambiguous as learning and research are also usually factored into these processes, meaning the proportion could be significantly higher.

This is important to bear in mind even in the simplest of systems, as the costs associated with systems for framework design, data collection, analysis and storage are not insignificant. These may include regular travel for certain members of staff, or capacity building with partners if they are doing monitoring and reporting for the project. Moreover, processing and analysis expertise will be required for dissemination, and the workshops for developing capacity and installing systems, the development of resources such as indicator guides, manuals, communication tools and spreadsheets can all be expensive parts of a project.

Monitoring the Right Things? Anthropology and Understanding Ebola

One of the challenges stemming from the complex designs of interventions is ensuring that sufficient breadth of data is given scope within a monitoring system, and including within it the opportunity to check assumptions that relate to how an intervention unfolds. There may be unintended consequences and effects of projects that are not monitored because they are not foreseen. The outbreak of the Ebola virus in West Africa in 2014 provides a strong example of how anthropological knowledge in the context of a public health emergency can support a better understanding of how a project is being received. It showcases the importance of monitoring approaches that provide space to ask different questions of affected populations, and include different methods and approaches that can help the exploration of unintended consequences of interventions.

The spread of the Ebola virus disease from late 2013 through several states in west Africa produced an international response that focused on isolation and containment to prevent the spread of infection, including multiple kinds of interventions which ran counter to local beliefs and practices. These included the forced removal of sick individuals, including children, from their families and treatment in medical centres where they were under the care of strangers and likely to die without any kin. Entire households were sometimes confined to quarantine, often without access to sufficient food and water and producing additional hardship and secondary illness (Abramowitz 2017). In Liberia, unmarked burials and cremation were widely implemented, despite the fact that locals considered these practices inhumane and grotesque ways of treating their dead.

The exacerbation of suffering by interventions was contrasted with the fact that burial rites are a key feature of social and cultural life in the region, and linked with secret societies (Parker et al. 2019). In contexts where there were already difficult relations with the state, distrust was exacerbated by acts of forced removal that were sometimes backed with threats of violence. In response to these measures, such was the scale of resistance and evasion that analysis of a single village in Sierra Leone found that only eight out of fifty-seven suspected cases were referred to the chief-dom or local authorities. As observed by some involved, "alienating people who are perceived as acting morally is likely to be counterproductive" (Parker et al. 2019). The scale of underreporting as a consequence of distrust of the response suggests that the scale of infection could well have been much higher than many official esti-mates. Those cared for locally were typically taken into the forest, where relatives drew on previous experiences of feverish illness, as well as new knowledge gleaned from contacts, to look after them. Not only did this allow what was perceived as dignity in dying and the continuation of important rituals, but many of those treated in this way survived (ibid).

One estimate puts the cost of anthropological involvement, mounted online (given issues of access) via professional networks and drawing on previously collated material, in total around 0.03% or \$3 million of the overall spend of \$10 billion on the response (Abramowitz 2017). This fractional cost contrasts with the kinds of important insights the work can yield.

Working in Hard-to-Reach Areas: Remote or Third-party Monitoring

The design of M&E systems is necessarily a function of who is involved and where. With Ebola, access was difficult, as it is in the contexts of many projects in human-itarian and conflict-affected or fragile states. These projects may require remote monitoring, passing responsibility for monitoring to local partners on the ground. In the Covid-19 pandemic from 2020 onwards, staff across the world were grounded and had to move work online, using web-based communications technologies that enabled everything from conferencing to data processing. Other situations where physical access is difficult include in the wake of a major disaster where infrastructure is damaged, and to places where for political reasons such as conflict, direct presence for monitoring work is difficult. Indeed one of the challenges humanitarian aid has faced in the last twenty years is the increasingly politicised nature of assistance. In an apparent paradox of presence, the risk aversion of major aid agencies can also mean that staff are hampered from doing their jobs in person, resulting in what has been termed the 'bunkerisation' of aid (Collinson and Duffield 2013). In many conflict areas, aid workers are isolated in secure compounds with armed protection, and increasingly separated from those outside, including their beneficiaries but also partner CSOs. In extreme situations, the bunkerisation of aid can, amongst other side effects, mean that "liability for negative outcomes can be avoided by claiming ignorance: reference to the security risks and obstacles involved in monitoring outcomes provides an alibi for not knowing" (ibid: v). In the most extreme conflict contexts where international staff are removed completely, work is left to national staff who may have less security protection than their expatriate counterparts. In contexts where activities are subcontracted or outsourced, lines of accountability can become blurred.

Yet monitoring is one part of the sector's renewed emphasis on localisation, whereby the implementation and monitoring of projects is done in partnership with and increased leadership and co-design by local partners. Such transitions and changes in power relations have historically been slow and difficult to achieve, given the institutionalised asymmetries of power within and across the aid chain. Indeed, promises of such shifts during the Covid-19 pandemic were much welcomed but not necessarily delivered as far as expected. Such processes may also be hampered by a lack of trust and time in which to build those relationships that rapidly emerging situations involve.

Case Study: Remote Monitoring in Syria

In an example of where many agencies withdraw completely, the long conflict in Syria forced many agencies to adopt new techniques for remote monitoring, some for the first time, and necessitated learning and sharing among agencies of what approaches could work as partners. The humanitarian organisation Alnap[3] (2014) notes the varied and sophisticated body of practice on remote M&E and of working through partners in the Syria response context. A number of specific challenges relate to the security situation, and responses have involved both people and technology, sometimes combined in new ways. Fundamental issues such as targeting and beneficiary identification were often hard to define in conditions of overwhelming need, and the evolving situation meant many new actors were brought into the work. Traditional methods for communicating with affected populations, either through project outreach or use of media such as radio, have been challenging or impossible in Syria, and underlines the inherent tension between the desire to be transparent and the security context in which information can endanger humanitarian workers (2014: 5).

Looking after staff, and giving them time out from stressful environments was important, including psychological support and security training. One agency developed a mentoring system via social media and complemented this by regularly bringing staff out to a neighbouring country for further training and support, while using a consultant in country to provide a backstop on technical issues. This is a labour-intensive approach suitable for smaller-scale interventions, but the technology can be more relevant at larger-scale efforts and programmes.

The uses to which new and adapted technologies can be put in places where staffing is difficult are constantly being revised. One agency, for example, developed a system for tracking commodities using scanned bar codes. Another did mass data gathering via questionnaires done on tablet devices, which were then uploaded to a central server, although noting security risks associated with carrying a tablet. Other agencies have contracted out elements of the monitoring systems with cost implications but advantages including drawing on an established networks of monitors and providing some independent perspectives.

Monitoring for Adaptive Management

The previous chapter discussed the appetite and need for adaptive management in the sector, particularly in more complex contexts and when change is not linear, which involves the ability to learn from monitoring data. This is sometimes referred to as happening via feedback loops, another concept from systems thinking, whereby parts of a system have effects on others, which then trigger unforeseen or unpredictable further effects. A good example of a number of elements of adaptive monitoring can be found in the work of a large project in Uganda that sought to integrate some of these new principles from the start.

The Northern Karamoja Growth Health and Governance programme was started in 2012 as a $55 million five-year development food assistance programme funded by USAID. It had three strategic objectives that were interlinked: economic growth, health system strengthening, and improved conflict mitigation and governance. The programme was designed to defy multiple traditional dichotomies in aid, such as those between short-term relief and long-term development, public versus private and market versus services (Allana 2014: 5). It was also designed to be driven by strategic and facilitative management, embodying a number of the strategies and techniques called for by the adaptive and complexity-informed shifts discussed in Chapter 4.

A critical factor in adaptive management is doing monitoring differently. Here this involved vigilant monitoring, including lots of discussions around the questions of 'what if' and 'how might we', that occurred both within and outside normal timeframes and working hours. A key focus, consistent with complexity thinking, was on emergent practice, instead of a 'best practice' model that helped define what to do and when. This was coupled with a culture of peer review with the project, and outside of it with talking to as many people as possible. These processes involved generating a few hypotheses and framing systemic changes that were open to review and critiqued constantly. Another critical feature was openness to admitting failure, allowing a space for learning where typical monitoring and performance management closes it down. This implies shifting the dominant professional culture of the contemporary workplace whereby admitting failure is 'bad', and with a crucial role for management in allowing that culture to be established.

A number of innovative tools and processes to support adaptive management are used alongside the program's theory of change. At the most regular and day-to-day level, these include a weekly report on progress, after action reviews and in-house studies. Focusing for a moment on the weekly reports, the most everyday or frequent monitoring turns monitoring into a reflective exercise. The weekly reports are described as an opportunity for accountability and "reflection on the week's work, and . . . to share day-to-day successes and challenges with management" (ibid: 16) that keep prescription to a minimum. These reports were briefs of under two pages for any given week, that describe which results are being targeted, what successes might look like, what actions and activities have been tried with what signs of progress or otherwise and with an account of why that has been the case. These reports also outline what is going to be tried next, other observations teams had access to each other's reports and all team leaders were copied in on submission emails. Senior management would then respond to reports from one to two teams each week, creating a dialogue around the work that linked the activities to the results chain.

The results chain, at the other end of the scale in terms of frequency of review, are 'higher level systemic change' that remains the constant goal of the programme. At an operational level, these results chains give senior management clarity on what each team is doing, sufficient to allow for accountability. The chains defined boundaries within which the intervention team experiments, and serves as the mission for it. One key result is around the animal health team, whose systemic change goal is "poor women and men in northern Karamoja have increased access to high-quality, affordable drugs and veterinary services through well-functioning drug shops, vets and health workers". The process of getting to this change and outcome is not prescribed. However, at lower levels the comment notes that the results chain "describes a causal logic in excruciating detail but lays out the team's assumptions of how change will occur and what the programme will contribute to the change process" (2014: 13). The chains produce important points for monitoring and learning, as they come with measurable indicators to confirm or disconfirm hypotheses. When approaches need to change, so can the indicators.

An example of a change to indicators is in relation to the veterinary products and services chain and goal. Keeping livestock healthy is essential for the largely pastoralist community, and the initial project plan was to support a network of community animal health workers to support animal health. However, when this failed to gain traction, because animal health workers were disparate geographically, and not necessarily well trained, the team changed tack and started working instead with two well-established licenced local veterinary medicine or drug shops. These were stable and managed by experienced veterinarians. With the change of tack came a shift to the original progress indicator in the results chain. This had stipulated measures for both "average working capital received by community animal health workers" and "quantity of drugs supplied to them". However when the work shifted to the drugs shops, so did the progress indicators on the revised results chain, which got a new indicator of "proportion of community animal health workers receiving embedded services from local drug shops". This shift, in connexion between community workers and the drug shops, was also associated with an improvement to the supply of medicines that led to a 20–30% price drop (ibid:14).

The authors also identify critical lessons and examples from building a culture of learning and adaptation in the project, which have ramifications at the level of management including HR. They include the observation that 'office culture is fundamental', describing a learning culture that "hinges on the behaviours and beliefs of the people on the team", including all management and employees, that allows for openly admitting failure, cultivating debating strategies and individual curiosity, and which transcends standard rules practices. Here informal structures need to take space alongside formal ones, but note that this takes time and effort to build. Managers need to be able to build trust and deal with ambiguity, significant shifts from the typical command-and-control systems in many organisations. Alongside this, they observe that tools and processes "support learning behaviour, they do not create it" (ibid: 3), meaning that management has a key role in ensuring this does happen.

The idea that monitoring systems that are driven by goals of data collection and aggregation with some minor analysis and then presented to donors do not facilitate learning is now fairly widely acknowledged. However, such data-driven processes remain as much a part of the norm, despite calls for their reinvention to systems that support more adaptive management. Some of these critiques look at collapsing the distinctions between monitoring and evaluation, and bringing in elements of evaluative analysis to the monitoring process that have implications for action. Structuring these means changing the way both monitoring and management are done. Regular reviews with an open dialogue with partners and stakeholders are not just time consuming, but it might mess up your logframe, not to mention your Gantt chart as well, and with likely budgetary implications meaning complicated discussions with the donor. The example from the IRC in Myanmar that follows shows how even when donors are willing to engage with adaptive processes, the bureaucratic accountability systems can get in the way.

Case Study: Adaptive Management by IRC in Myanmar (from Mercy Corps & IRC 2016)

The Three Millennium Development Goal (3MDG) health project in Kayah state in eastern Myanmar was led by the International Rescue Committee (IRC) with a consortium of agencies, including the United Nations Office for Project Services (UNOPS) and International Office on Migration (IOM), a local organisation representing six local health groups and liaising with the state health department. Funded by seven donors, the project needed to work effectively in a context where decades of civil war have led to ongoing conflict, as well as one where ethnic diversity has been coupled to political exclusion, low levels of economic progress, and cultural and social repression.

The goals centred around improving access to basic quality health care, with a particular focus on the most vulnerable, including new and expectant mothers, newborns and child health. One of the key things done differently was to have a six-month inception period that was spent building trust and understanding local health priorities, and carrying out stakeholder mapping and network analysis. One of the things that stakeholder mapping revealed was where trust existed between actors and partners, and this information was used to build an understanding of where opportunities might arise and where tensions needed to be managed, producing a way to strengthen relationships over the course of the project.

However, the original logframe did not reflect these complex and nuanced relationships and approaches, and proved something of an obstacle rather than a help for local work. One donor representative noted that:

> progress doesn't happen at a constant rate or necessarily in line with program implementation work plans. It rather is a start-stop process with slow periods, sudden spurts forward as well as some steps back.
>
> (2016: 3)

One flexible funding stream was created and proved essential for opportunistic programming to complement the core activities for the project, and meant they were able to respond to heterogeneity, developing opportunities in work in response to local requirements. However, getting new budgets for organisation-specific health plans that reflected communities' diversity was difficult to agree on with donors and required no less than 10 iterations. Overall, the fact that a good working relationship with community representatives had been developed proved a sustainable legacy of the approach, and when a deadly cyclone hit, this enabled an effective joint response.

Flexibility in Dutch CSO Projects

In a different kind of case study, that explores the challenges that the wrong kinds of accountability structures can produce for adaptive management, Gutheil (2020) considered the impact on CSOs in a programme where M&E were left fairly open and flexible. The work involved an approach informed by adaptive critiques, and experiences of CSOs involved in a programme led by the Dutch Ministry of Foreign Affairs to support civil society. The Dutch 'Dialogue and Dissent Theory of Change 2.0' approach incorporates an understanding of the non-linear nature of social change, recognising both power asymmetries and goals of social transformation. In this paradigm, CSOs were seen as political actors and partners of embassies and the Ministry, who received funding through consortiums headed by Dutch CSOs. Acknowledging multiple elements of newer adaptive paradigms, the project aimed for local ownership, embeddedness and legitimacy, with three central innovations. The first was working in partnership with shared responsibilities, aligning efforts between the Ministry, embassies and CSOs based on equal and reciprocal relationships. Second, the approach used a flexible theory of change with room for local adjustment as part of the paradigm. Third, flexibility was also given on monitoring and evaluation processes, with minimal reporting and an emphasis on learning.

Gutheil's conversations with CSOs that participated in this programme underlined the mixed and complex nature of implementing such shifts. She found that although practices for joint collaboration were welcomed by CSOs, they noted that the relationships were still largely transactional, and relied on personal relations, reflecting the fact that money and power asymmetries retained a unidirectional kind of character. CSOs were also reluctant to criticise the Ministry openly, suggesting limitations to which power shifts could be realistically delivered. While the flexible theory of change was welcomed, there was discrepancy as to what difference this really made; in some cases, it wasn't presented beforehand. There were also issues with the fact that advocacy tends to come with smaller budgets than service delivery, and some organisations struggled with the reduced money for overheads, and had less flexibility to finance their own institutional priorities. While the freedom in monitoring evaluation processes was welcomed, the challenge of producing written artefacts for the donor include the fact that writing seemed to reflect hierarchies more than meetings, and many noted that they struggled to turn the information they received from partners into presentable forms that did justice to its complexity (2020: 136). Gutheil notes that this underlines the extent to which 'learning and knowing are social activities' (ibid), a relevant reminder about the challenges of learning in organisations that are structured through socially constituted hierarchies.

This case study concludes that while the discretion and space for flexibility were broadly welcomed, institutional parameters, relationships and financial responsibilities shaped how individual actors encountered these processes. Tools are thus implemented within social webs and communities of meaning. Gutheil discounts Mosse's (2005) idea that projects are instances of policy, and that aid workers translate what happens into authorised versions of this. Instead she suggests that we need more research on how different actors respond to the institutional realities within which policy innovations are nested.

Beyond the Manuals: Escaping Technocracy?

Indeed, it is one of the central challenges to arise from the results agenda that while time, space and dedicated staff for monitoring and evaluation functions have all grown, M&E resources have tended to be allocated to upwards accountability to donors rather than learning. When M&E staff spend more time collecting reams of quantitative data, opportunities to support reflection and learning on various assumptions in support of adaptation that might improve the way development happens are lost (Figure 5.4).

The acknowledged gap between theory and practice in monitoring still needs to be closed in many cases, to shift away from indicator- and data-driven M&E to systems that are geared towards learning (Brock et al. 2016; Wild and Ramalingam 2018; Woodhill 2011). This would necessitate some blurring of task boundaries across specialist teams, and involve including M&E staff in discussion with strategic planners and decision makers. However, not all managers are willing to do this, nor do donor systems invite it (Honig 2018), meaning that many managers persist in seeing M&E as

> number counting and dull reporting, . . . a disengagement [that] becomes a self-fulfilling prophecy as the lack of management orientation during the M&E design stage will certainly make it ineffective in terms of that function.
>
> (Woodhill 2011: 4)

Figure 5.4 Beware of machine-like monitoring

Source: Silva Ferretti

A few key problems in this discussion include the fact that because of the division of tasks, and the reduction of M&E to collection and aggregation of data, the fact it is considered dull and repetitive is perhaps not surprising, given that many who do it consider it onerous and as meeting donor demands rather than programmatic ones. Management needs to think monitoring is important as well, but because M&E is often parcelled out to technical specialists who may sit in a hub of 'number crunchers' or alone, those involved with high-level strategic work may not see the potential it has to radically reshape management. Instead, we see the disciplinary effects on aid workers' time, through systems that often prioritise donor accountability. So the shift to an integrated system where monitoring is regularly providing feedback loops to management and new knowledge for learning has been slow to arrive and in many places never happened.

The metrics with which large agencies feel they are judged in a competitive marketplace for voluntary and donor funding can also mean that resources are geared towards generating numbers that suit this top level of understanding. Instead of fostering the kinds of dynamics that rights-based approaches to impact assessment, such as involving stakeholders including children in monitoring and evaluation, marketing and competitive fundraising environments have led instead to the development of systems counting aggregeating numbers of all beneficiaries. This has directed significant effort and time towards counting numbers of individual people who are reached by programmes, counting anyone who has received any kind of service or material output and focusing at the level of output instead of impact (see Scott 2016). This focus on short-term and quantifiable metrics is part of the results agenda and distracts from longer-term and systemic thinking. While long-term impact is invariably difficult to assess, just because things are difficult that doesn't mean they're not worth doing.

A related challenge is that a metricised view of M&E is the displacement of other kinds of knowledge. As outlined earlier in the book, the project's effects as an instrument of governmentality are nowhere more apparent than in the heavily technical domain of M&E. Observing the ways M&E demands have altered the practices of NGOs in South Africa, Mueller Hirth (2012) argues that this new domain of knowledge has been made possible by the calculated creation of new spaces for technical expertise. She cites a USAID PEPFAR[4] manual, which suggests that a successful M&E unit needs expertise in epidemiology, social science analysis, data processing, statistical analysis and data dissemination (ibid: 652). To bring together all this is far beyond what many NGOs can provide, excluding many smaller NGOs from participating in large aid grants and contributing to the chain of 'fundermediaries' mentioned in the previous chapter. In so far as they can and must adopt the use of this specific language to participate at any level, even if a lower rung and delivering indicator information to a grant holder, we see the extension of this domain of neoliberal rationality and technical approaches into new spaces.

Moreover, and given that indicators have become highly technical and complex systems for data gathering and aggregation, the opportunities for bottom-up shaping of indicators have been significantly reduced. Girei (2016) describes negotiations over indicators with a local NGO in Uganda, reporting on local staff protestations that the proposed quantitative indicators on which they had been asked to report had no meaning locally. However, there was no space for contestation. Instead, she identifies the reach of metrics, and the wider management systems in which they were embedded, as forced upon those who wish to receive the donor money, in a hegemonic manner.

So some of what might have been known or discussed informally, experimentally and negotiated with local knowledge and experience is now second place to the quantifiable, verifiable knowledge that is framed as appropriate and relevant for M&E and management.

These examples also suggest some of the disciplining effects of these forms of knowledge. As outlined earlier, the data and requirements for indicators and M&E more generally constitute a broad and demanding set of knowledges, data and behaviours. Indicators and their categories constitute the subject of much professional debate, around for example the precise difference between an output and outcomes. But those debates have often been closed down by the time project development and implementation is taking place, as in Girei's example. The specific indicators to be fulfilled are already specified. These in turn depend on quite specific categorisations of inputs, resources and other definitions, and indicator guidance that tells people in projects what things to count and how, and when, can run to many pages. Even identifying the numerator and denominator are far from straightforward, and decisions have to constantly be made about what constitutes the right knowledge and where to establish boundaries around the categories being defined. Such demands are often supported by 'capacity building', but this is rarely building capacity to debate, but simply to follow instructions, according to logic and categories that may have been determined very far away. What is counted and how matters in development, but it is in the minutiae of some of these processes that our very understanding of what is or isn't being achieved is shaped.

Conclusions

Monitoring is, in theory, about ensuring that a project is running smoothly and delivering according to schedule and budget. Indicators play a central role in such monitoring, but it's worth bearing in mind, particularly before developing too many, what indicators can and *cannot* tell us. Indicators can tell us to what extent a project's objectives have been met, what progress a project has made, the extent to which targets have been met or that a specific change is happening. But, the clue is in the name: indicators only provide specific information and make indications; they cannot tell us many other important things, such as why a project has made a difference or why and how change occurs.

As we saw in the discussion of indicators, choosing and using appropriate indicators can be difficult because the logic that distinguishes between different types of effects is subtle, has come from other contexts, and requires both technical training and disciplining to work properly. A combination of political pressures and tight timelines often leads to fudges to ensure that the right criteria are met, particularly important for establishing project success and payment by results. Therefore disciplining demands that at least some compliance is made with the rules of the game, while also trying to make things have some bearing on reality. Even in the Myanmar case study where some adaptive management was possible, and indeed essential for project success, the requirements of donor reporting were experienced as time consuming and burdensome (Mercy Corps/IRC 2016: 5).

Monitoring should and can be about adapting work to the feedback that indicators provide, about being accountable and responsive to local stakeholders and perspectives, and about learning from the processes of doing work. Adaptive management, as explored here, allows for recognition and understanding of complex contexts in which linear pathways are not predetermined but mapped out according to a hypothesis of change and then developed according to feedback loops. Such innovations offer new ways for development to be more responsive and flexible with project design and management. Moreover, NGOs and other agencies are pressed to do monitoring differently in challenging humanitarian contexts, and have shown that many uses technology can be put to.

However, the examples from both the IRC and Dutch CSOs underline some of the challenges that remain for the aid sector. All organisations and staff reliant on funding are ultimately guided by a need to sustain that funding, as an imperative for survival in the competitive world of aid and charity finance. As per the example reviewing the use of adaptive management in northern Karamoja, management processes and the accountability systems with which they work need to be aligned to different ways of working for adaptive approaches to function. The questions of upward accountability and giving management the space and freedom to be flexible depends then also on internal cultures of organisations, their funding structures and the extent to which organisations and their managers or leaders are comfortable with relaxing their own standard rules and procedures.

The discussion of monitoring highlights the challenges produced by the importation of abstract concepts from project management brought into development from corporate sectors. Despite the rise of adaptive and flexible approaches, development planners have to try to reconcile the complex realities on the ground with the demands for upwards accountability. As such, monitoring systems can be seen as a form of surveillance, that endeavour to create conditions for careful and constant scrutiny of work, which thanks to technology is possible even if it is far away. On the ground and in between levels of the aid chain, workers need to be prepared and ready for accounting rituals of verification (Power 1999). As the development of good monitoring systems shows, such audit works to shape both the present and the future (Scott 2022).

Notes

1   USAID (2017) Program Cycle Monitoring toolkit Template Performance Indicator Summary table, p. 2.
2   The PPR column is an internal reference.
3   www.alnap.org/ is 'a global network of NGOs, UN agencies, members of the Red Cross/ Crescent Movement, donors, academics, networks and consultants dedicated to learning how to improve response to humanitarian crises'.

4   The President's Emergency Plan for AIDS Relief is a large grant-making programme for HIV/AIDS started in 2003, led and run by the Department of State and managed across seven departments of the US federal government.

References

Abramowitz, Sharon 2017 Epidemics (Especially Ebola), *Annual Review of Anthropology*, 46, 421–445, https://doi.org/10.1146/annurev-anthro-102116-041616.

Allana, Amir 2014 *Navigating complexity adaptive management at the Northern Karamoja growth, health, and governance program*, Toronto: Engineers without Borders Canada (EWB) for Mercy Corps (MC).

ALNAP 2014 *Workshop summary remote monitoring, evaluation and accountability in the Syria response*, Peer Learning Event, 27 June 2014. https://www.syrialearning.org/system/files/content/resource/files/main/alnap-dec-syria-workshop-summary-final.pdf Accessed 20 March 2023.

Bond 2012 *Assessing effectiveness in empowerment programmes thematic paper – draft for consultation*, London: BOND, March.

Brock, Karen, Cathy Shutt and Alison Ashlin 2016 *Learning for change in accountable governance programming*, Brighton: IDS.

Collinson, Sarah, Mark Duffield, Carol Berger, Diana Felix da Costa and Karl Sandstrom 2013 *Paradox of presence: Risk management and aid culture in challenging environments*, Overseas Development Institute. www.odi.org.uk/hpg.

Girei, E. 2016 NGOs, management and development: Harnessing counter-hegemonic possibilities, *Organization Studies*, 37(2), 193–212.

Gutheil, Lena 2020 Why adaptive management will not save us: Exploring management directives' interaction with practice, *Public Administration and Development*, 40(2), 129–140.

Honig, Dan 2018 *Navigation by judgment: Why and when top-down management of foreign aid doesn't work*, Oxford: Oxford University Press.

IFRC 2011 *Project/programme monitoring and evaluation (M&E) guide*. www.ifrc.org.

Kusters, Cecile & Batjes, Karen & Wigboldus, Seerp & Brouwers, J. & Baguma, Sylvester 2017 *Managing for Sustainable Development Impact*. Rugby: Practical Action Publishing, DOI: 10.3362/9781780449807.010.

Mosse, D. 2005 *Cultivating development: An ethnography of aid policy and practice*, London: Pluto Press.

Mercy Corps & IRC 2016 *Adapting aid: Lessons from six case studies*. www.mercycorps.org/research-resources/adaptive-management-case-studies.

Mueller-Hirth, N. 2012 If you don't count, you don't count: Monitoring and evaluation in South African NGOs, *Development and Change*, 43, 649–670. https://doi.org/10.1111/j.1467-7660.2012.01776.x.

Organisation for Economic Co-operation and Development – Development Assistance Committee (OECD-DAC) 2002 *Glossary of key terms in evaluation and results-based management, working party on aid evaluation*, Paris: OECD-DAC. www.oecd.org/dataoecd/29/21/2754804.pdf.

Parker, Melissa, Tommy Matthew Hanson, Ahmed Vandi, Lawrence Sao Babawo and Tim Allen 2019 Ebola, community engagement, and saving loved ones, correspondence, *The Lancet*, 393 (29 June), 2585. www.thelancet.com, Published Online 10 June 2019. http://dx.doi.org/10.1016/S0140-6736(19)31364-9.

Power, Michael 1999 *The Audit Society*: Oxford: Oxford University Press.

Rugh, Jim 1995 *The Rosetta stone of logframes*. Comparisons between terminologies of different donor agencies for results/logical frameworks, *Compiled for CARE International and InterAction's Evaluation Interest Group*, http://awidme.pbworks.com/w/page/36051640/The%20Rosetta%20Stone%20of%20Logical%20Frameworks, accessed 20.03.02023.

Scott, Caitlin 2022 Audit as confession: The instrumentalisation of ethics for management control, *Critique of Anthropology*, 42(1), 20–37. https://doi.org/10.1177/0308275X221074834.

USAID 2017 *Program cycle monitoring toolkit template*, Washington, DC: USAID. https://usaid-learninglab.org/monitoring-evaluation-and-learning-toolkits.

Wild, Leni and Ben Ramalingam 2018 *Building a global learning alliance on adaptive management*, Report, London: ODI, September.

Wodhilll, Jim 2011 M&E as learning: Rethinking the dominant paradigm, in J de Graaft, J. Cameron, S. Sombatpanit, C. Pieri and J. Woodhill, eds. *Monitoring and evaluation of soil conservation and watershed development projects*, Boca Raton, FL: CRC Press.

6 Evaluation and Impact

In theory, evaluation processes mark the end of a project cycle, the final stage of the loop, whereby management comes full circle. Evaluations provide an important opportunity to assess a project's performance against its stated objectives, and to learn about what went well and less well, so that future project designs can incorporate knowledge about relevant improvements. Evaluations, or impact assessments, will be carried out on the project to produce scientifically reliable estimates of its effects. This will typically be done by one or more evaluation professionals using a sophisticated range of tools and approaches. Project staff will be consulted about the project's performance and to share data, and project baseline and monitoring data will be reviewed to assess how progress unfolded, as well as new evidence of final impact collected. Approaches that promise 'gold standards' such as randomised controlled trials will produce robust findings and establish reliable data for future planning. Sites to visit will be chosen according to a specific research design, to test the project theory of change or logframe hypothesis. Choices may be influenced by an interest in comparing results from sites with specific characteristics, such as rural and urban or according to varied ethnicities of project participants. Ideally the research design overall will involve both qualitative and quantitative evidence so that claims regarding specific project effects can be supported by data explaining how this change happened. Project staff will emerge from the process with a better sense of what has gone well, and less so, and these lessons will be shared internally as well as published on an organisational website. Ideally, the findings should be of sufficiently high quality so that they can contribute to future programmes as well as systematic reviews, which synthesise established evidence on a particular field.

In reality, only some projects are subjected to a comprehensive evaluation. Many are reviewed through a brief internal process or subject to a design that the donor or senior management feel is suitable. These may involve collecting quantitative data on what changes have occurred using surveys, meaning many questions about why certain things happened are not given an adequate explanation, and assumptions about causation remain untested. The evaluation might be done by an external consultant who flies in for 10 days and visits pre-arranged sites that purportedly offer a good cross section of communities, but which may not offer a comprehensive view of the full diversity both within and between communities. Some important project data will not be available, including a baseline, because there was no time for it at the

DOI: 10.4324/9780429427411-6

start and it wasn't demanded by the donor. Moreover, much of the monitoring data will be quantitative and not explain why certain work failed to produce effects. The evaluation consultant will talk to some project staff, but not all will be available and some will have moved on to other work. There may be very little or no consultation with the community, because the survey is designed beforehand to collect specific data of interest to the evaluation design, which has little interest in community views. In the end, the consultant may find some significant problems but have to make judgement calls about how to avoid embarrassing the project implementers. In order that everyone gets work again in the future, the report will be carefully coded not to embarrass those who commissioned the evaluation.

Introduction

The theory of how evaluations should be done, and learnt from, are the subject of a great deal of academic and practitioner discussion. The question of demonstrating and proving the right results has come to dominate much of the aid agenda, with engaged debate over which methods offer the best levels of statistical reliability and understanding local realities amongst the spectrum of concerns. This high-level theory, however, misses out on the reality through which the situated practice of evaluations takes place. Although the nominal goal of evaluation is to find out what happened, with a view to improvement and learning, and with learning tacked into many job titles in the industry over the last decade to demonstrate this concern, it is also a politically sensitive field. Theories of evaluation need to grapple with institutional parameters of praxis, and confronting the question of the extent of the use of evaluation in policy making. Where a scientific approach would presume the importance and logic of evidence-based policy making, political realities mean data is often only one part of the picture (Pritchett 2002; Szekely 2015).

This chapter explores some of the evaluation approaches that have received significant attention in recent decades, changing in terms of both breadth and quality. A major growth in investment in and use of evaluations has been part of the 'results agenda', supported by the OECD aid effectiveness agenda, which constituted a marked effort by the global aid system to improve the effectiveness of aid design and delivery (Eyben et al. 2015). To deliver the desired evidence of impact for this, robust, reliable evaluations should test programme hypotheses and gather impartial data that can guide evidence-based planning and policy making.

This starts with an exploration of some of the core rubrics that govern contemporary project evaluation. We first look at the key criteria for evaluations, as defined by the OECD and used widely in the sector. We then consider a range of both quantitative and qualitative methods, and consider the case for how both kinds of data in a mixed-methods approach can not only help produce robust findings, but also explain them in relation to a range of project logics. This includes some of the more cutting-edge and creative approaches to evaluation, including the evaluation of advocacy and campaign work, which produces challenges when it comes to evaluation criteria such as attribution.

The merits of different evaluation methodologies are hotly contested. Moreover, despite the fact that evaluation and monitoring have grown vastly in recent years as professionalised areas of project management, and the existence of a large industry and literature on evaluation, the use of systematic evaluation methods and incidence of the carrying out of rigorous evaluations is lower than might be expected (see Camfield and Duvendack 2014). Evaluation, done correctly, is methodologically demanding, time consuming and expensive. It can also be embarrassing, revealing failures that are at odds with demands for high professional standards. In addition to evaluations for donors, many major development organisations have their own internal systems for project evaluation or results tracking, which may aim to use more participatory methods or focus on organisation-wide indicators such as total reach, in addition to specific aggregate indicators for each area of work. And most projects, as noted earlier, are focused on delivering according to predetermined quantified outcomes.

Defining Questions: What Is Evaluation and What Does It Involve?

In the previous chapter we looked at the processes and methods used to monitor and assess progress during a project life span, that aim to enable learning and adaptation to manage delivery to effective ends. Evaluation, in the sense primarily used here, is different. It is *ex post* – that is, at the end of a project.[1] Where single-loop learning allows for adjustments in the way a problem is being addressed, evaluation should allow for double-loop learning, that can look back and assess not just success or failure, but the nature and character of the effects achieved in the course of a project. Evaluation at this point focuses on understanding a project's effects and impacts in relation to the project's stated outcomes and goals.

A fairly widely recognised definition of evaluation in the sector is from the OECD (2002), whereby evaluation is:

> The systematic and objective assessment of an on-going or completed project, programme or policy, its design, implementation and results. The aim is to determine the relevance and fulfilment of objectives, development efficiency, effectiveness, impact and sustainability.

An evaluation is thus a formal assessment of a project, typically an end-of-line analysis that looks back at a project and considers to what extent it achieved its stated objectives. It can ask and answer questions such as what changes has it delivered, how many of the objectives has it fulfilled, by how much and where?

Evaluations also usually consider other aspects of a project, such as the design – if not all of the objectives have been fulfilled, or less than was anticipated, why was this? Was there a flaw in the approach, or perhaps in the delivery? They can consider everything from a project's original justification to its final impact and many steps along the way. A theory of change can be examined, for example, and questions asked about how valid the original assumptions and ideas were, as well as the approach that was employed.

In these ways, and its regularity or periodicity, evaluation differs from monitoring. Where monitoring is often done internally, evaluation is typically done by external actors, often specialist consultants, to ensure impartiality and objectivity in reviewing the project and to avoid principal agent complicity, the idea that those directly involved in a project will have too many vested interests to be able to give an unbiased approach or judgement. Evaluation also uses different methods, asking questions that require new and different kinds of data than that collected for monitoring purposes. The definition also sets out a few key terms or standards – systematic and objective – that are key to how evaluation is done. As we will look at later, debates over what methods to use often centre on ensuring the highest possible standards of objectivity and using them in a systematic way that ensures rigour and validity. To this, the OECD further adds six evaluation criteria that are commonly used as core to an evaluation's remit: Relevance, Coherence, Effectiveness, Efficiency, Impact and Sustainability (Figure 6.1).

The question of *impact* is a core one and asks whether the project has made a difference, as per the prior discussion. *Relevance* is about the extent to which the solution proposed was relevant and useful to the community and a suitable model to achieve the stated outcome/goal. An associated question is whether the intervention is doing relevant and useful things in relation to the needs and priorities of local people. *Effectiveness* asks whether the intervention is achieving its own objectives – note, this may not be the same as impact. This can and should be asked across diverse parts of the population to take account of difference. *Efficiency* demands that

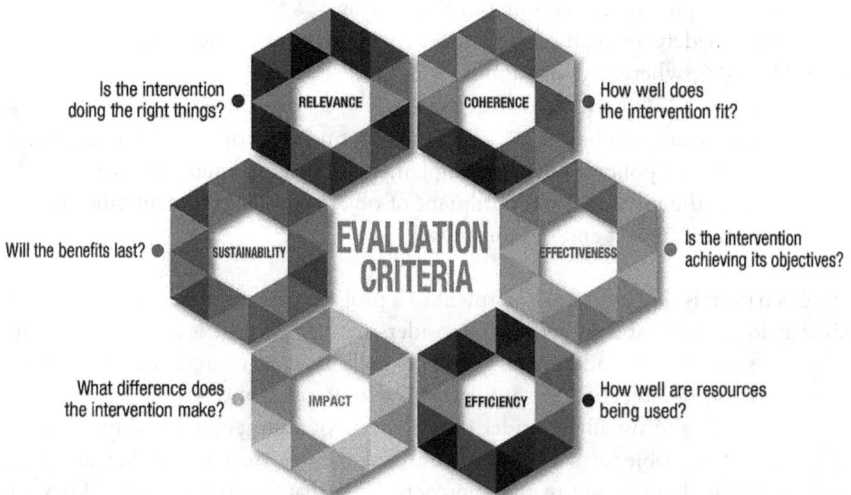

Figure 6.1 OECD evaluation criteria and questions
Source: OECD 2021

the question of how well resources are being used is asked. If a project design or implementation has been poor, resources may have been wasted on activities that have not been successful in gaining attention locally, for example, or inputs that are not used for their intended purposes, such as toilet blocks used as storage sheds (Lansbury et al. 2016).

The question of *coherence* has been added more recently, in line with the SDG agenda, and relates to the extent to which an intervention is compatible and complementary to other initiatives in the same sector, in that location (OECD 2021: 45). *Sustainability* relates to the likelihood of the intervention enduring, once the project delivery time period has completed, rather than environmental sustainability – although that of course should be an aim of any project in the contemporary climate emergency. Sustainability is an important question but one that is sometimes difficult to answer, given that many evaluations take place shortly after a project has finished. At this stage some project impact may be apparent, but a few years down the line, it may have disappeared. OECD guidance suggests looking at conditions for such longer-term sustainability in an evaluation, by identifying factors in the operating environment that could favour sustainability (ibid: 74). An operating environment has many factors, however, and what may seem stable at that moment can quickly be shifted by unforeseeable changes in political contexts, such as the withdrawal of US and allied troops from Afghanistan and the takeover of the government by the Taliban or a pandemic such as Covid are but two recent examples.

In some cases, qualities such as equity and Value for Money (VfM) are also assessed, and to these we may also add criterion of unintended effects – positive, negative or other (Stern 2015: 5). Evaluations also need to ask broad questions, and if part of a sectoral review, an evaluation might also explore questions on whether another project approach might have given the same or perhaps better results. Given this broad range of questions, evaluators need to draw on a large body of methods and options for generating the data to answer them.

Methods and Methodologies

The demands that evaluations be valid, reliable and impartial set a high benchmark or standard of quality and scientific credibility. A goal for many is that evaluations can inform policy, as part of an evidence-based agenda for action and governance, and in line with the use of learning that informs subsequent iterations or adaptations of a project. The methods used to gain the data upon which evaluations make their claims thus need to be able to withstand criticism and challenge.

Evaluation is concerned with making a connection between things happening in the project environment and the project itself. It is thus focused on determining attribution or contribution and the extent to which changes identified can be said to be the result of or influenced by the intervention (Stern 2015). Attribution of a direct causal link is the standard usually aspired to, whereby it can be said that statistically it must be the case that changes can be attributed to a specific intervention. This is more likely in some kinds of project than another, for example a vaccines intervention. In cases where work is centred around policy or advocacy change, it is a contribution to change that is more realistic, given the number of possible influences that may be impacting upon decision makers as they design a new policy.

For many, impact evaluation also specifically requires a rigorous counterfactual, involving an experimental or quasi-experimental design to assess the impact of the intervention alongside a control group where there is no intervention. Randomised controlled trials (RCTs) are amongst the most well-known approaches as experimental methods and which seek proof of causation through statistical means. These involve providing counterfactual evidence from a control group and the randomisation of subjects to either a control or treatment comparison groups. RCTs hold a hotly debated status as a scientific 'gold standard' within many evaluation quarters, largely because randomisation is held to offer the highest standard of rigor and validity. Randomisation can avoid the risks of bias in the selection of samples, and by neutralising all factors other than the dependent and independent variables, allow for direct inference of causality.

Establishing a counterfactual within an evaluation design is not suitable for all circumstances, however, particularly areas such as advocacy or governance where it is unrealistic to expect to be able to fully isolate project work from wider dynamics in the field of intervention. There can also be ethical challenges with randomisation, such as withholding treatment of a largely proven intervention from groups who could benefit from it.

Other approaches such as quasi-experimental designs offer alternatives and may be more useful where a comparison group is used but without randomisation. Both approaches test a hypothesis about the effect of the treatment upon a population, but the quasi-experiment compares effects on the two groups against each other and controls for bias by ensuring the control and treatment groups are as similar as possible (White and Sabarwal 2014).

Quantitative methods have had a dominant role in much evaluation practice for a number of reasons. Some of these are related to the results agenda as discussed earlier, and the general sense that numbers have a possibility for robustness and verifiability, such that policy makers tend to feel comfortable with 'hard' data that sets out statistical points of argument. The underlying issue of proving causality to a high degree of certainty is important in debates about attribution and contribution. Donors, policy makers and project managers all want to know as exactly as possible whether or not the project intervention has caused a particular effect. By removing all other possible causes, this gives as clear as possible evidence of causality and thus, attribution, so that project and donors feel they can be sure that a change can be attributed to a project.

However, the complex realities of many development contexts can make it very hard to dive into these fields with as much rigor as supposed for the kinds of certainty promised by RCTs. Additionally, much contemporary aid work is about awareness raising and campaigning, in which case interventions are made in a more indirect way to a group of people and have focused attention on contribution rather than attribution. We return to this point later.

If we want to know more than just about *if* change happened, and answer questions about *why* and *how*, evaluations can deploy methods that can get at subtler dynamics and ask questions about processes as well as 'hard' results. Where large 'n' number statistical methods looking at large numbers of beneficiaries seek to establish causation through statistics, small 'n' methods tend to build up evidence of causality through the weight of evidence, strength of argument (drawing on theory) and absence of other plausible explanations. They also look to have a high standard of validity, indeed that used in a court of law – beyond reasonable doubt – but do this in a different, yet systematic way by reviewing different types of evidence.

If for a long time development has been largely wedded to the idea of using statistical means, there has been significant debate within recent years about the potential value of mixed methods, as well as battles over which paradigms are more suitable and robust for evaluation (Bryman 2006; Camfield and Duvendack 2014). These evaluation debates do not always take place within the confines of development, but also engage development specialists in dialogue with those assessing public policy around the world in a range of contexts.

Core Evaluation Approaches

In this section we explore a selection of tools and approaches to give an overview of the kinds of approaches being used. This is bearing in mind that evaluators' methodological toolkit is now quite ample with some twenty-six standard or common approaches (Aston 2022), and a toolkit which is regularly growing as new approaches are added to the repertoire.

The first set of approaches considered are those using statistical analyses (Khandker et al. 2010). As introduced earlier, the basic logic of statistical approaches to impact evaluation is that they are looking to consider the average treatment effect of a project for a certain group of individuals. Let us start with person Y, for Yan, a farmer whose village has been targeted for a crop improvement programme. If we take Y_i as the outcome for Yan with treatment, we can write this as $Y_i(1)$, and without is $Y_i(0)$ – as Yan was before the treatment. In very simple terms, evaluation seeks to assess the difference between $Y_i(1)$ and $Y_i(0)$. To express this mathematically is $E = Y_i(1) - Y_i(0)$. So for example the difference between $Y_i(1)$ is Yan *with* the effects of the project to improve his output – and hopefully income – and $Y_i(0)$ is before the intervention. One way of estimating the effects is to find someone similar to Yan, say Xavier in another village, and compare individuals who participated with those who did not.

A range of options follow from this proposition. RCTs are commonly used in medical and other scientific trials where it is important to test the effectiveness of one treatment against a control group. These involve preselecting 'treatment' and 'control' groups chosen to be comparable, aside from intervention. RCTs have come into widespread use in development on the back of their perceived rigour. The fact they offer a good experimental design that includes a counterfactual, as discussed before, has led to them being heralded as a 'gold standard', and whose fervent advocates have even earned the nickname 'randomistas' (Bryman 2006; Camfield and Duvendack 2014; Jones et al. 2009; Quinn Patton 2008).

The basic logic of an RCT is that a given group of people are assessed according to a set of criteria, for example age and income, for selection into the group for the experiment. So Yan and other villagers might be in a village designated for intervention, and a highly comparable control village nearby is selected for monitoring but not given the intervention. Details of relevant variables within these are noted, and from here they are allocated either to the intervention group or to the control group. For ideal conditions the participants are blind to the facts of whether they are in a control or treatment group. The groups are compared before and after the intervention, and analysis is performed that assesses to what extent the intervention made a difference. Variables can be brought into consideration that may help explain why some and not others experienced effects.

If we wanted a simpler approach, and only to consider the effects of the change to Yan and neighbours over time, a simple **comparison before and after (CBA)** approach could suffice. In this we look at Yan's locality and typical productivity before the intervention and that after the intervention. A reliable baseline survey here will, as in an RCT, be essential, one that gives us sufficient data to be able to make good comparisons after the fact, and so draw valid conclusions (and to populate the baseline box of the indicator lines in the results framework). We hope to see the impact that the intervention has made and be able to measure it according to a range of indicators – a core one is likely to be the overall objective of the project, typically stated at the top of the logframe, which could well be something like percentage change income from crops, with a sub-objective around productivity and outputs indicators around use of the new techniques. Such conclusions will say something about change but not explain either mechanism of causality, or thus certainty about it. Other factors could have caused changes, but without a counterfactual element in the design, we cannot be sure. Another option is a **difference in difference** approach, which takes assessment data on control and treatment groups at two time points, once before and once after the intervention; as with CBA, questions around the intervention would also need answering.

Although these approaches sound simple, they involve collecting significant amounts of data to verify the key indicators. Evaluations also need to contribute to answering a wider set of questions. Returning to the OECD criteria set out earlier, the evaluation must also ask questions about how relevant this intervention was – did Yan and others think the crop yields were a problem in the first place? On what basis and data was the project initially justified? In relation to efficiency, we may well need to ask – depending on the donor, different methods may be required – and estimate the costs to output or outcome. Has this been a cost-effective approach?

Longer term we might want to know more about impact. How hardy have these new varieties been? Has any income rise been sufficient to offset any new costs, such as those of the varieties and any new fertilisers that have to be used with them? Moreover, how equitable have these impacts been? We would need some careful consideration of methods to address the question of equity in an evaluation. Projects can have varied effects across and within communities, and for example, inadvertently exclude women or other groups marginalised by social dynamics that without social and cultural context analysis designers might have missed, but we need to know about differences within the community and who has benefited and how from the project. If it has just helped those with land rights or ownership, social connections and status, all of which motivated and enabled them to participate, the project may risk elite capture and unwittingly further entrench inequality within a community.

The question of sustainability would demand that we ask how long and within what contexts these changes endured – are the costs of the new varieties manageable, are the crops that produce still wanted in the market – has the market for the crops held up given the increases yield, or has the growth in supply meant the price for the crop has gone down (as per supply and demand theory).

Case Study on Nutrition Programming: Flawed Assumptions, the Benefits of Varied Approaches and a Cautionary Tale of the Impact of Evaluation

An example showing how both qualitative and quantitative approaches are important comes from the Bangladesh Integrated Nutrition Programme (BINP), which was the subject of various evaluations and reviews and significant debate in the 1990s and 2000s.[2] The case also refers to several other approaches and methods to consider alongside those discussed earlier.

The programme responded to high levels of child malnutrition, as evidenced by stunting (or impaired growth and development) in Bangladesh, building and scaling up from two prior projects in the region. Launched in 1995, the project involved three core activities: a national nutrition programme, community-based nutrition and developments such as creating vegetable gardens and keeping poultry. The community-based interventions were at the core of the pro-gramme, as it was through these that children were given supplementary feeding if underweight or malnourished, and were weighed regularly at health centres to monitor their progress. The feeding was complemented by nutrition education, with the argument made by core funders at the World Bank that income-based improvements alone were inadequate. This was based on the assumption that 'bad practices' in child feeding in the community were a major part of the cause of malnourishment, rather than a simple lack of food. As evidence for this, the Bank put forward their own analysis of 'unprecedented' rates of decline in malnutrition in one of the starter projects that incorporated this in its design. However, subsequent reviews doubted the quality of the data and analysis on which these claims were made and challenged the basis on which the project was due to be scaled up to a much larger population and geographical coverage. In a report poignantly titled 'Thin on the Ground', Save the Children (2003) questioned this logic based on analysis of its own data that showed there was no difference between the communities receiving the intervention and those not, and lobbied against its expansion as wasteful.

The case threw up debate about what was considered sufficient evidence. Both the SC study and Implementation Monitoring and Evaluation Department (IMED) of Bangladesh's Ministry of Planning used difference estimates of nutri-tional impact after the intervention (see White 2006). These used a single differ-ence approach, mentioned earlier, a quasi-experimental design that compared project and control villages (thanas). However, critics challenged the validity of the findings because of the range of other factors not taken into account or controlled for (White 2005). Similarly, the BINP project evaluation undertook three surveys, at the start as a baseline, a mid-term review and an endline or ex post. However, there were problems of comparability on account of differences in survey design, the survey taking place at different times of year, as well as with the small size of the control group, especially at the baseline, which constituted further grounds to question the validity of the findings. A subsequent review (White and Masset 2007) looked at the data again and found that the control groups were too small and that compressions of the data used in the studies ignored selection bias because these included some non-project children, who were likely to have different characteristics such as different household incomes.

It was argued that in order to properly situate the project's effects, the project needed a comparison group whose characteristics were identical to characteristics of the project group before project implementation, or they would in simple terms not be comparing like with like. The review results showed that the impact was small. Although there was some improved or higher knowledge of nutrition practice in project areas, and some spillover effects into neighbouring areas, the effects on malnutrition were low and disappointing, showing only a 2% reduction or no significant impact on nutritional status, although there was a positive impact on the most malnourished children (White and Masset 2006; Rogers 2014).

These poor results meant that questions needed to be asked about the approach and the logic and assumptions on which it was based. The core component of the project's community element was to work with the mother, with nutritional counselling targeting pregnant and lactating women and adolescent girls with the goal of changing the nutritional behaviour of primary child caretakers. This included advice regarding the value of colostrum after birth and the importance of including vegetables in food preparation. The programme logic chain basically presumed that the right people (i.e. those making decisions regarding under-nourished children) were targeted → that these people participated in project activities, and so were exposed to these messages → exposure led to acquisition of the desired knowledge → acquisition of the knowledge leads to its adoption (i.e. a change in practice) → the new practices make a substantial impact on nutritional outcomes.

Here they found some significant flaws. In the communities where the project was working, as in fact elsewhere in Bangladesh, the children's mothers were targeted with the messages about colostrum and vegetables. However, they did not necessarily have much power over what food was purchased for the family to eat. This is because men do the majority of the shopping and take a lead in deciding on health matters, as did mothers-in-law, who in many cases also reside with the families. So effectively, assumptions that women were in charge of food and child health informed the project and ultimately also derailed it. Economists and other planners had failed to understand who made what decisions and who did the shopping in the communities, in a finding that underlines the concerns about the lack of attention to culture and context discussed in Chapter 3. The research also found that many of those going to growth-measuring sessions did not get the messages they were supposed to, as these were noisy and sometimes chaotic events with lots of people gathered and not an opportune space to deliver health messages; of those getting supplementary feeding, one-third were found to have received no message at all. This suggests too the ways in which very simple prosaic day-to-day aspects of life are somehow beneath the large and policy-important questions that project designers ask themselves. Despite the fact the evaluations found no evidence of impact, and the protestations of NGOs such as Save the Children, the World Bank pressed ahead to fund the projects without impact for some years (White 2009).

One of the challenges this series of evaluations around this nutritional programme showed is the importance of unpacking the assumptions underlying the logic chain in a project. Most large 'n' statistical methods do not have the goal or the means to check and address the question of implied causality, only a concern with proving whether or not an effect was noted. It is in the realm of small 'n' methods that more attention has been given to project theories of change, and used these to provide a more nuanced exploration of pathways of change within projects.

Small 'n' Approaches and Qualitative Methods

Although impact evaluation is often associated with the experimental and quasi-experimental methods discussed earlier because of their perceived 'objectivity' (Eyben 2013: 20, in Cornwall 2014), there are many occasions in which the conditions necessary for large-scale statistical analyses are not present. Given the costs associated with developing control groups and experimental designs, small 'n' methods can also be useful in smaller-scale projects. However, it also applies where project outcomes are considered emergent. Here, what are sometimes referred to as small 'n' approaches (White and Phillips 2012) can be used, alone or in combination with quantitative methods.

Small 'n' approaches draw on methods including case studies, interviews, life histories, and focus or small group interviews and discussions, that are frequently used in social science disciplines such as anthropology and sociology. These methods are designed to elicit interviewees' and participants' views and perspectives on a situation, allowing for contextually grounded interpretations of events. These interpretive methods are sometimes referred to as 'soft' methods, in an apparent contrast with the 'hard' numbers that quantitative approaches yield, but such semantics should not obscure the real value of such methods in understanding not only effects but also in allowing for the unpacking of social processes in complex contexts where a fuller understanding of project impact requires more than numbers. These methods can also be complemented by participatory approaches, using some of the methods discussed in Chapter 3, including the family of approaches in participatory appraisal such as mapping and timelines.

Small 'n' approaches can broadly be grouped into two kinds of approaches, on the basis of how they attempt to establish causality and answer evaluative questions (White and Phillips 2012). The first are those that seek to develop explanatory theory and draw on tools such as the theory of change for this task. These approaches, including realist evaluation (RE) and process tracing (PT), look at contexts and other relevant factors around a project intervention to constitute plausible hypotheses that they then explore and test using a range of methods. The second group are banded under participatory approaches and include most significant change (MSC), participatory process evaluation and other approaches that draw on qualitative data generated through participatory means to consider how members of the community have experienced the process. They can analyse cause and effect through developing understandings that come from the community of their experiences of the role the programme has played in changes at community and individual levels. These approaches have the benefit of allowing evaluative research "to explore a richer picture of what 'success' might mean to different kinds of people, one that would provide opportunities along the way for reflection that could spur further action" (Cornwall 2014: x).

Theory-Based Evaluation Approaches

As discussed in Chapter 4, theories of change are in common use today in development planning, and having clarity about the expected chain of causality can play an important role in impact assessment. A number of approaches to impact evaluation draw in different ways on project theories of change, as looking at a project's theory of change allows the evaluator to look at the steps that the project imagined it would follow, and then have a basis for considering how things panned out in practice. Two approaches which draw on this and which are considered here include realist evaluation and process tracing. Attention to theory can also help you determine what the best way to evaluate an intervention is, including what to focus on. One question this can help to answer is whether a project can be scaled up without changing its outcomes. To know this, you need to be able to assess to what extent the theory depends on the context.

A lighthearted example of this is the 'dishy David Beckham hypothesis', as outlined by Pawson and Tilley (2004). Concerned with the health implications of the fact that teenage girls in the UK didn't like exercise very much, policy makers also noted that girls were influenced by the magazines they read (this is before the era of computers, social media and smartphones). So the idea was developed that if they showed images of 'dishy' (British slang for 'good-looking') sporting heroes instead of unhealthy rock or TV stars in the magazines that girls read, this might inspire the girls to do more sport. However, cause and effect were not necessarily clear in the adult minds of the people doing the planning, as the following extract from an interview with a teenage girl shows:

Interviewer: Do you think the fact that these good-looking blokes [men] are footballers has any effect on girls' attitude to playing football?

Girl: No, I think it has more effect on them *watching* football, well not the
                 football – the guys (*to general laughter and agreement*) (Mitchell 1997,
                 cited in Pawson and Tilley 2004)

There was a reaction, then, to a trigger, but it did not have the intended effect. The
simple assumption that girls would respond to images of sporting heroes was correct, but it did not then cause the specific change in behaviour that was imagined.
This suggests there was not enough understanding of the factors upon which girls
make decisions to exercise, or of what ways the girls would approach these images
and ideas about sport, such as the context in which sports is considered uncool
and to be avoided for other reasons, such as unflattering gym clothes and a dislike
of sweat. It seems the age and gender approaches to sport specific in this instance
were a bit beyond the planners' scope of thinking. This example also suggests that
we need more understanding of what are called generative mechanisms, the factors
which generate a change in behaviour, the responses that are triggered to understand
such dimensions of change. For example, contraceptive counselling does not prevent
unwanted pregnancies on its own, but the knowledge acquired through counselling
could help, as could the shedding of taboos in talking about family planning and the
confidence it gives women to negotiate and be assertive in sexual issues and relationships. All of these topics can be explored through qualitative research.

One approach which attempts to draw connections between the contexts in
which changes happen, the mechanisms for these and the outcomes and that is
growing in popularity is realist evaluation. **Realist evaluation** is a theory-based
approach, but distinctively founded on critical realism. Its methods (see Pawson
and Tilley 2004; Westhorpe 2013; Greenhalgh et al. 2009) look at various possible
causal mechanisms that help to explain *how* programmes work. More specifically
these mechanisms explain the reasoning in response to resources introduced by the
programme. Pure realist approaches test various hypotheses to try to establish how
these mechanisms are influenced by context. This involves exploring how context
mechanism outcome (CMO) configurations work in a given project. The process
starts by understanding the theory of the programme, the target population and
context along with the theory or hypothesis of change, and then mapping out various plausible CMO configurations that allow exploration of how contexts might
produce different outcomes. This is followed by building an outcome 'enquiry' that
gathers qualitative and quantitative data for evidence and then defining the theories
using the CMO trajectories.

An example of this approach (Westhorpe 2013) comes from a realist evaluation
of a multi-component early years intervention in South Australia which *worsened*
outcomes for the most disadvantaged children. The author used empirical research
and realist synthesis to understand why. By developing and analysing various CMO
statements, she found that where parents are resource and time-poor (Context), programmes that use a parent training model, but do not negotiate content or methods
with parents (Context) are experienced as burdensome, which increases parental
stress (Mechanism), increasing negativity towards children and demands of parenting (M), resulting in less sensitive parenting (Outcome), which generates insecure
child attachment (O) and worsens child development outcomes (O). Where it was
expected that parent training should help parents with the tasks of parenting, here

a misinformed appraisal of existing parenting overlooked the fact that parents were time and resource poor. As a result, instead of being experienced as helpful, the intervention was experienced as yet another burden on parents' time. The original positive intervention hypothesis has been much tested in many parenting interventions programmes since the success of the Sure Start programme in the 1960s in the US. But in her analysis of this programme, which involved multiple therapies and interventions from social, medical and psychological professionals, Westhorpe drew on a range of theories which explored social capital, inclusion, social judgements and attachment theory. By so doing she was able to develop a tentative theory that took account of how negative social judgements intensified parents' negative attachment behaviours towards children, leading to withdrawal from support and networks, and led to increased isolation and stress, producing worse outcomes for children. Combining theory-based pathways to draw out possible explanations coupled with interviews and discussions with participants allowed the researcher to build a new hypothesis that explained unforeseen and damaging outcomes. It is worth noting, however, that although helpful, the complicated nature of pure realist approaches has led to other 'realist-inspired' methods (Punton et al. 2020).

Process Tracing and Assessing the Impact of Advocacy and Campaigns

Some kinds of intervention are not suited to either randomised or control approaches that produce statistical outcomes. In collective campaign work, attribution of effects to single interventions or organisations is difficult, and indeed counter to the ethos of collective work. It can also be a significant challenge to map out influence in complex multi-stakeholder political environments, and thus requires different approaches. This is often the case with the impact assessments or evaluations of advocacy and campaign work. Here some of the more creative and exploratory methods are more suitable, such as process tracing, which starts with outcome and works backward to prove contribution. To do this, evaluators construct various hypotheses about how the outcome might have been achieved and the kinds of cause and effect mechanisms that may have generated these changes. They then define what evidence they would expect to find in each of those hypothetical cases. They then need to set about building a case archive of 'diagnostic' evidence, drawing on qualitative and quantitative data from project records and other relevant sources. This data is then subjected to quality control processes, ensuring for example that the source of data was close to the events but not unduly biased.

The data is then used to test hypothesis for the predicted pathways, using the four 'Bennett's tests' to verify its confirmative value (Bennett 2010). In ascending order these go from a 'straw in the wind', which if passed merely confirms the relevance of certain evidence, to the highest and doubly decisive nature, the 'smoking gun' whereby it is both necessary and sufficient as an explanation.

Although there are lengthy debates amongst evaluators about varieties of causal inference, the complexity of the methodology and other issues (see for example Befani and Stedman-Bryce 2017, Bennet and Checkel 2014, Schmitt and Beach 2015, Wauters and Beach 2018), it can be a very useful approach for evaluation of advocacy and campaigns, as the case study below shows.

Case Study Using Process Tracing: OXFAM's Healthcare Campaign in Ghana

A useful example of a process training approach comes from the review of Oxfam's campaign for universal healthcare in Ghana. The campaign sought to effect change to the Ghanaian health system, including to the lack of health infrastructure and inequalities in access to these and medicines, the lack of awareness amongst the population about their health rights, amongst others. At the time, Ghana had a national healthcare insurance scheme (NHIS) that involved charging users for services; locally it was called 'cash and carry' (Stedman-Bryce 2013: 5). This was widely viewed by civil society groups to be failing to deliver for many parts of the population, which led to the campaign to propose improvements. A key part of this campaign was getting hold of the right data to disprove the government's promotion of the NHIS as a 'success'. According to the original logic model, this data was one of the strategies to address the basic problems, that included lack of health infrastructure and uneven distribution of resources, amongst others. The logic model suggested that media attention, collaboration amongst civil society and capacity building amongst healthcare workers would help produce an improved level of public awareness of the right to healthcare, reduced maternal mortality rates and a new national policy paper. Ultimately, these outcomes were expected to deliver a platform that delivered healthcare for all.

However, when the evaluation process got underway, it was soon found that the logic model was not in fact used or revisited after drafting and, as such, was "not an up-to-date representation of the aims and objectives of the Campaign strategy document" (ibid: 12).

As in many projects with goals linked to political change, the aims and objectives had shifted with changes in contexts and changed understandings of how the project was interacting with context during the course of the campaign. Some of the planned activities and strands of strategy, such as around access to parliamentarians, either did not take place or were difficult to fully realise. Without a good model of what the project had been doing, the process review thus had to take a different approach to think about what had happened.

The process tracing method involved eight steps, starting with a consideration of this programme logic but then questioning it via a more careful examination of a few key outcomes, as follows:

1. Reconstruct the theory of change and the assumptions which accompanied it
2. Work with stakeholders to identify *up to three* **intermediate or final outcomes** considered to be significant for the evaluation
3. Systematically assess **what was done** by the intervention to achieve these

4. Identify the *extent to which the* **outcomes materialised** and any unintended outcomes
5. Undertake 'process induction' to identify causal explanations
6. Use 'process verification' to assess the extent to which these explanations are supported by the evidence
7. Write a report documenting the above processes
8. Summarise the narrative analysis by allocating contribution scores to outcomes on a 1–5 scale, with 1 being strong and 5 meaning zero or no impact

After completing step 1, they revised the logframe they produced in the new diagram, as shown in Figure 6.2.

As per step 2, they then decided to focus on three intermediate outcomes to verify what had happened. The three outcomes chosen for consideration were raising consciousness amongst Ghanaians that the current system was ineffective, the political support for universal access and improved coordination amongst civil society. Here we will look at the process they followed to explore the first of these outcomes, showing that the NHIS system was an ineffective vehicle to deliver free universal healthcare in Ghana.

Evaluators looked at key events that had helped to realise this outcome. A key piece of work was identified as the publication of a campaign's report that showed that the government agency implementing the NHIS, the National Health Insurance Agency (NHIA), had been inaccurately reporting the number of people covered by the NHIS. In relation to this, key informants claimed that the report was successful in showing the NHIS to be an ineffective vehicle to deliver free universal healthcare in Ghana, and that as a result of the campaign, the NHIA was forced to revise its methodology for calculating active membership of the NHIS, which was subsequently much closer to Oxfam's. The evaluators reviewed conducted interviews with key actors and project documentation to find evidence that this could indeed have been a strong factor in the NHIA decision to revise its methodology.

This process was not without challenges. Amongst the evidence reviewed was that put forward by the NHIA that they had always intended to revise their methodology, and that the timing was coincidental. However, much evidence pointed to the contrary, including some senior figures from the Ministry of Health. Because of issues of bias, the review wanted to find a truly impartial figure who would determine one way or the other; in other words, a 'smoking gun', or an incontrovertible piece of evidence, that would provide the highest level of confidence. This came from a Ghanaian delegate to a WHO and World Bank meeting, who was interviewed and stated:

I'm sure you all know about what has been come to be known as "the Oxfam Report". This report declared that coverage of the NHIS was as

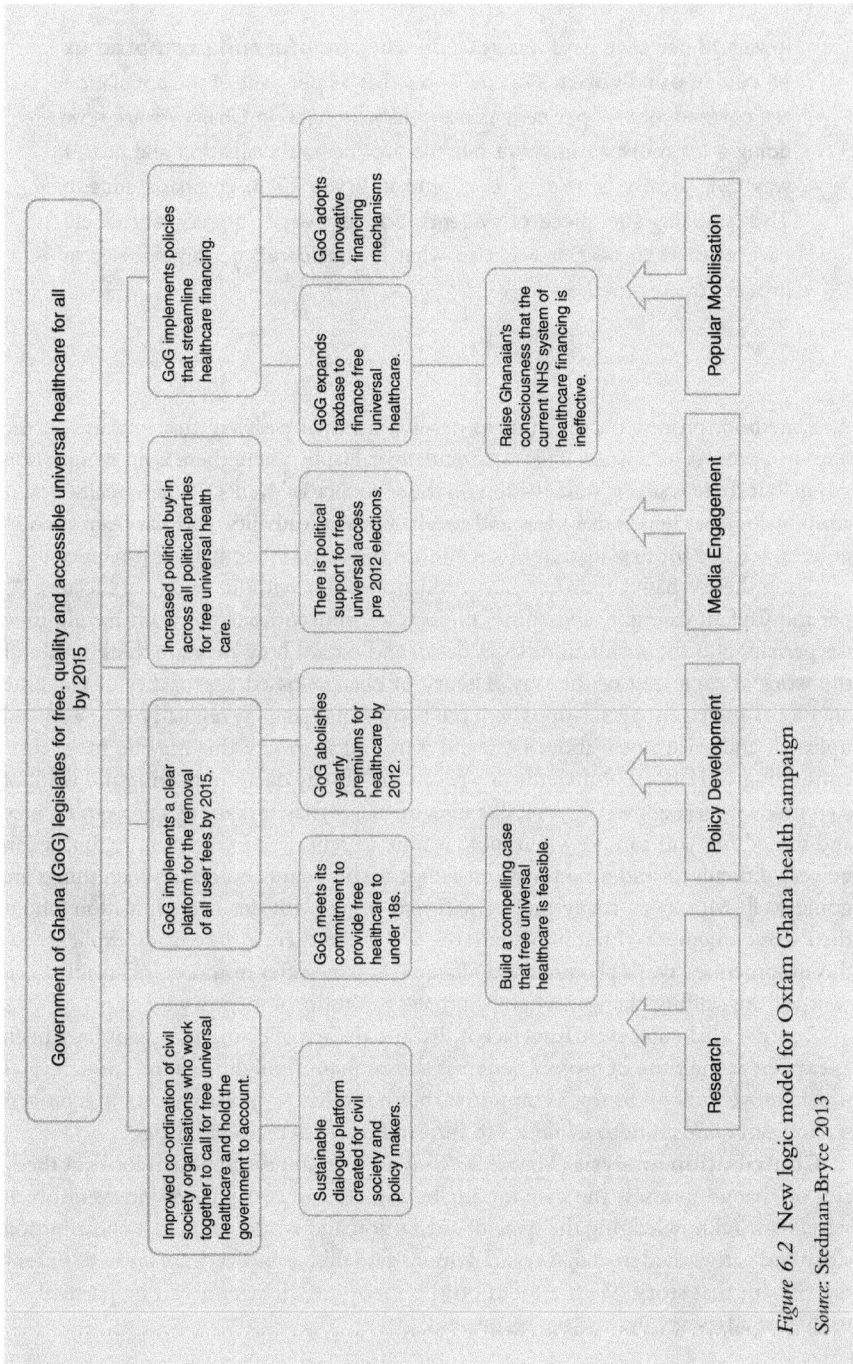

Figure 6.2 New logic model for Oxfam Ghana health campaign

Source: Stedman–Bryce 2013

low as 18 per cent. This was **actually very helpful and prompted us to revise our figures**. We now know that 34 per cent of the population are covered, not 67 per cent as previously thought. In Ghana we are now doing a lot more to improve our monitoring and evaluation and in this way civil society is helping us. (Stedman-Bryce 2013: emphasis added). This 'smoking gun' piece of evidence was just what campaigners would have wanted to hear. It was also what is considered doubly decisive in process tracing methodology.

As a method, process tracing aims to develop a causal pathway that explains all the steps in a process of change. This is particularly valuable where there is no comparison group, but there is strong information on the sequence of events. As with realist evaluation, it looks at generative ideas and mechanisms of causality, and has been used in political science for explanation of key historical events or anomalies (deviant cases).

Using theory-based approaches to evaluation is not without potential hiccups. As per the Oxfam example, sometimes projects are run without the team having time (or perhaps also the inclination) to sit down and record how they are thinking about the work at each step of the way. Theory of change–based approaches to planning envision a management set-up where the theory of change is regularly reviewed and updated, and with notes about how and why, but in reality this may be more time consuming and laborious than the fast-paced day-to-day decision making and work of a complex project allows. It's a bit like updating a journal or diary of a project: it's nice and something you can do when there is time to reflect and contemplate, but it can be very difficult to find time for when things are busy and also often when things are going well. Moreover, many project staff may work with detailed stipulations about their work schemes written into contracts, and unless there is time made explicitly for this in someone's work planning and schedule, it may suffer from lack of an author, as well as from staffing changes whereby project institutional memory is lost.

Another challenge evaluators face is that the theory of change may not have been as explicit at the time of project design as the evaluation might require. In such cases it may prove difficult to test assumptions, but nonetheless approaches such as process tracing can contribute to evidence to inform future theories of change.

Contribution analysis (Mayne 2008) is another approach which looks at theories of change to assess the case for attributing change to a project intervention. It starts with acknowledging the issue of attribution and works to build a contribution story and gather evidence that could demonstrate this, as well as in relation to potential risks in that story. With a focus on the theory of change, it can be particularly useful for advocacy evaluation (Kane et al. 2017).

Participatory Evaluation Approaches

A series of alternatives to theory-based evaluations are participatory evaluation approaches (White and Phillips 2012) that seek to understand the views of beneficiaries and others about what has happened as a result of a project. These approaches use qualitative and quantitative data generated in a participatory manner to analyse the cause and effect of perceived changes that a project has yielded at community and individual levels. An example is most significant change (Davies and Dart 2005), which involves collecting and selecting stories of significant changes that have occurred around a project.[3] Such approaches centre on important localised perspectives of what has happened. Rather than ceding the definition of what is important to external actors, such as the donor or a team of project managers, these methods allow for examination of what those affected think and observe about significant changes. Another example of these is outcome harvesting, one of a range of approaches which takes a participatory approach to considering what important outcomes have been.

Outcome Harvesting: Participatory Approaches to Understanding Outcomes in Complex Situations

As discussed in Chapter 4, projects which are deemed complex, where there are too many interacting parts and issues to have clear trajectories towards impacts, can be challenging to evaluate. In contrast to those methods which look to build a case going forwards through a classic predictable linear process of change, such as process tracing, outcome harvesting works backwards, with implementers collecting evidence about what has been achieved "to determine whether and how the project or intervention contributed to the change" (Wilson-Grau and Britt 2013: 1). Methodologically, it applies a series of questions including around what happened, who did it (or contributed to it) and 'How do we know this?', along with 'Is there corroborating evidence?' (ibid). Following on from these questions, the approach uses a range of qualitative and participatory methods to gather data about project outcomes.

An example of an evaluation using this method is of Oxfam Novib's Global Programme of work from 2005–2008 (Majot et al. 2010). The evaluation could not compare achieved outcomes or what happened in reality with what was planned in terms of outcomes, because the programme did not report consistently on these, and they also changed from year to year. So they instead worked backwards and drew on underlying theories of change that influenced the work during this period, to reconstruct a sense of what happened around nearly 200 important outcomes generated through a participatory process. A subsample of sixty-six of these were verified and substantiated. This yielded strong results on work building participation and strengthening civil society, and a deeper understanding of cooperation and spheres of influence of partners, amongst others (Majot et al. 2010). It is held to be particularly useful for knowing more about what happened in terms of results than concern with details of the process of project delivery, or 'achievements rather than activities'. Amongst its strengths are the possibilities of looking at and for the unintended outcomes of interventions. Where standard approaches look for data associated with indicators, casting a wider net for data and views about impact and outcomes provides space in which unforeseeable and unintended effects can be gathered. A further advantage of this method is that it is relatively accessible and intelligible, as it uses a common-sense approach with which informants can quite easily engage.

Case Study: Participatory Process Evaluation of a Nutrition Project (Drawing on Cornwall 2014)

For many agencies and aid workers, the principle of participation is not only ethically and politically important, but it can also yield some of the most important findings that questions predesigned at a distance may not get to. A good example of this comes from a participatory evaluation conducted by the anthropologist Andrea Cornwall and colleagues. They set out to assess an integrated government nutrition project addressing malnutrition and stunting in a rural community in central Kenya. The evaluation took place two years into the program, when the funders, a 'progressive Nordic donor', felt it would be useful to review. The project was already proving a success, according to statistical analysis, with lower numbers of underweight children. Moreover, change was visibly evident in new vegetable gardens in the community. However, more questions needed to be asked and data collected about how and why the planned work was having an effect, to generate a full account that could explain the process.

Cornwall notes that this participatory approach was used "against a backdrop of . . . hegemony of experimental forms of impact evaluation in which all that counts is that which can be counted" (2014: X). It was designed to consider intended results as well as unintended outcomes, and in addition to talking to people at the headquarters about what had and hadn't gone well, they undertook a three-step participatory process. This started with stakeholder analysis and conversations to generate a set of key interviewees. Exercises were then done with card, paper and string to map out expectations and experiences about the programme, which generated illuminating points about the process that a standard approach would not have asked, such as about local perceptions of the project process. A third stage involved sorting the positive and negative outcomes and using them as a basis for further discussion. The approach also varied in some important ways from typical evaluation processes. The team visited a random list of project sites, rather than those selected by a project manager because they were doing well, as can typically happen, and demonstrating the potential of participatory approaches to include randomisation, a point overlooked by many randomistas (Shutt, personal communication). They then used participatory techniques, such as timelines, social mapping, Venn diagrams and other PRA techniques (discussed in Chapter 3), to facilitate discussions with children and parents in communities.

One of the startling findings was that at the project's start, when the baseline data on height for weight and arm circumference was being gathered by teams of enumerators visiting individual households, rumours were sweeping around the community that a cult engaged in sacrificial rituals was looking for children to abduct. This threw the project plan off track, and local leaders had to be engaged to clarify and reassure local populations. But for Cornwall, most significant were the "incommensurability of knowledge systems, the lack of trust of outsiders and the failure to adequately countenance what was needed to establish the basis for informed consent" (2014: 14). Baselines and other development research conducted for operational purposes may seem perfectly logical and justifiable to those designing development projects, but, as explored in Chapter 3, development has a tendency to assume a great deal about how people should respond to their apparently benevolent interventions. Too often there is totally inadequate recognition of the ways of thinking that exist before-hand, as well as how to make project work amenable to cultural contexts. The emphasis Cornwall places on trust is indicative of the importance of ethics in development projects and practice.

Some other findings of the evaluation underlined the importance of the par-ticipatory approach, such as discovering stakeholders' sentiments towards the project had a significant impact on their reasoning and how they engaged with it. Whereas the project had hoped children would take messages home from school in songs, local people noted that this only worked with girls, because boys didn't want to sing. Project staff also learned that children couldn't just take messages home from school, but that parents had to be involved. In other words, the project repeatedly changed tack and responded to problems through incorporating participatory monitoring-type activities within programme design. As a result of needing to gather communities to explain the baseline survey pur-pose, and to share its findings, opportunities were created for new dialogue. One mother noted,

> When we started with the activities, I thought what has this got to do with malnutrition – there is still no food. But later I came to realise that there are lots of causes of malnutrition like disease, water and not eating the right foods.

Here, participatory research became pedagogy – communities took over the message-spreading activities, in ways which the project's staff found surprising, but which generated new spreading of knowledge and its own dynamics, which locals felt was irreversible.

The example shows just some of the ways in which standard evaluation ques-tions and designs may fall short of asking questions that are central to gaining an in-depth understanding of what does and doesn't work in project design. It underscores not just the importance of participation from an ethical point of view, and as a method to ensure project efficacy, but its functional utility to generate new knowledge for evaluators as well.

Key Debates and Issues: Qualitative, Quantitative and Mixing It Up

Development evaluation is neither a quiet nor a static field, as debates and disputes about methods and about the wider purpose of evaluation, and political contexts of this, are on-going and lively. These debates involve academic departments, development agencies and the grey area in between of influential think tanks, including the International Initiative for Impact Evaluation (or 3ie),[4] that seeks to expand the knowledge basis and use of high-quality evaluation for development. At the core of these debates are arguments about methods, for despite significant progress including a diverse and ever-expanding range methods in the evaluator's toolkit, certain biases continue to prevail and shape dominant understandings of what rigour and the standards of a good project evaluation should be.

When it comes to evaluation this has played out in terms of RCTs being judged by some as the best methods to establish certainty at the highest level, a claim that is contested by those who favour some of the theory-based and participatory approaches outlined earlier. Differences of opinion surface in what some have termed the 'paradigm' or 'zombie' wars within evaluation (Bryman 2006; O'Donnell 2019; Patton 2008), a debate about paradigms which is a zombie because it never seems to be quite dead and over. Patton suggests the myopia which places RCTs as a 'gold standard' is the product of the view amongst education specialists in the US in the 1960s and 1970s over what contexts were appropriate for federal investment, which focused on those that offered an experimental design (2008: 423–425[5]). The status of RCTs as a 'gold standard' relates to the view that they are "the only method that can convincingly establish causality between observables" (Camfield and Duvendack 2014: 4). A focus on this has led to a secondary importance being given to other factors, such as the many and diverse range of contexts in which they are not suitable (Jones et al. 2009). This includes cases which are complex and non-linear in nature as well as other situations in which RCTs are not practicable, ethical or relevant.

Methodologically contexts such as education in which whole schools are in treatment or non-treatment groups are rarely able to offer the same double- or even single-blind conditions as in medical RCTs, for example, and social contexts mean that it can be hard to separate treatment and control groups, resulting in what are referred to as 'spillover' effects; but humans moving between villages or school communities are not substances leaking from petri dishes, and the risk with such language and conceptualisations of development is that complex human behaviour can be so isolated and defined or generalised about.

As feminist epistemologies tell us, there is no such thing as disembodied or impartial knowledge: all knowledge and data are collected by and for a purpose, and in evaluation as in any other research or intervention, every action has a consequence. As the example from communities concerned about people coming in to assess their children shows (in Cornwall 2014), people and communities need to be treated with dignity and respect that actors would expect from anyone coming into their own communities. A challenge with many quantitative approaches is that because so much faith is placed in scientific ideas of rigour, there is insufficient examination of what effects defining things in particular ways to be counted has – what is left out, whose views are privileged over others. Ultimately, clear ethical decision making should be coupled to methodological openness and pragmatism, and determining methods in relation to the kinds of questions that need to be answered should guide good evaluation. This should guide what is done, not a commitment to either or, as the earlier discussion of conflict situations suggests.

The Case for Mixed Methods

The design of evaluations necessarily responds to the questions that it needs to answer, but as discussed previously, what questions a donor or project team want answered will be a function of what they think is important. This may be in relation to the DAC criteria discussed at the start of the chapter, or it may expand to consider theories of change, equity and local views of the project. Echoing wider practice, decisions about the terms of reference and what methodology to use are often part of a team discussion, but may also be influenced by a political economy of methods, whereby the perceived 'hard' statistical data derived from methods such as RTCs that offer compelling concepts such as 'rigour' can have significant sway over decisions. Practitioners around the sector will often aim to offer the highest possible standard to donors, or those commissioning evaluations feel they must showcase their knowledge of scientific quality and so focus on methods that offer this, at the expense of methods which might answer other important questions of how change happens (Shutt and McGee 2013). As summarised by Garbarino and Holland (2009),

> An impact evaluation that combines qualitative and quantitative methods can generate both a statistically reliable measure of the magnitude of the impact as well as a greater depth of understanding of how and why a programme was or was not effective and how it might be adapted in future to make it more effective.

This is sometimes referred to as the black box problem of causation or the understanding about why and how -with as much precision as possible – change happens. If we go back to the logframe and the assumptions that are buried underneath the 'if . . . then' implications of causality, a statistical approach alone cannot unpack why that particular causation has happened. As with a detailed theory of change approach, unpacking and detailing what the expected steps and links are not only helps planning but can then be assessed in an evaluation that considers those progressions and processes with detailed contextual data.

One of the challenges of RCTs and experimental methods is that their focus "is too narrow to tell us 'what works' in development, to design policy, or to advance scientific knowledge about development processes" (Deaton 2009: 6). If development is always looking for broader lessons, an evaluation which cannot speak to variables around culture and context is of limited use in the search for replicable lessons. The low external validity and low levels of generalisability of findings of RCTs limit their potential for use in design for different contexts. A mixture of methods can thus allow evaluation to address a wider range of research questions and topics, and improve the quality of the data by using different methods for different questions, units of analysis and groups of respondents. Framing the work of impact evaluations as those which involve a counterfactual element, recent work by Dixon and Bamberger (2022) argues that these are most useful when complemented by factual evaluations that look at issues of implementation, such as process evaluation.

The benefits of mixing methods are multiple and include the possibility of comparing findings across different methods via triangulation, and allowing the strengths of one method to fill in the gaps of weaknesses of others. Qualitative data can provide rich and nuanced information that helps illuminate questions of why and give depth to understanding that are more rigorously based in an understanding of effects in relation to context. The question of the generalisability of findings can be aided with qualitative approaches, such as case studies that are done within a large survey sample, to develop theories of how interventions work that are potentially applicable to that population.

A related challenge is that despite the wide array of tools available, whether these translate into the production of reports that are then used for learning and to build knowledge across the sector is debatable. Learning should be enabled and facilitated, which is also a question of how evaluations are utilised. As proponents of utilisation-focused evaluation (UFE) argue, evaluations should be assessed by how useful they are (Patton 2008, 2012; Ramirez and Broadhead 2013). UFE starts by identifying who will benefit from and use findings and ensuring that they have some ownership of the process so that they are more likely to do so. This can help close the gap at the top of the project cycle, as discussed earlier in the book.

Conclusions: Remaining Challenges of Evaluation

As noted at the outset of this chapter, evaluations are – in theory – an important part of the process of learning in the last stage and at the end of a project cycle. Evaluations offer an opportunity to assess project impact, often by an external team of experts to minimise the risk of bias in assessing results, but also to draw on specific forms of knowledge that professional evaluators offer. These should be via a design which offers robust evidence and may be experimental in design to offer a counterfactual. This should enable learning not only about what change happened as a result of a project, but why and how.

However, in reality, there can be an excessive focus on quantified outcomes and results at the expense of understanding processes of change, the views of project staff and last but not least the perspective of participants and intended beneficiaries. As noted in the chapter, there are a range of methods open to evaluators and others involved in assessments that allow for participatory and theory of change–based methods. The case study of the BNIP and the Kenyan nutrition programme shows the importance of methods and research design in evaluation. From involving communities in elucidating their experience to the importance of questioning assumptions around culture, theories of change and participatory approaches can yield important kinds of learning for development actors and agencies.

Such approaches have been championed by some of the techno-normative actors in the sector. Ways of ensuring that monitoring is more progressive include looking at what feminist principles would involve. Oxfam has identified several strands to this, including ensuring there is co-production in planning, the use of participatory and rights-based tools – and ensuring that barriers to participation are acknowledged and dealt with, and self-awareness amongst staff, amongst others (Wakefield and Koerppen 2017). However, these approaches need champions, and the approaches within institutions are varied, from agencies that are very open to experimenting with new methods and ensuring that processes are part of what is to be measured to those where an economistic perspective privileges quantified and statistical data. It is also true that despite the clamour for rigour and the impact of the results agenda in sharpening a focus on results, funding for a fully independent and full evaluation of a project that responds to the OECD criteria described at the outset can be expensive and time consuming. This means that not all projects are subject to such assessment, despite the growth of the practices around this in the last twenty years.

But a critical set of faults remains around how and where evaluations should be used. Observers note that the 'paradigm wars' detract from the core purpose of evaluations and thinking about who can use evaluations, where and for what (Guijt and Roche 2013). Evaluations are often held to be about accountability for and to donors, and thus primarily about explaining what effects funds have achieved, but they should also be framed to enable improvements in practitioner responses. However, linking to the culture of audit and accompanying fetishisation of metrics in some western countries across governance and within the aid sector (Shore and Wright 2015; Muller 2018) evaluation frameworks and their scientific rendering inevitable privilege certain forms of knowledge over others. When experimental methods exclude consideration of the mechanisms through which change is enacted, and disavow consideration of context, the problems of ignorance of locality and context that projects start with can be reproduced. This can leave us with insufficient knowledge to answer wider questions of effectiveness.

Notes

1 There are other forms of evaluation, such as ex ante, but which for space reasons we do not consider here.
2 See Hossain et al 2005 and WB 2005.
3 For more on MSC, see https://mande.co.uk/wp-content/uploads/2018/01/MSCGuide.pdf
4 www.3ieimpact.org
5 There is a great deal more to this debate than can be reviewed here, including engagement by the American Evaluation Association in grappling with the and against the dominance of one gold standard approach; see more in Patton 2008.

References

Aston, Thomas 2022 Method evangelists and zealots need not apply, *blog April, Medium.com.*

Befani, B., and Stedman-Bryce, G. (2017). Process Tracing and Bayesian Updating for impact evaluation. Evaluation, 23(1), 42–60. https://doi.org/10.1177/1356389016654584

Bennett, Andrew 2010 Process Tracing and Causal Inference Henry Brady and David Collier, eds, *Rethinking Social Inquiry*, London: Rowman and Littlefield

Bennett, A., and Checkel, J. (Eds.). 2014 *Process Tracing: From Metaphor to Analytic Tool* (Strategies for Social Inquiry). Cambridge: Cambridge University Press. doi:10.1017/CBO9781139858472

Bryman, Alan (2006) 'Paradigm Peace and the Implications for Quality', *International Journal of Social Research Methodology*, 9:2, 111 - 126 DOI: 10.1080/13645570600595280

Camfield, Laura and Maren Duvendack 2014 Impact evaluation – are we 'off the gold standard'? *European Journal of Development Research*, 26, 1–11. DOI: 10.1057/ejdr.2013.42.

Cornwall, Andrea 2014 *Using participatory process evaluation to understand the dynamics of change in a nutrition education programme*, Working Paper 437, Brighton: IDS Sussex.

Davies, Rick and Jess Dart 2005 *The 'most significant change' technique: A guide to its use.* mande.co.uk.

Deaton, Angus 2009 Instruments Of Development: Randomization In The Tropics, And The Search For The Elusive Keys To Economic Development, *Proceedings of the British Academy* 162 , 123–160, London: The British Academy.

Dixon, Vibecke and Michael Bamberger 2022 *Incorporating process evaluation into impact evaluation: what, why and how*, 3ie Working Paper 50, London: International Initiative for Impact Evaluation.

Eyben, Rosalind, Irene Gujit, Chris Roche and Cathy Shutt eds 2015 The Politics of *Evidence and Results in International Development: playing the game to change the rules?* Rugby: Practical Action Publishing.

Garbarino, *Sabine and Jeremy Holland 2009 Quantitative and Qualitative Methods in Impact Evaluation and Measuring Results*, Birmingham Governance and Social Development Resource Centre (GSDRC). www.gsdrc.org.

Greenhalgh, Trisha, Charlotte Humphrey, Jane Hughes, Fraser Macfarlane, Ceri Butler and Ray Pawson 2009 How do you modernize a health service? A realist evaluation of whole-scale transformation in London. *The Milbank Quarterly*, 87(2), 391–416.

Guijt, Irene and Chris Roche 2013 (2014) Does impact evaluation in development matter? Well, it depends what it's for! *European Journal of Development Research*, 26, 46–54. DOI: 10.1057/ejdr.2013.40.

Hossain, S.M., Duffield, Arabella and Taylor, Anna. (2005). An evaluation of the impact of a US$60 million nutrition programme in Bangladesh. *Health policy and planning*, 20, 35–40. 10.1093/heapol/czi004

Jones, Nicola, Harry Jones, Liesbet Steer and Ajoy Datta 2009 *Improving impact evaluation production and use*, Working Paper 300, London: Overseas Development Institute.

Kane, Robin, Carlisle Levine, Carlyn Orians and Claire Reinelt 2017 *Contribution analysis in policy work: Assessing advocacy's influence*. www.evaluationinnovation.org/publication/contribution-analysis-in-policy-work-assessing-advocacys-influence/.

Khandker, S. R., G. B. Koolwal and H. A. Samad 2010 *Handbook on impact evaluation: Quantitative methods and practices*, Washington, DC: World Bank Publications.

Lansbury Nina, Angela Dean, Helen Ross and Tari Bowling 2016 Sanitation projects will go down the toilet unless we ask people what they really want, *The Conversation*. https://theconversation.com/sanitation-projects-will-go-down-the-toilet-unless-we-ask-people-what-they-really-want-69144.

Majot, Juliette, Wolfgang Richert and Ricardo Wilson-Grau March 2010 *Evaluation of Oxfam Novib's global programme 2005–2008 for aim 1 and 4 GloPro's strategic positioning and counterparts' outcomes*, Oxfam Novib. www.outcomemapping.ca/download/simonhearn_en_Evaluation%20of%20Oxfam%20Novib.pdf.

Mayne, John 2008 *Contribution analysis: An approach to exploring cause and effect*, ILAC Methodological Brief. https://beamexchange.org/uploads/filer_public/f5/55/f5553494-f9cf-4f2f-90ee-105877dddd71/contribution-analysis.pdf Accessed 12 September 2022.

Muller J.Z. (2018) *The Tyranny of Metrics*. Princeton: Princeton University Press.

O'Donnell, Michael 2019 *The Nobel prize or the Zombie returns*, blog, Save the Children UK. www.savethechildren.org.uk/blogs/2019/the-nobel-prize-or-the-zombie-returns.

Organisation for Economic Co-operation and Development – Development Assistance Committee (OECD-DAC) 2002 *Glossary of key terms in evaluation and results-based management, working party on aid evaluation*, Paris: OECD-DAC. https://www.oecd.org/dac/evaluation/daccriteriaforevaluatingdevelopmentassistance.htm.

Organisation for Economic Co-operation and Development – Development Assistance Committee (OECD-DAC) 2021 Evaluation Criteria, Paris: OECD-DAC, https://doi.org/10.1787/543e84ed-en.

Patton, Michael Quinn 2008 *Utilization-focused evaluation*, 4th edition, London: Sage.

Patton, Michael Quinn 2012 *Essentials of utilization-focused evaluation* London: Sage.

Pawson, Ray and Nick Tilley 2004 *Realist evaluation*, London: UK Cabinet Office. https://assets.publishing.service.gov.uk/government/uploads/system/uploads/attachment_data/file/1004663/Brief_introduction_to_realist_evaluation.pdf.

Pritchett, Lant 2002 It pays to be ignorant: A simple political economy of rigorous program evaluation, *Policy Reform*, 5(4), 251–269.

Punton, Leanie, Isabel Vogel, Jennifer Leavy, Charles Michaelis and Edward Boydell 2020 *Reality bites: Making realist evaluation useful in the real world*, Brighton: Centre for Development Impact Practice Paper Number, 22 March 2020.

Ramírez, Ricardo and Dal Brodhead 2013 *Utilization focused evaluation: A primer for evaluators*, Penang: Southbound Press.

Rogers, P. 2014 *Theory of change, methodological briefs: Impact evaluation 2*, Florence: UNICEF Office of Research.

Save the Children 2003 *Thin on the ground: Questioning the evidence behind world bank-funded community nutrition projects in Bangladesh, Ethiopia and Uganda*, London: Save the Children.

Schmitt, J., and Beach, D. 2015 The contribution of process tracing to theory-based evaluations of complex aid instruments. *Evaluation*, 21(4), 429–447. https://doi.org/10.1177/1356389015607739.

Shutt, Cathy and Rosie McGee 2013 *Improving the Evaluability of INGO Empowerment and Accountability Programmes*, Brighton: Centre for Development Impact (CDI).

Shore C and Wright S (2015) Audit Culture Revisited: Rankings, Ratings, and the Reassembling of Society. *Current Anthropology* 56(3), 421–444.

Stedman-Bryce, Gavin 2013 *Health for all: Towards free universal health care in Ghana*, End of Campaign Evaluation Report, Oxford: OXFAM GB.

Stern, Elliot 2015 *Impact evaluation a guide for commissioners and managers*, London: BOND.

Szekely, Miguel 2015 Closing the evaluation cycle, *Journal of Development Effectiveness*, 7(4), 453–461.

Wakefield, Shawna and Daniela Koerppen 2017 *Applying feminist principles to program monitoring, evaluation*, Accountability and Learning, Discussion paper Oxfam, USA July 2017. www.oxfam.org.

Wauters, B., and Beach, D. 2018 Process tracing and congruence analysis to support theory-based impact evaluation. *Evaluation*, 24(3), 284–305. https://doi.org/10.1177/1356389018786081.

Westhorpe, Gill 2013 Developing complexity consistent theory in a realist investigation, *Evaluation*, 19(4), 364–382.

White, Howard 2005 Comment on contributions regarding the impact of the Bangladesh integrated nutrition project, *Health Policy and Planning*, 20(6) (November), 408–411. https://doi.org/10.1093/heapol/czi061.

White, Howard 2006 *Impact evaluation: the experience of the Independent Evaluation Group of the World Bank*. Washington, DC: World Bank.

White, Howard 2009 *Theory-based impact evaluation: Principles and practice*, International Initiative for Impact Evaluation London: International Initiative for Impact Evaluation. https://www.3ieimpact.org/.

White, Howard and Edoardo Masset 2007 The Bangladesh integrated nutrition program: Findings from an impact evaluation, *Journal of International Development*, 19, 627–652.

White, Howard and Daniel Phillips 2012 *Addressing attribution of cause and effect in small n impact evaluations: Towards an integrated framework*, London: International Initiative for Impact Evaluation May. https://www.3ieimpact.org/.

White, H. and S. Sabarwal 2014 *Quasi-experimental design and methods, methodological briefs: Impact evaluation 8*, Florence: UNICEF Office of Research. www.unicef-irc.org/KM/IE/img/downloads/Quasi-Experimental_Design_and_Methods_ENG.pdf.

Wilson-Grau, Ricardo and Heather Britt 2013 *Outcome harvesting*, brief, Ford Foundation, MENA Office. https://outcomeharvesting.net/outcome-harvesting-brief/.

World Bank 2005 *The Bangladesh Integrated Nutrition Project Effectiveness and Lessons*, Bangladesh Development Series – paper no.8, Dhaka: The World Bank Office, December 2005, www.worldbank.org.bd/bds

7   Conclusion

Through the successive chapters examining the various phases of the project, this book has explored the many tools with which projects function. This review is and could not be exhaustive, but it is hoped that the reader will feel significantly more familiar with what might be involved in working with a development project. Over the successive decades and indeed generations in which aid practitioners have engaged with development projects, they have developed new tools with which to render these projects feasible, to improve the methods via which data is collected for baselines, to plan in more flexible ways, and bringing new approaches for measuring the impact of these interventions. Reviewing the life span of the project as a form at the World Bank, Picciotto (2020) observes how the project's malleability and adaptability has been a key part of its longevity. The tools may have changed, as have some of the language of management, but the form itself has remained, as a neat, efficient and privileged particle of development across the world. The project's functionality as an adaptable means of organising work and funding underpins its ubiquity. Such processes to change the project need to grapple with the wider politics of development, whereby projects align to donor imperatives, which are in turn subject to political decision making. Despite the many variations and attempts at improvement that have been made to the ways projects are done, by both techno-normative and techno-managerial approaches, challenges with this endure, some of which we may see as intrinsic to the form itself. The process of projectisation and rendering technical involve taking complex social problems and turning them into fundable accounts of how to solve issues that can be targeted with a few years intervention, and fit within the structures of the aid chain. The project for all its variants, is a servant of power, not a master.

Throughout the book we have seen just how carefully calibrated and constructed projects must be to function in this system. At each turn and stage, there are tools that determine what can and should be said, in what form, about what issues. In each of the chapters of the book we saw different examples of these tools, the variants made according to different moments of the progressive insertion and fastening of the project to the centre of development aid operations. We also considered the theory and the reality in each stage of the project cycle, and in Chapter 2 we saw how this was in a supposed virtuous cycle, with phases of the project cycle connected and joined together by learning. Specific historical processes and developments have

DOI: 10.4324/9780429427411-7

accompanied the project management techniques into aid, and their evolution since, including the NPM that has so shaped the aid sector in the last twenty years. These have shaped the management systems that the tools must align with and support, and where techno managerial imperatives of results based management and the logics of managerialism dominate. In the book we have seen how techno normative reformist efforts, such as the theories of change, adaptive management and participation, have endeavoured to move projects on from their industrial origins to more flexible, adoptable and realistic processes that reflect the complex and immensely varied contexts in which projects operate. Yet such changes tend to be accommodated within existing structures, rather than change them.

In considering project inceptions in Chapter 3, and the different dynamics and processes through which projects come about, the roles of both institutional preferences and funding are apparent, as are the ways in which certain topics and themes come to the fore of the aid agenda. These themes and key concepts set preferences and trends within aid that shape which projects can get funding. Focusing in on such topics, many projects are furthermore formulated on the basis of the specific kinds of data about issues that project forms demand, isolating this data from the wider context. Unfortunately, time pressures and a lack of humility means that insufficient attention goes to the views of local people, to culture and history, as apparent when anthropologists comment on the mistakes poorly informed aid can make. Even where some dynamism has been brought in, through some variants of PEA, exploring what political and economic factors are important to consider in any given context, the institutional space for it remains a challenge and at the discretion of higher authority than most project designers.

Indeed even when attempting to embed participation in management, as per the ActionAid case study, reconciling different forms of power and how it is understood and enacted in different spaces can be difficult. The political thrust behind participation, acknowledging not just the practical but ethical importance of local interest and knowledge, underlines the importance of attention to culture. Specific and recognised identification of cultural factors as something to be worked with, and responded to, rather than solely being the object of change, could prove a corrective to an area of significant oversight. Such attention might also change the tendency for culture to be blamed as the cause of poverty-related problems, omitting attention to structural factors. However for this to happen it would require development to take more seriously an understanding of how social progress has been achieved in the global north, including the role of social protest in demanding more just societies.

The assumptions and understanding developed in the project inception phase feed into planning for the intervention, as explored in Chapter 4. In this planning stage of the project cycle, the key terminology of the project begins to take shape, as goals, outcomes, outputs and inputs are identified. The role of the logframe and subsequent variants such as results frameworks demonstrate some of the ways in which the sector has evolved new tools, each seeking to improve upon and correct weaknesses of those that came before. These restrictive tools for planning have given way to some extent to theories of change based approaches, which surface and question some of the many assumptions, including flawed cultural ones, that underpin the logframe. If for some a 'lockframe' (Gasper 2000) beloved only of planners in air conditioned offices, the logframe is also symptomatic of wider trends in the sector. 'Logframitis' (Sriskadaraja 2015) characterises a situation in which donors demand that long term and systemic change be squeezed into narrow, quick and quantified outcomes. Other tools in, such as the Gantt chart, underline the extent to which the project uses tools articulated in spaces that are predictable, governable and neat, where spheres of control are extensive or even comprehensive, rather than limited.

Project monitoring, as practiced in some parts of aid, reflects the desire to extend control and confirm only whether or not something has taken place in a single-loop learning model. The simplistic goal of checking on delivery often takes precedence and produces huge demands of staff time as even in simple forms, monitoring processes can be complicated and expansive, given the range of different indicators that are often required by results frameworks, or fourth-generation logframes. From a governmentality perspective, this amounts to erecting systems for surveillance of work, focused on donor accountability rather than learning. Yet in more flexible formats, it can facilitate adaptive planning and be a key source of double-loop learning, and provide grounds for revisiting a theory of change or action. A good M&E system needs to allow for space to identify even unforeseen elements, as suggested by the review of anthropologists' contributions to understanding complex interactions of communities and the medical interventions in the context of Ebola.

The attention to careful accounting for project progress in fourth-generation logframes is due to a combination of the results agenda and managerialism, alongside significant attention to what happens at the end of projects. In discussion of evaluation approaches in Chapter 6, the dominance of quantitative data reflects the privileging of certain kinds of knowledge over others. The sometimes fractious area of debate over differing epistemologies has often served to limit understanding to the verification of certain kinds of project effects. Attention to issues amenable to survey techniques rather than those which elicit views of communities undermines our ability to understand more about how change happens and is experienced by recipient communities. These apparently methodological challenges should not just be the purview of elite technocrats and meticulous academics, for these are more than technical or procedural. The results agenda has shown that what you decide to count means changing what people do, narrowing the ends of development, and led to a sometimes dangerous focus on specific indicators rather than systemic progress. Combined with risk aversion, this has produced unhelpful tendencies within development, meaning that projects, with their pre-stated goals and clearly set out means to achieve these, become an instrumental tool for organising resources to a limited set of specific ends.

Disciplining Tools of Projects

As argued at the outset, the tools of project design and management have a disciplining effect, aligned to specific modes of governmentality. The exploration of the tools showed how this very word and notion is rooted in the proposition that these processes are comparable to mechanics. This linguistic sleight of hand normalises and makes mundane and ordinary the very technocratic approaches which it describes. This technocratic veil is also pulled across the disciplinary functions that project toolkits and concepts exert, as project logics are transmitted through the reams of manuals and guidance which direct practitioners to support project functions in specific ways. When we only observe the disconnect between the theory and the reality – the gap that is one of the more obstinate problems of development – the disciplining effects of the tools of project management may not be apparent.

The fact that these tools do not produce an entirely effective form of control over the outcomes on the ground of project delivery is not necessarily what matters. Discipline has achieved in shaping so much of what is possible, that even if there is a gap on the ground, the control around funding and thinking have been achieved. As I have shown, the tools shape the categories of objective, goal, output and what we count for different indicators. They also shape how we think about what matters as we sit down at our desks and flick the computer on in the morning. What kinds of key performance indicators (KPIs) are aid workers working to? What will the next project they work on entail? How will the success of their grant appeal or a project's results shape both their future and that of the organisation they work for? The gap between plan and outcomes is also managed via close performance management of staff, as audit regimes enacted through systems of indicators and tracking shape the day-to-day of aid work, filling the time of monitoring and evaluation teams, keeping thematic advisors busy trying to align project outcomes to institutional objectives, and shaping the dialogue that is had between workers and communities. While following these codes, these rules for the tools, other qualitative judgments may be excluded. Through these tools, projectification colonises our very imaginaries, to the extent that sometimes aid workers struggle to imagine how they might do it differently. This may be a specific effect of this long-term compliance to these forms within the sector. As a review of results-based management at the Swedish agency SIDA found, the arrival of NPM techniques here led to more focus on compliance than policy or knowledge development, as one observer noted that " 'it has not enabled people to think more, but rather less'" (Vähämäki 2015: 148).

Objecting to managerialism can be difficult, not least because audit purports to encompass an ethical stance (Strathern 2000), claiming virtues of efficiency and economy in the name of public accounts. These questions of accountability inform the tools and apparatuses for tracking and tracing aid spending through every activity and output according to a matrix of time and money, in what amounts to a system of surveillance. These systems are based in notions of the need for discipline and control to prevent corruption given the presumptions about human nature that underpin managerialist views of the subject, as one prone to self-interest and requiring close management. The Hayekian rationality of selfishness that underpins the public choice and principal-agent theory within management today is based on a bleak assessment of human nature, one without controls of contract or culture (Udehn 2002). Yet these questions of efficiency are answered primarily in relation to donors and project logics, rather than those of beneficiaries. These are therefore specific kinds of institutional formulations of ethics and about accountability that is almost entirely upwards rather than to the communities which might benefit from it (Scott 2022; Ebrahim 2003; Wallace et al. 2007).

At the same time, the fact that development projects have drawn on tools and processes and concepts designed for use in military industrial contexts is not widely grappled with, nor are its problematic legacies. Amongst these issues and legacies are the hierarchies of power to its project forms typically subscribe. There are also subtler points with the project's hegemonic nomenclature, disguising the peculiarity of certain kinds of practices, such as the conversion of human labour into a time-managed commodity, under the apparently scientific rubric of quantified inputs. The hierarchies in which organisations are positioned within the aid chain also shape the way in which they must adhere to the use of these tools. The extent to which work is prepacked and delineated according to techniques and process standards and to which individuals are held accountable as owners of work creates technologies of agency and enforcement that reduce scope for manoeuvre.

Another aspect of the structuring of power projects bequeathed to development is the division of roles within a team, such that staff can function in relative isolation, functionalities often echoed within organisations as professional silos. Moreover the linking of many worker contracts to short-term project funding arrangements is another effect of the project and means that like other members of the globalised workforce today, aid workers are subject to the disciplining mechanisms of the market, and forced to fashion themselves as entrepreneurial selves who can market their professional identities successfully as they move between contracts. This short-termism is combined with high levels of geographic mobility that can distance workers from the complex political realities of successive locations.

Projects thus shape the thinking about what can happen in aid, to structure the categories through which the future is imagined, as a set of small, specific and concrete changes, rather than fundamental systemic change that addresses the many more profound and historical drivers of inequity and poverty, or to create a more inhabitable planet, for example.

Future and Contemporary Trends

The project's inner workings and technologies have been ignored for too long as boring and arguably irrelevant aspects of this small particle of development, considered lowly by those concerned with the higher power echelons of policy. But policy is enacted not just by actors but also through systems and tools for its transformation into everyday practice. It has long been argued, but without an effective resolution, that we need alternatives to the project as a mode of disbursing grants and loans in aid. This will, it seems, require some imagination. Some parameters of the current debate that this needs to engage with are discussed as follows.

A first is the need to decolonise aid and to think through how the hierarchies of the aid chain can be reconfigured, as a core mechanism of control and discipline in the sector. At the same time, uneven progress with the localisation agenda suggests that there is work to be done in extending trust within the sector, linking back to questions of what view of humanity informs collaboration. Analysis of how vectors of control function and could be re-configured would also need to consider the accountabilities of bilateral aid mechanisms. That such efforts need to counter nationalistic agendas and the tying of aid to more directly and explicitly to specific political interests does not make the task easier but arguably more urgent.

Practitioners also need to be politically savvy (Gujit 2015). This could include that rather than presume that the tools that come with market logics are necessarily suitable for aid, practitioners ask questions about where these tools have come from, who wrote them, why and whose ends they serve. A reflexive practitioner needs to look into the tool bag they carry to work, not just accept what is in there as the standard kit that they must adopt. They may very well find these tools unsuitable, and that similar to the absence of culture from development planning, the tools miss and evade certain central questions and make many assumptions. Aid agencies may also want to question the underlying basis on which they promote the use of these tools and think about how workers interact with these tools on a daily basis. Much work looking at this topic, in relation to tools and areas such as logframes and evaluation (Girei 2016; Wallace et al. 2007), identifies numerous challenges, as discussed in these pages.

New forms also need to take accountability for global realities in new directions, as linked to climate change and the need for projects and aid to be directed towards supporting those experiencing its worst effects. There is a need to ensure that the way projects are packaged does not privilege those who speak the language of project management best and are most adept at using the latest buzzwords, or most able to compete in this commodity market (Freeman and Schuller 2020), but rather provide an agile and flexible response. This approach also needs tools that are development from the bottom up, not designed from afar and imposed, but co-created, as vehicles for voicing diverse realities and allowing these to shape how and what initiatives might be most useful. Many aspects of a broader, less hierarchical approach exist in the myriad forms of more complexity-aware and adaptive approaches, which could not only be effective (Shutt 2016) but also offer more progressive and inclusive forms of development practice.

Where many aid agencies were once managed by a generation who saw development as linked to goals of liberation, who came of age in an era of socialist revolutions and could advocate for participatory methods and goals, today's aid workers are more likely to be functionaries in vast development machines who have grown up in the 'end of history' era, where market capitalism knows no ideological competition. This political imaginary is particularly pertinent given the now very evident destruction of the planet that growth-derived economic models are inducing, and yet, to quote Fisher (2008), it is easier to imagine the end of the world than the end of capitalism. Unless a more cogent grappling and unpacking of this issue is undertaken, progress is difficult. Only by confronting its past can the development management process as enacted through the project confront the future.

References

Ebrahim, A. 2003 Accountability in practice: Mechanisms for NGOs, *World Development*, 31(5), 813–829.

Fisher, Mark 2008 *Capitalist realism: Is there really no alternative?* London: Zero Books.

Freeman, Scott and Mark Schuller 2020 Aid projects: The effects of commodification and exchange, *World Development*, 126, 104731.

Gasper, D. 2000 Logical frameworks potential and problems. *Teaching Materials for ISS Participants*. http://hdl.handle.net/1765/50949.

Girei, E. 2016 NGOs, management and development: Harnessing counter-hegemonic possibilities, *Organization Studies*, 37(2), 193–212.

Gujit, Irene 2015 Playing the rules of the game and others strategies, in R. Eyben, I. Gujit, C. Roche and C. Shutt, eds. *The politics of evidence and results in international development*, Rugby: Practical Action Publishing.

Picciotto, Robert 2020 Towards a 'new project management' movement? An international development perspective, *International Journal of Project Management*, 38, 474–485.

Scott, Caitlin 2022 Audit as confession: The instrumentalisation of ethics for management control, *Critique of Anthropology*, 42(1), 20–37. https://doi.org/10.1177/0308275X221074834.

Shore C., and Wright S. 2015 Audit Culture Revisited: Rankings, Ratings, and the Reassembling of Society. *Current Anthropology* 56(3), 421–444.

Shutt, Cathy 2016 *Towards an alternative development management paradigm?* Sweden: Report for EBA.

Sriskadaraja, Danny 2015 Message from the secretary general, Civicus. *State of civil society report 2015*. Johannesburg: Civicus Alliance.

Strathern, M. 2000 Introduction: New accountabilities, in M Strathern, ed. *Audit cultures*, London: Routledge.

Udehn, Lars 2002 The changing face of methodological individualism, *Annual Review of Sociology*, 28, 479–507.

Vähämäki, Janet 2015 The results agenda in Swedish development cooperation: Cycles of failure or reform success? in R. Eyben, I. Gujit, C. Roche and C. Shutt, eds. *The politics of evidence and results in international development*, Rugby: Practical Action Publishing.

Wallace, T., L. Bornstein and J. Chapman 2007 *The aid chain: Coercion and commitment in development NGOs*, Rugby: Practical Action Publishing.

Index

Note: Page numbers in *italic* indicate a figure and page numbers in **bold** indicate a table on the corresponding page.

Accountability Learning and Planning System (ALPS): case study 66–68
ActionAid: case study 66–68
activities 83
adaptation 114–116, 120, 124, 136; flexibility in Dutch CSO projects 132–133; *see also* adaptive management
adaptive management 78–79, 103–108, *103*, **105**, 110–111; case study 131; changing planning 108–109; and core elements of project planning 81–82, *81*; and fourth-generation results frameworks 90–91; and Gantt charts 91–92, *92*; and the logframe 82–89, *86–87*, *89*, 93–96, *95*; and the logics of planning 79–81; monitoring for 128–130; and systems theory 103–108, *103*, **105**; and theories of change 96–103, *97*, *99*, *101*; and trafficking myths 109–110
advocacy 152–156, *155*
aid sector 22–23, 40–41; and management science 23–28; manuals, toolkits and the search for technocratic perfectibility 32–35, *34*; and project cycle management 28–32, *29*; and project delivery 35–40, *37*
analysis *see* tools of analysis
anthropology: anthropological insights 8–11; and monitoring 125–126
area of intervention 14
assessing impact 152–156, *155*

baselines 120
beneficiaries 14
budget process: case study 58–59

campaigns 152–156, *155*
case studies: ActionAid and ALPS 66–68; adaptive management 131; 'the budget as theatre' approach in Malawi 58–59; nutrition programming 147–149; OXFAM 153–156, *155*; participatory process evaluation 158–159; remote monitoring 127–128; State Accountability and Voice Initiative (SAVI) 106
change *see* theories of change
child trafficking 109–110
civil society organisations (CSOs) 12, 100, 106, 127, 132–133, 136
comparison before and after (CBA) approach 146
complexity 103–108, *103*, **105**; participatory approaches 157
contexts 11–13, *12*
contribution analysis 156
coordinated actions 28–32, *29*
Covid-19 52, 126–127, 143
critical perspectives 5–8
CSOs 132–133
culture 17–18, 32–36, 46–47, 129–130, 167; absence of tools for assessing 70–73

delivery 35–38, *37*; direct 15
Department for International Development (DFID): and project inceptions 48–51, 56–59, 63–66; and project management 25–27, 31, 39; and project planning 87, 91, 106
depoliticising 2, 8–9, 40

development: key characteristics of projects in 13–15; projects and tools in 1–3; *see also* international development
development planning 93, 96, 98, 171; absence of tools for assessing culture in 70–73
difference in difference 146
direct delivery 15
disciplining tools of projects 168–170
Doing Development Differently (DDD) 105–108

Ebola 125–126
evaluation 139–141, *142*; case study 147–149, 153–156, 158–159; challenges of 162–163; core approaches 145–147; defined 141–143, *142*; evaluating impact 82; key debates and issues 160–161; methods and methodologies 143–145; and mixed methods 161–162; participatory evaluation approaches 157; and process tracing 152–156; small 'n' approaches 149–150; theory-based evaluation approaches 150–152

factory production systems 23–28
flexibility 132–133
Foreign Commonwealth and Development Office (FCDO) 25, 31, 36–37
Foucault 3, 6
fourth-generation results frameworks 17, 90–91, *92*, 108, 168; *see also* results

Gantt charts 91, *92*
Ghana 153–156, *155*
goals 13, 81, 83

healthcare campaign 153–156, *155*
humanitarian projects 15

impact 82, 139–141; case study 147–149, 153–156, 158–159; challenges of 162–163; core approaches 145–147; defined 141–143, *142*; key debates and issues 160–161; methods and methodologies 143–145; and mixed methods 161–162; participatory evaluation approaches 157; and process tracing 152–156; small 'n' approaches 149–150; theory-based evaluation approaches 150–152
inceptions *see* project inceptions

indicators 114–116, 117–119, *118*, 130, 134–136; assembling 119–122; M&E systems 122–125, *123–124*; and monitoring 116–117
inputs 15, 83–86
Institutional and Governance Review (IGR) 60
institutionalisation 57, 60, 63–64
international development 25–26; defining projects in contexts of 11–13, *12*
international non-governmental organisations (INGOs) 5, 12, 15–16, 27, 36–37, 48, 51
International Rescue Committee (IRC) 131, 136

learning 114–116, 119, 122, 124–130, 132–134, 136
local views 70–73
logframes 1–3, 167–168, 171; and core elements of project planning 81–82; evaluation and impact 139, 146, 154, 161; and fourth-generation results frameworks 90–91; and the logics of planning 79–81; and monitoring 114–122, 131; problems with 93–96; and project management 24–32; and project planning 78–79, 82–89, 106–108, 110–111; and theories of change 96–99, 102–103
logics of planning 79–81

Malawi 58–59
management *see* adaptive management; management science; project management
management science 6, 23–28, 39
M&E systems 122–125, **123**, *124*
manuals 32–35, *34*, 133–135, *133*
McNamara, Robert 24
methods/methodologies 15–16, 143–145; *see also* mixed methods
mixed methods 17, 145, 161–162
monitoring 82, 114–116, 122, **123**, 124–125, 135–136; for adaptive management 128–130; flexibility in Dutch CSO projects 132–133; and indicators 116–119; monitoring the right things 125–126; remote or third-party 126–128; and technocracy 133–135, *133*
monitoring, evaluation and learning (MEL) 114–115

Myanmar 131
myth 33–34, 109–110

Netherlands 132–133
New Public Management (NPM) 3–7, 26, 38, 40, 167, 169
Nigeria 106
non-governmental organisations (NGOs) 5, 12, 15–16; and monitoring 135–136; and project inceptions 48–54, 65–68; and project management 36–41; and project planning 95, 99–100, 106
nutrition projects: case studies 147–149, 158–159

objectively verified indicators of achievement (OVI) 86
objectives 81, 83
OECD 56–57, 116, 140–143, 146, 163
outcomes 83, 120–122
outcomes harvesting 157
outputs 83
OXFAM 153–156, *155*

participation; case study 66–68, 158–159; and top-down planning 64–70
participation evaluation approaches 157
Participatory Rural Appraisal (PRA) 60, 65–69, 158
perfectibility 32–35, *34*
planning *81*; changing 108–109; logics of 79–81; *see also* development planning; project planning; top-down planning; work planning
political economy analysis (PEA) 56–60; challenges of institutionalising 63–64
problem 166–169; 2–4, 7–9, 14; challenges of using tools 62–64; framing 52–53, 56, 58, 60; logframe 93–96; and project inceptions 45–47, 74; and project management 27–30; and project planning 79–80; theories of change 102–103
Problem-Driven Governance and Political Economy (PGPE) framework 60
problem tree 60–62, *61*
process tracing 152–156, *155*
progress indicators 120
project 1–3; delivering project in the aid chain 35–38, *37*; disciplining tools of 168–170; in international development contexts 11–13, *12*; key characteristics 13–15; origins 47–49; as series of coordinated actions 28–32, *29*
project cycle management 28–32, *29*
project inceptions 45–47, 73–74; and the challenges of using tools 62–64; and participation 64–70; and political economy analysis 56–60; and the problem tree 60–62; project origins 47–49; and situation analysis 50–53; and stakeholder analysis 53–56; and tools for assessing culture 70–73; and top-down planning 64–70
projectisation 15, 18, 108–110, 166
project management 22–23, 40–41; management science 23–28; manuals, toolkits and the search for technocratic perfectibility 32–35, *34*; project cycle management 28–32, *29*; project delivery 35–40, *37*
Project Management Institute (PMI) 4, 25
project origins 47–49
project planning 78–79, *86–87*, **105**, 110–111; changing planning 108–109; and core elements of project planning 81–82, *81*; and fourth-generation results frameworks 90–91; and Gantt charts 91–92, *92*; and the logframe 82–89, *86–87*, *89*, 93–96, *95*; and the logics of planning 79–81; and systems theory 103–108, *103*, **105**; and theories of change 96–103, *97*, *99*, *101*; and trafficking myths 109–110
purpose 13

qualitative data 169; evaluation and impact 139–140, 149–152, 157, 160–162; and project inceptions 51–53
quantitative data: evaluation and impact 139–140, 144, 149–152, 160–161; and monitoring 133–135; and project inceptions 51–53, 73; project management 24–25

realist evaluation 151
remote monitoring 126–127
resource 83–86
results 3–5, 15–18, 167–169; evaluation and impact 139–148, 157, 162–163; fourth-generation results frameworks 17, 90–91, *92*, 108, 168; and monitoring 114–115, 119, 129–130, 133–136; and project management 22–27, 30–33, 37–39; and project planning 78–87, 103–108

results-based management (RBM) 4, 28, 33–34, 108, 111

situational analysis 50–53, *51*
small 'n' approaches 149–150
'special circumstances' 15
stakeholder analysis 53–56, *54–55*; critical reflections on 62–63
State Accountability and Voice Initiative (SAVI) 106
strategies 81
sustainability 13–15, 103, 141–143, 146
Syria 127–128
systems theory 103–108, *103*, **105**

technocracy 133–135, *133*; technocratic perfectibility 32–35, *34*
technologies 26–27, 32–33, 71, 126–128, 136–137, 170
theories of change 96–99, *97*; problems with 102–103; visualising 99–102, *99*, *101*
theory *see* systems theory; theories of change; theory-based evaluation approaches
theory-based evaluation approaches 150–152
third-party monitoring 126–127
time frames 14

tools and toolkits: 1–5, 15–18, 166–171; anthropological insights 8–11; for assessing culture 70–73; challenges 62–64; critical perspectives 5–8; disciplining tools of projects 168–170; evaluation and impact 145, 160–163; and monitoring 115, 129–130; political economy analysis (PEA) 56–60; problem tree 60–62; and project inceptions 45–47, 49–50, 64–67, 70–73; and project management 22–29, 32–35, *34*, 39–40; and project planning 78–82, 88–97, 106–110; situation analysis 50–53, *51*; stakeholder analysis 53–56, *54–55*
top-down planning 5, 29, 49; problems with 64–70
trafficking 109–110
trends 170–171

Value for Money (VfM) 143
vision 81; *see also* goals
visualising a theory of change 99–102, *99*, *101*

work planning/workplans 22, 24, 81, 91, *92*
World Bank 11, 25, 28, 49–51, 57, 63–65, 147–149

For Product Safety Concerns and Information please contact our EU
representative GPSR@taylorandfrancis.com
Taylor & Francis Verlag GmbH, Kaufingerstraße 24, 80331 München, Germany

www.ingramcontent.com/pod-product-compliance
Lightning Source LLC
Chambersburg PA
CBHW070340270326
41926CB00017B/3926

9 781138 384828